Distant voices

Ideas on democracy and the Eurozone crisis

Rostra Books – Trondheim Studies in History
Series editor: Professor Per Hernæs

Executive editorial committee:
Professor Tore T. Petersen
Professor Ola S. Stugu
Professor Steinar Supphellen

Contact address:
Professor Per Hernæs
Department of Historical Studies
NTNU
NO-7491
Trondheim
Norway

E-mail: per.hernaes@ntnu.no

Lise Rye (ed.)

Distant voices

Ideas on democracy and the Eurozone crisis

akademika"
publishing

© Akademika Publishing, 2013

ISBN 978-82-321-0354-6

This publication may not be reproduced, stored in a retrieval system or transmitted in any form or by any means; electronic, electrostatic, magnetic tape, mechanical, photocopying, recording or otherwise, without permission.

Layout: Type-it AS, Trondheim
Cover Layout: Mari Røstvold, Akademika Publishing
Paper: Munken Lynx 90 g
Printed and binded by: AIT Oslo AS

Cover: Reconstruction works over Parthenon, Athenian Acropolis. Wikimedia Commons.

This book has been published with funding from the Department of Historical Studies, Norwegian University of Science and Technology (NTNU),
the Norwegian Research Council (NRC) and the Norwegian Ministry of Foreign Affairs.

We only use environmentally certified printing houses.

Akademika Publishing
Oslo/Trondheim
www.akademikaforlag.no

Publishing Editor: andreas.nybo@akademika.no

Table of Contents

Acknowledgements 7

Contributors 9

Distant voices. Ideas on democracy and the Eurozone crisis: Introduction 11
by Lise Rye

Democracy or demagogy? The Greek political actors on the sovereign debt crisis 23
by Anna Visvizi

Going further peripheral? Portugal, democracy, and the crisis 51
by Cláudia Toriz Ramos

EU membership and the question of Hungary's sovereignty: Ideas of the European Union before and following the crisis 75
by Anna Molnár

The EU membership yet to come? Turkish civil society speaking in times of crises 105
by Ülkü Doğanay, Özlem Erkmen and D. Beybin Kejanlıoğlu

A threat to democracy and independence? Perception of the EU in Icelandic discourse 137
by Eiríkur Bergmann

Crisis and convergence: Norwegian parliamentary debate on the EU .. 161
by Lise Rye

Identifying the crisis 187
by George Chabert

Acknowledgements

Distant Voices is a product of Beyond Borders: Transnational movements through history – a research project run by the Department of Historical Studies at the Norwegian University of Science and Technology (NTNU) in the period of 2010-13 and financed by the Norwegian Research Council (NRC). Distant Voices was also supported by the Norwegian Ministry of Foreign Affairs (Tilskudd til europapolitisk forskning 2013). I would like to acknowledge both institutions for their financial support. I would also like to acknowledge the staff at the Centre Franco-Norvégien en Sciences Sociales et Humaines in Paris, the staff at the Mid-Norway European Office in Brussels, and Elise Hov at NTNU for practical assistance in connection with the organization of two workshops in 2012. Finally, I thank the contributors to this volume with whom it was my pleasure and privilege to work.

Trondheim, October 2013
Lise Rye

Contributors

Anna Visvizi is Postdoctoral Research Fellow at the Central-East Europe Institute (Lublin, Poland) and Associate Professor in Economics and Political Science at DEREE – The American College of Greece (Athens, Greece).

Cláudia Toriz Ramos is Professor of Politics at Fernando Pessoa University (Porto and Ponte de Lima, Portugal).

Ülkü Doğanay is Associate Professor of Politics at Ankara University (Ankara, Turkey).

Özlem Erkmen is Phd Candidate and Research Assistant at Doğuş University (Istanbul, Turkey).

D. Beybin Kejanlıoğlu is Professor of Communication Sciences at Istanbul Aydin University (Istanbul, Turkey)

Anna Molnár is Associate Professor of Politics at the University of Pannonia (Veszprém, Hungary).

Eiríkur Bergmann is Professor of Politics at Bifröst University (Bifröst, Iceland).

Lise Rye is Associate Professor of Contemporary European History at NTNU – Norwegian University of Science and Technology (Trondheim, Norway)

George Chabert is Professor of Cultural History at NTNU – Norwegian University of Science and Technology (Trondheim, Norway).

Distant voices.
Ideas on democracy and the Eurozone crisis:
Introduction

Lise Rye

Since 2009 the European integration process has taken place in a context of crisis. Triggered by the sovereign debt crisis that was laid open in Greece in autumn that year, a series of European countries are facing deep social distress as they struggle to unite austerity measures with the fostering of new growth. Along with dire social consequences, the crisis has had many political consequences. A two-digit number of national governments have lost office as a direct effect, most noteworthy in Greece and Italy in autumn 2011, where elected governments were dismissed for the benefit of appointed governments dominated by technocrats. On the EU level the initial attempts to tackle the problems of the economic and monetary union have been described as 'too little, too late'.[1] As the Union has taken up a more vigorous role, attention has turned to the democratic implications of its actions. German philosopher Jürgen Habermas (2012) argues that the EU has entered a state of *post-democracy* characterized by the execution of power by bodies of questionable democratic legitimacy. Against the backdrop of crisis the Franco-German leadership has, Habermas says, established a system where power has shifted from the people into the hands of institutions such as the European Council, which has engaged in politics without the authorization to do so. In a blueprint presented at the end of 2012, the European Commission depicts a *crisis of confidence* and acknowledges the need for increased democratic legitimacy.[2]

In this volume, the focus turns from the EU centre and towards countries that form part of its periphery – from the decision-making core to countries where the role as receivers of EU policy has been prominent. The purpose is to examine

---

1 Jacques Delors, quoted in *The Guardian*, 3 December 2011.
2 'A blueprint for a deep and genuine economic and monetary union. Launching a European Debate' (European Commission, 2012).

whether, in a context of Europeanization and at the juncture of crisis, shifts in ideas about democracy have taken place.[3] Keeping a dual focus on *ideas of democracy in the European Union* and *ideas on the impact of Europeanization on national democracy*, the volume presents, in the form of individual chapters, qualitative analyses of political party and civil society discourse in six countries: Greece, Portugal, Hungary, Turkey, Iceland, and Norway.[4]

The study of the role of ideas in the process of European integration advanced with the emergence of new institutionalism in the 1990s and has produced seminal contributions to our understanding of its development.[5] Inspired by this ideational turn, *Distant Voices* reflects the opinion that ideas as conveyed by discourse are objects of research in their own right, informing us of the ways a given actor in a given setting chooses to present a given topic. The actor's power, representativeness, or opinion-forming capacities will be factors that in turn may add to or reduce the societal significance of the ideas in question. Rather than a quest for truth or correctness, the analysis of political discourse is primarily a search for *patterns in communication*. Distinguishing the particulars from the general, and continuity from change, requires contextual insight. Each of the country-based chapters in this volume therefore includes a section that places the European connection of the country in question in historical perspective and introduces readers to the instance of Europeanization on which it focuses.

Scholarship on the role of ideas in the European integration process constitutes a many-sided category, covering studies that emphasize the *constitutive* role of ideas, studies with a stronger focus on the *interactive process of discourse*, and studies of the *causal* role of ideas. This variety is also reflected in this volume. For example, in the chapter on Iceland, Eiríkur Bergmann traces the Icelandic lack of interest in EU membership back to the power of the idea of the sovereign Icelandic nation. To acknowledge that ideas may have a causal role does not imply a contradiction between ideational approaches and analyses focusing on material interests. Rather than conceiving of these approaches as competing, research has moved towards

---

3   For the purpose of this study, we use a definition of ideas that covers different levels of generality, including *policy ideas* (specific policy solutions), *programmatic ideas* (that frame or underpin the specific policy solutions), and *fundamental ideas and values* that has been referred to as 'public sentiments' (Cambell, 2004, quoted in Schmidt, 2008) that 'sit in the background as underlying assumptions that are rarely contested except in times of crisis' (Schmidt, 2008: 306).

4   Discourse is defined here as *text in context* – as the substantive content of ideas and the ways and circumstances in which they are conveyed.

5   See for example Frank Schimmelfennig's article on the eastern EU enlargement, published in 2001, or the volume edited by Hansen and Wæver on how the Nordic states relate to the European integration process, published in 2002. For a discussion of new institutionalism, see Rasmussen (2009).

considering them as complementary (Checkel, 2006; Pollack, 2006). This is also the case in this volume. Within the ideational approach, *discursive institutionalism* has been depicted as less static than the three older types of new institutionalism and consequently as more capable of explaining change (Schmidt, 2008). However, to prove empirically that ideas are truly transformative and not merely reflections of material interests is a demanding exercise. Such an approach has been used in research where all other factors are accounted for (Berman, 1998; Parsons, 2003). However, it is not the objective of the research presented in the present volume. *Distant Voices* investigates the impact of the Eurozone crisis and country-specific instances of Europeanization on ideas of democracy as conveyed by political and civil society discourse. The fact that some of its chapters demonstrate the impact of ideas on stands on European integration should be seen as a bonus.

The six countries in question make strange bedfellows in several ways, perhaps most conspicuously with regard to their geographical location and size, which ranges from 320,000 Icelanders in Europe's north-western corner to 75 million Turks in the south-east. In economic terms, the group includes some of the poorest and some of the richest countries in Europe. While some of them are currently in deep economic crisis, which is the case for Greece, Portugal, and Hungary, others enjoy economic growth, which is the case in Turkey, Norway, and more recently in Iceland. The difference in quality of democracy is yet another central dividing line of relevance for this study. In 2012, Norway and Iceland headed, as numbers 1 and 3 respectively, the group defined as 'full democracies' in *The Economist*'s Democracy Index.[6] The index for that year, subtitled *Democracy at a Standstill*, was an assessment of democratic standards in 167 countries as of ultimo 2012. As indicated by the subtitle, the overall conclusion was that 2012 did not bring significant progress or setbacks for global democracy. (By contrast, the 2011 index was subtitled *Democracy under Stress*.) However, the report emphasized that the year 2012 was marked by the crisis as well as by weak political leadership and the continuous decline in trust in political institutions in many European countries. The index ranked Portugal as number 26, at the top of the group of countries categorized as 'flawed democracies'. The latter category also comprised Greece and Hungary, ranked as numbers 33 and 49 respectively. Turkey was ranked as number 88 in the category classified as 'hybrid regimes'. Lastly, the six countries in

---

6 The Economist Intelligence Unit's Index of Democracy operates with four types of regimes: full democracies, flawed democracies, hybrid regimes, and authoritarian regimes. The index is based on five categories: electoral process and pluralism, civil liberties, the functioning of government, political participation, and political process (*The Economist*, 2013).

this volume have dissimilar institutional relations with the EU: Greece, Portugal, and Hungary are full members since the southern (1981 and 1986) and eastern (2004) enlargements, whereas Turkey and Iceland both are candidate countries (since 1999 and 2009 respectively); and Turkey is linked to the EU by means of the 1963 Ankara Agreement, whereas Iceland and Norway are part of the European Economic Area (EEA), regulated by the 1994 EEA Agreement.

What then, are the reasons for bringing together these countries, which differ in many important respects? First, they all form part of an EU periphery. 'Peripheral' may seem an odd description of a group that includes, for example, central European Hungary. However, the term 'peripheral' is applied primarily in a chronological and political sense, and refers partly to the fact that none of the countries are founding members of the European Union, partly to the fact that in terms of practical politics they have not influenced the process of integration and EU crisis management in ways that matches the influence exerted by core players such as Germany and France. During the crisis, the term 'peripheral' has become synonymous with 'southern'. For the purpose of this volume, 'peripheral' contrasts the notion 'EU core', in turn defined as the six founding members and the UK. In shifting the focus towards the relatively less researched periphery, the volume complements existing research on the effect of the Eurozone crisis on political discourse in the core countries, thereby contributing to a more complete picture of the effect of the crisis on political ideas.

Previous research underpins the relevance of the present study. The divide between pragmatic and normative discourse is central in research on political discourse in the EU (Eriksen and Fossum, 2004; Sjursen, 2007). *Pragmatic discourse* is characterized by an emphasis on the EU as a 'problem-solving entity promoting free markets and regional security' (Schmidt, 2012: 170). This way of presenting the European integration process has traditionally been associated with Great Britain, the Scandinavian countries, and the Eastern and Central European countries. By contrast, *normative discourse* is characterized by the emphasis on the EU as a 'value-based community ensuring solidarity' that has been connected with the founding members, particularly France and Germany (Schmidt, 2012: 170). Research on elite discourse in the EU core has established that the crisis has entailed significant discursive shifts. As for traditional carriers of normative discourse, this is particularly the case for Germany, where the transition from financial crisis to sovereign debt crisis was accompanied by a more pragmatic discourse on the part of Chancellor Angela Merkel. By contrast, the discourse of former French President Nicolas Sarkozy's has been compared to the pro-European discourse of François Mitterrand and as a result has been interpreted as more true to form. With regard to Great Britain, the crisis has entailed instances of highly untypical calls for deeper integration. However, these have been interpreted as pragmatic attempts to 'save Britain from economic contagion from the Eurozone' and as disconnected from the more fundamental programmatic ideas that appear unchanged (Schmidt, 2012: 176).

If the crisis has caused distinct shifts in the communicative discourse of the decision-making elite, how have the attempts to handle it affected the discourse in countries that to considerable degrees are the objects of decisions they have little room to influence? Previous research on ideas of Europe in countries within and outside the EU core demonstrates that historically the surrender of sovereignty has been a more contested issue in new member states, candidate countries, and EEA member countries than in founding member states (Ramos, 2011). This finding accentuates the question of how the periphery has reacted to recent surrenders of sovereignty.

Our second reason for bringing these six peripheral countries together is that regardless of their current association with the EU they are all countries that have been and continue to be the objects of considerable Europeanization. We define 'Europeanization' as national change in consequence of regional integration in Europe (Tallberg et al., 2010). Europeanization thus captures change *in* a country that follows *from* that country's association *with* the EU. Three of the countries discussed in this volume are full members of the European Union. The process leading up to full membership is perhaps the foremost illustration of Europeanization, as it includes the candidate country's acceptance of the EU's *acquis communautaire* – that which has been agreed upon. The *acquis communautaire* may also be translated as 'the EU as it is': it is the EU treaties and regulations, declarations and opinions, international agreements that the EU has entered into, and the rulings of the European Court of Justice (ECJ). Accepting the EU *acquis* means accepting the EU as one finds it. The degree of Europeanization that this entails will thus depend on the original distance between national and EU law. If this distance is considerable, the degree of Europeanization will be considerable too, provided that the candidate country implements and complies with EU law. With the introduction in 1993 of the accession criteria – the Copenhagen criteria – the demands made on prospective members were extended beyond the demands that Greece and Portugal had faced in the southern enlargement. From then on, countries seeking to join the EU had to demonstrate stable institutions guaranteeing democracy and the rule of law, and respect for minorities and human rights. They had to have a functioning market economy and a public administration capable of handling the practical aspects of EU membership. It is up to the EU to decide when a country has completed these conditions and when it is ready to accept that country as a new member.

When Greece, Portugal, and Hungary joined the EC/EU, they also became members of the EC/EU decision-making institutions, thereby assuming formal roles in the formulation and adoption of the regulations to which they are subjected. However, under the current crisis both Greece and Portugal have been subjected to new supremacy, as the bailouts to which they have resorted condition austerity measures that leave national authorities with little room for manoeuvre. The situation raises a dilemma between economic necessity and national sovereignty, which has also been experienced by Hungary. In 2008 Hungary received an IMF bailout that was financed in conjunction with the EU. Two years later the then new Prime Minister Viktor Orban chose not to renew Hungary's agreement. When returning to the IMF one year later, Orban told listeners to Hungarian radio that he would seek an insurance-type agreement with the fund but not one that implied the surrender of Hungary's economic sovereignty.[7]

Despite their positions as non-members, Turkey, Iceland, and Norway have been the objects of substantial Europeanization too. In the case of Turkey, EU conditionality was particularly conspicuous in the five-year period leading up to the opening of formal negotiations with the EU in 2004, when a series of constitutional reforms were accomplished, aiming to bring the country in line with EU standards as formulated in the Copenhagen criteria. Two years later, the European Council decided to suspend 8 out of 35 chapters in the negotiations, following Turkey's refusal to extend the Ankara Agreement to the Republic of Cyprus. As shown in the chapter on Turkey, domestic support for EU membership has since declined and the idea of the EU as unjust has gained ground.

After coming to power in April 2013, the new right of centre government in Iceland put EU negotiations on hold. As in Turkey, support for membership has dwindled, in this case in pace with the country's recovery from its financial meltdown in 2008. In the meantime, Iceland, in common with Liechtenstein and Norway, is closely connected with the EU through the EEA Agreement. This agreement ensures the three EFTA countries' access to the EU internal market on (almost) equal terms as EU member states. However, the access is conditioned on their adoption, implementation, and compliance with EU internal market legislation. In practice, the honouring of this obligation implies the export of considerable law-making from elected national representatives to EU institutions in which the EFTA-countries have no formal say. In her book on democracy in Europe, Vivien Schmidt claims that the real problem for EU member states is not so much that their democratic practices have changed as that national ideas and discourse

---

7   Viktor Orban, quoted in *The New York Times*, 18 November 2011

about democracy have not (Schmidt, 2006: ix). Ideas on democracy have certainly proved remarkably resilient, in both Iceland and Norway. In the case of these countries there is, however, no doubt about the fact that the changes in democratic practice that follow from their relationship with the EU are genuinely problematic, as the transfer of law-making to the EU level is not compensated for by participation in EU-level democracy.

Our final reason for bringing the six countries together is the centrality of arguments about democracy in the processes that have brought them into or kept them on the outside of the EU. On the one hand, there is Greece, Portugal, and Hungary, where membership represented a transition from dictatorship and state socialism to democracy and market economy. On the other hand, there is Turkey, which is not democratic enough for the EU, and there is Iceland and Norway, which seem to consider themselves too democratic for the EU. It is against this backdrop that the following chapters identify, contextualize, and discuss ideas about national and EU democracy as they have been communicated in a context of crisis, conditionality, and the weakening of national democratic institutions.

Anna Visvizi examines how ideas of democracy and democracy itself have been influenced by the sovereign debt crisis and the way of addressing it. Given that questions of democracy and democratic consolidation have always played significant roles in discourses framing Greece's membership in the EC/EU, her chapter demonstrates that the concept of *democracy remains a powerful political resource in contemporary Greece*, whereas *ideas of democracy are fundamental in delineating the dividing lines on the Greek political scene*. The detailed discussion of specific ideas of democracy that transpire through discursive interventions of key Greek political actors is located in a broader argumentative framework that links the sovereign debt crisis to a persistent structural imbalance between the rule of law and democracy in Greece. Although, in this context, the consolidating impact of the EC/EU on democracy is questioned, Visvizi also suggests that the crisis presents an opportunity to rejuvenate democracy and the mechanisms that underpin it.

Cláudia Toriz Ramos analyses ideas about the economic crisis and its relation to Europeanization in Portugal. On the basis of elite discourse (parliament, presidency, government, and political parties), her chapter demonstrates that the government and its supporting majority acknowledge the impact of conditionality upon sovereignty. The government traces Portugal's situation to major structural imbalances dating back to the origins of Portuguese democracy. The structural problems are in turn linked to the unfortunate consequences of European economic integration on Portugal that include exaggerated expansion of trade and services and construction combined with the decline of the agricultural sector. While the government continues to present the EU as *central for the country's transition to a more robust economy*, opponents frequently present the austerity measures as part of a *domination strategy* of the European centre over peripheral economies. Ramos concludes that the crisis has strengthened Portugal's identity as peripheral. Portugal's pre-crisis relationship with the EC/EU was one of optimism and willingness to converge into a better quality of life and into better politics. The crisis has accentuated the question of whether this convergence will continue.

Anna Molnár examines Hungarian standpoints on the European Union, with a particular focus on the debate between the Hungarian government and EU institutions on Hungary's political situation and quality of democracy following its 2010 general elections. Drawing on public opinion polls, political documents, speeches and secondary sources, the chapter demonstrates how the original idea of membership as a vehicle to a possibly prosperous, democratic and European Hungary has given way to increasing Euro-scepticism. The conflict between the EU and Hungary is interpreted as a conflict between fundamental EU values on the one hand and Hungarian sovereignty on the other, in which each party considers the behaviour of the other a *violation of European values*. The case of Hungary also serves as an instance depicting the emergence of a European public space, where domestic affairs of a member state become an EU issue, fuelling heated debates among politicians in different institutions at the EU level. The author links Hungary's crisis to the speed with which an immature democracy and inexperienced market economy had to adjust to EU standards and policies. Disappointment with its EU membership has in turn maintained the country's identity as peripheral, the difference being that Hungary has moved 'from the centre of the European periphery to the periphery of the European centre'.

Ülkü Doğanay, Özlem Erkmen, and D. Beybin Kejanlıoğlu investigate how civil society actors that have been active in areas directly related to Turkey's harmonization process to the EU conceive of the EU as a democratic entity, the EU's ongoing economic crisis, the future of the EU, and Turkey's bid for EU membership. The source material consists of in-depth interviews with actors based in Istanbul, Ankara, and Izmir, presenting a panorama of civil society's positioning between pro-EU and anti-EU perspectives. The authors describe a dual process, where *the accession process has furthered the development of civil society*, and where the ensuing organizations have acted as *catalysts and controllers* in the process of making and implementing legal-institutional regulations for harmonization with the EU. The authors demonstrate how the 2006 decision to suspend negotiations with Turkey gave prominence to the arguments that the EU is *discriminatory* and thus *undemocratic*, also within civil society organizations known to be favourably disposed towards the EU. The economic crisis, which is interpreted as a crisis of governance, has fuelled the idea of the EU as unfair, accepting countries such as Bulgaria and Romania 'while it has been testing Turkey for years'. The chapter includes evidence of an eclectic and sometimes contradictory discourse, most remarkably within the pro-European group. The overall conclusion is that alongside shrinking domestic support for Turkish EU membership, Turkish civil society continues to believe in the EU as an economic, social, and political project.

Eiríkur Bergmann analyses political discourse in Iceland on the intertwined concepts of sovereignty and democracy, on democracy in the EU, and on the democratic consequences of EEA participation and full membership respectively. Based on parliamentary debates on the Icelandic association with Europe from 1968 until today, the Icelandic case testifies of striking discursive continuity as well as of an increasing gap between ideas and realities. Demonstrating the value of a long perspective, the chapter documents how contemporary political discourse makes active use of the myths created during the 19th century struggle for independence that is conceived as everlasting, despite the fact that it resulted in full independence from Denmark in 1944. Illustrative of this point is the debate on the application made in 2009 to join the EU, when both supporters and opponents argued their case for the need to protect Icelandic sovereignty. The author claims that the significance of Iceland's post-colonial identity has been neglected in research on Iceland's relations with the EU, which cannot be fully understood without taking into consideration the idea of how EU membership threatens the sovereign, independent, and democratic Icelandic nation.

Lise Rye analyses Norwegian political discourse with a view to establishing whether central ideas of the EU and Norway's relationship with it have changed in the dual context of crisis and Europeanization following the country's association with the EU. Using parliamentary debates on EU and EEA affairs as an empirical basis, the author argues that while Norway's entry into the EEA necessitated a discursive shift on the part of the EU membership supporters, from a pragmatic discourse with emphasis on access to markets to a normative discourse with emphasis on the EU's role as a peacekeeping and democracy-fostering community, the crisis has not led to conspicuous shifts in the ways Norwegian political parties present the EU. The supporters of EU membership maintain the idea of supranational integration as a *necessity* and the one of the EU as a *democratising and solidary power*. The opponents continue to present the process of integration as a *threat to national democracy*. However, indirectly, the crisis has resulted in a rallying round the EEA association, which is noteworthy given the fact that this agreement is hardly anyone's preferred solution. Norwegian political discourse testifies of well-developed *pragmatism* and of politicians with ambitions that are limited to following the prevailing majority opinion, rather than leading the way.

George Chabert rounds off the visit to the periphery with an essay in which he argues that the crisis resides in the absence of a European political community. Chabert depicts a Europe that has embraced individualism at the expense of a common identity, in turn impeded by the continent's history of internal conflict. Taking the reader on a journey through Europe's history of political organization from the city-state state via the empire to the nation-state, the author argues that as the nation-state developed it contained the beginning of its end, as the individualism that it hailed contradicted the exclusivism of nationality, transforming man as kin into man as an individual. Adding to the inheritance of the enlightenment, the guilt resulting from Europe's past as a colonial power has, Chabert claims, fed into a normative multiculturalism devoid of content. Based on the assumption that the national model of integration is exhausted, his essay ends on a positive note, suggesting the development of European constituencies as a means to create new European social bonds.

Presenting dissimilar cases, the purpose of *Distant Voices* is not to prepare for cross-country comparisons as in a Eurobarometer survey but to offer an *in-depth understanding* of ideas of democracy in countries where democratic concerns have been central for whether they have gained EU membership or remained outside the EU. By so doing, the book aims to illustrate the value of thick descriptions that devote adequate attention to national contexts and that concentrates on *actual* rather than formal associations with the EU. Finally, and arguably most importantly, it questions the idea that EU membership equals democratic consolidation as well as the assumption that non-membership may serve as a means to protect national democratic institutions.

References

Primary sources

European Commision (2012), 'A blueprint for a deep and genuine economic and monetary union, Launching a European Debate', Com (2012) 777 final/2, http://ec.europa.eu/commission_2010-2014/president/news/archives/2012/11/pdf/blueprint_en.pdf

'Eurozone was flawed from the start, says Jacques Delors', *The Guardian*, 3 December 2011.

'Hungary Turns to I.M.F. for an 'Insurance' Pact', *The New York Times*, 18 November 2011.

The Economist (2013), The Economist Intelligence Unit's Index of Democracy 2012, www.eiu.com

Literature

Berman, S. (1998), *The Social Democratic Movement: Ideas and Politics in the Making of Interwar Europe*, Cambridge: Harvard University Press.

Cambell, J.L. (2004), *Institutional Change and Globalization*, Princeton: Princeton University Press.

Checkel, J. (2006), 'Constructivism and EU politics' in K. Jorgensen, M. Pollack and B. Rosamond, *Handbook of European Union Politics*, London: Sage, pp. 57–76.

Eriksen E.O. and Fossum, J.E. (2004), 'Europe in search of legitimacy: Strategies of legitimation assessed' in *International Political Science Review*, Vol. 25, No. 4, pp. 435–459.

Habermas, J. (2012), *The Crisis of the European Union: A Response*, Cambridge: Polity Press.

Hansen, L. and Wæver, O. (eds.) (2002), *European Integration and National Identity: The Challenge of the Nordic States*, Oxford: Routledge.

Parsons, C. (2003), *A Certain Idea of Europe*, Itacha: Cornell University Press.

Pollack, M. (2006), 'Rational choice and EU politics' in K. Jorgensen, M. Pollack, and B. Rosamond, *Handbook of European Union Politics*, London: Sage, pp. 31–56.

Ramos, C. (ed.) (2011), *Ideas of Europe in National Political Discourse*, Bologna: Societa Editrice Il Mulino.

Rasmussen, M. (2009), 'Supranational governance in the making: Towards a European political system' in W. Kaiser, B. Leucht and M. Rasmussen (eds.), *The History of the European Union: Origins of a Trans and Supranational Polity 1950-72*, Oxford: Routledge, pp. 34–55.

Schimmelfennig, F. (2001), 'The community trap: Liberal norms, rhetorical action, and the Eastern enlargement of the European Union' in *International Organization*, Vol. 55, No. 1, pp. 47–80.

Schmidt, V.A. (2006), *Democracy in Europe. The EU and National Polities*, Oxford: Oxford University Press.

Schmidt, V.A. (2008), 'Discursive institutionalism: The explanatory power of ideas and discourse' in *Annual Review of Political Science*, Vol. 11, pp. 303–326.

Schmidt, V.A. (2012), 'European member state elites' diverging visions of the European Union: Diverging differently since the economic crisis and the Libyan intervention?' in *Journal of European Integration*, Vol. 34, No. 2, pp. 169–190.

Sjursen, H. (2007), 'Enlargement in perspective: The EU's quest for identity', Recon Online Working Paper Series, Working Paper 2007/15, http://www.reconproject.eu/projectweb/portalproject/RECONWorkingPapers2007.html

Tallberg, J., Aylott, N., Bergström, C.F., Vifell, Å.C., Palme, J. (2010), *Demokratirådets rapport 2010. Europeiseringen av Sverige,* Stockholm: SNS Förlag.

Democracy or demagogy?
The Greek political actors on the sovereign debt crisis

Anna Visvizi

The Eurozone crisis that has been unfolding since late 2009 has attracted enduring attention worldwide and triggered two interconnected debates. The economically inclined commentaries focus on fiscal consolidation, austerity programmes, the reform process, and the role of the European Union (EU) institutions in advancing economic governance at the EU level (Subacci & Pickford, 2012; Visvizi, 2012d). The second debate that is unfolding oscillates around questions of democracy, solidarity, social justice, sovereignty, and popular discontent with the 'policies of austerity' implemented across the EU member states as a means of addressing the crisis (Sen, 2012; Habermas, 2011; Mazower, 2012). In this context, Greece represents a special case because several developments in the timeline of the sovereign debt crisis in Greece seem to have been aligned with the broader EU-level debates on the appropriateness of the economic policy responses to the crisis and their impact on the state of democracy in the EU member states. In this regard the Greek case offers an insight into the question of how the way of addressing the crisis influences conceptualizations of democracy and what it tells us about the state of democracy itself. The objective of this chapter is to discuss these issues.

A great number of factors need to be taken into consideration to understand the complex causes and mechanisms behind the emergence and escalation of the sovereign debt crisis in Greece. Essentially, a set of endogenous variables (including delayed structural reforms, overregulation, and the abusive role of the state in the economy) and exogenous factors (including the secondary consequences of the global financial crisis in 2008) led Greece to the brink of losing access to financial markets in early 2010 and contributed to the escalation of the crisis thereafter (Visvizi, 2012a). In this sense, it is useful to consider the Greek predicament in terms of three overlapping crises that have beset the country since 2008, which include: the demand crisis and the liquidity crunch (2008–2009) caused by the global financial crisis, the sovereign debt crisis (2010 to the present) related to a specific course of action taken by the Greek government in autumn 2009, and the progressing economic recession (which started in 2011) that resulted from an inappropriate policy mix implemented since 2010 by the Greek socialist government (PASOK) under the aegis of the Troika of Greece's creditors, namely the International Monetary Fund (IMF), the European Central Bank (ECB), and the European Commission (Visvizi, 2012b).

As a means of addressing the crisis, two financial assistance and reform programmes for Greece have been launched since 2010. Two debt restructuring schemes followed. The major objectives of the adjustment programmes – framed by two Memoranda of Understanding (MoUs) – were to restore Greece's fiscal balance, ensure its solvency, modernize its economy, and revive growth. Since the official level of unemployment in Greece reached 28% in May 2013 and macroeconomic indicators displayed a fifth successive year of economic recession (−7% GDP in 2011 and −6.4% GDP in 2012), questions need to be raised about the appropriateness and efficiency of the adjustment programmes for Greece. In looking for the culprit behind the programmes' failure, it should be stressed that irrespective of research suggesting that 'expenditure-based adjustments are not recessionary and tax-based ones create deep and long lasting recessions' (Alesina et al., 2012: 26), the 'Troika' and the government of PASOK opted for a tax-based fiscal adjustment process. On top of it, the 'Troika' downplayed the notion of fiscal multipliers (Blanchard and Leigh, 2013).

Thus, rather than tackling the expenditure side of the public finance, which would require the politically costly necessity of restructuring and downsizing the public sector, the burden of fiscal adjustment has been channelled through the private sector of the economy since 2010. As a result of tax-based fiscal adjustment, significant contractionary effects have occurred in the Greek economy, and general government revenues have plummeted. Neither exports nor domestic demand could offset these contractionary effects. In a path-dependent manner, by virtue of Greece's legal commitments specified in the MoUs of May 2010 and March 2012, the coalition government formed in June 2012 under the leadership of Antonis Samaras has had a marginal space for manoeuvre to reverse the faulty policy mix designed to address the crisis in Greece in 2010. Even though Standard & Poor decided to raise its rating for Greece to B minus from selective default in December 2012 (Bernard, 2012), and the primary government deficit (January–November) shrank to EUR 1.5 billion (0.8% GDP) against EUR 6 billion (2.9% GDP) one year earlier (IOBE, 2013: 5), it is questionable whether these developments will translate in growth and the creation of new places of employment in short term or medium term.

In order to legitimize the particular policy mix, in 2010 the government of PASOK launched a communicative campaign in which the largely constructed (as far as its size and impact on the public finance are concerned) notion of tax evasion in Greece was presented as the main culprit behind Greece's economic meltdown. Seemingly confirming the pre-existing negative stereotypes about Greece abroad, during the period 2010–2012 the debate on tax evasion acquired a mythical size. Notably, the political establishment and public opinion abroad uncritically admitted to the socialist government claims on tax evasion and its role in triggering the sovereign debt crisis in Greece. The paradox is that, as in a self-fulfilling prophecy, as a result of massive increases in taxation over the period 2010–2012 that caused an exponential contraction of the private economy, data for 2011 and 2012 may reveal heightened levels of tax evasion as well as growth of the grey sphere of the economy (Visvizi, 2013).

As domestic political debate on the crisis and the ways of addressing it are dominated by discourses centred on usually unfounded assertions of tax evasion and to a lesser extent on corruption scandals in the public sector, little space is left in parliamentary discourses for a focused debate on the content of structural reforms necessary for overcoming the crisis. In this context, ideas of democracy remain largely implicit in discourses framing the crisis, whereby the notion of liberalizing the Greek economy has fallen hostage to the debate on tax evasion and the hunt for the alleged tax dodgers. Against this backdrop, the objective of this chapter is to focus on the debate centred on the two successive MoUs of May 2010 and of March 2012 and to extract and examine ideas of democracy entailed therein.

The argument is structured as follows. In the following section, the nature of the relationship between Greece and the European Communities (EC)/EU – dubbed as contingent and difficult – is discussed, and the notion of democracy therein is revisited. Then, the empirical focus of the discussion turns to the Greek political scene and its specificity. Against this background, the debate on the MoUs is examined in view of the ideas of democracy that it contains. A discussion on the meaning of this debate for the state of democracy in Greece follows.

The European connection: democracy and (self-imposed) constraint in the relationship between Greece and the EC/EU

One of the major threads in the discussion of Greece's membership in the EC/EU is defined by the issue of Greece's 'return to democracy'. In this line of argumentation it is stressed that Greece's membership bid was conditional upon the ending of the colonels' regime, and that in turn Greece's membership of the EC/EU was essential for the consolidation of democracy in the country (Verney, 1987; Valinakis, 2012). In fact, Greece signed an Association Agreement with the European Economic Community (EEC) in 1961, with the prospect of joining the EEC at the latest by 1984. The Agreement was partly frozen for the period 1967–1974, but it was resumed immediately once the New Democracy (ND) government was established in Athens in 1974 (Tsinisizelis, 2008: 14). Consequently, Greece joined the EC in 1981.

Frequent analogies are drawn between Greece and other countries of Southern Europe in view of the impact of the EC, including its institutions and policies, on sustainability of their democratic systems. Given the variability inherent in the specific cases of Greece, Portugal, and Spain as regards democracy and the nature and origin of their authoritarian regimes as well as their duration, many of these comparisons remain unfounded. In the case of Greece, the point that deserves emphasis is that the 'democratic order' that prevailed in Greece post-1974 failed to establish a structural balance between the rule of law and democracy, thus affecting the functioning of the state, undermining the possibility of efficient implementation of laws, and hence curbing the pursuit of a reformist agenda (Diamandouros, 2012: 17). In fact, in the 1980s, the rising divide between the principle of the rule of law and democracy triggered the development of a perverse political system. Although by all book-definitions democratic, this system proved highly susceptible to the maladies of nepotism, cronyism, and abuse of executive authority. This system proved defenceless against the emergence of powerful groups of interest, including trade unions and members of the ruling socialist party, benefiting from the weak state and determined to maintain their privileges at all cost.

The above-described specificity of the Greek political system has had a profound impact on the nature and quality of the relationships that developed between Greece and the EC/EU, and on the emergence of an image of Greece as Europe's 'odd man'. The ills of the Greek domestic political system hampered the impact of the EC/EU on Greek policies, polity, and politics, repeatedly prompting questions about the virtues of Europeanization of Greece. It determined the role that Greece assumed at the EU forum. Today, it affects Greece's position vis-à-vis the 'Troika' and conditions the coalition governments' ability to embark on a truly reformist agenda. The following paragraphs shed some light on these issues.

The EC membership bid launched in the 1970s by Konstantinos Karamanlis, leader of the centre-right ND constituted an attempt to restate Greece's position in the West and create new geopolitical prospects for the country rather than economic ones. Nevertheless, ND – the party that promoted and successfully negotiated the country's entry into the EC – lost the general elections in 1981, as did other small parties in favour of Greece's membership in the EC. The winner of the elections was PASOK, a political movement that 'had made its anti-communitarian rhetoric a central element of its political platform' (Mitsos, 2000: 53).[1] Indeed, having risen to power, the PASOK government submitted the 'Greek memorandum' and sought to renegotiate Greece's EC Accession Treaty. Consequently, even if in the first years of Greece's membership of the EC the Greek authorities did not treat it in a hostile manner, their attitude towards the EC was at least defensive, focusing on a narrowly defined Greek interest and the promotion of Greek 'distinctiveness' (Mitsos, 2000: 61). The EC was employed as a political resource in political competition at home, while the EC itself and the process of European integration did not constitute a political priority for successive Greek governments. Overall, in the first years of its membership of the Communities, Greece remained an introverted country, a receiver of European policies, emphasizing Greek exceptionalism, yet – due to an almost exclusive focus on the intergovernmental and bilateral fora of decision-making – incapable of promoting its national interest in the EC and unwilling and/or unable to adjust to the broader logic of cooperation within the grouping.

In the mid-1980s, a qualitative shift in Greece's attitude towards the EC took place. Since it did not constitute a political resource for the PASOK government any longer, a more constructive attitude towards the EC was affordable. In particular, the launch of the Integrated Mediterranean Programmes (IMPs),[2] an addendum to the Structural Funds, created an opportunity for Greece to adopt a more

---

[1] The main slogans of the electoral campaign included: 'Out, out! The EEC and NATO are the same syndicate' and 'Greece for Greeks'.

[2] The IMPs, adopted by the Council of the European Communities in 1985, aimed at preventing any worsening of possible regional imbalances caused by the Community's enlargement on the accession of Spain and Portugal. For that reason, in June 1985 the Council adopted a regulation providing for the commitment up to the end of 1993 of ECU 4.1 billion: ECU 2.5 billion from the Structural Fund and ECU 1.6 billion under a specific budget heading intended to support multiannual development programmes in Greece, Italy, and the French Mediterranean regions. Furthermore, the funds were to be supplemented by additional Community loans estimated in the regulation at ECU 2.5 billion (http://europa.eu/rapid/press-release_IP-89-808_en.htm).

'communitarian' approach. Nevertheless, hopes for an enduring improvement in Greece's attitude towards the EC did not last too long, as political instability in Greece over the period 1988–1991 made the country resort to a passive position at the Community level. Although a major recipient of budgetary resources (via structural and agricultural funds), Greece was absent from European developments, whereby 'the Community was used both as a shield and as an offensive weapon in solving internal difficulties' (Mitsos, 2000: 68).

Following the end of communism in 1989, Greece ceased playing the role of the flank of the Western democratic world. This epochal change in the geostrategic location of Greece, largely misunderstood by Greece's European partners, served as a new source of tension in the relationship between the EC and Greece. The disintegration of Yugoslavia, and then specifically the 'Macedonian problem'[3], exacerbated Greece's marginalization and isolation on the European scene; specifically, 'Greece's position vis-à-vis the "Macedonian problem" did not just diverge from its partners but remained completely inexplicable in their eyes' (Mitsos, 2000:70). Admittedly, Greece failed to take advantage of its geographical proximity to the Balkans and to assume the role of a regional power.

In the negotiations leading to the Treaty of Amsterdam in June 1997 and to the Agenda 2000, the Greek Government opted for an active, albeit low-key, participation and for a strongly 'federalist' orientation. By reinforcing the image of a credible moderate interlocutor, Greece was in a position to capitalize on its lowest level of economic development in the EU in order to increase Community transfers to regions in need. Adopting the same moderate approach to EU matters, Greece succeeded in changing the negative attitudes towards itself. Regardless of the initial hesitation of its EU partners, Greece was eventually considered as a candidate and then admitted as a member of the Eurozone in 2001. Greece continued its active yet toned-down performance in the EU, assuming a very important role during its presidency of the European Council for the first half of 2003 in view of completing the 'big bang' enlargement of the EU in 2004.

The year 2004, a very successful year for Greece due to the hosting of the Olympic Games in Athens, winning the European Football Championship, and coming third in the Eurovision Song Contest, contributed to the emergence of a new image

---

3   The 'Macedonian problem' is a political problem that concerns issues of national security and territorial claims. Following the break-up of Yugoslavia in 1991, in an effort to legitimize its existence, today's FYROM (Former Yugoslav Republic of Macedonia), a political unit that was artificially created by Josip Broz Tito, started raising claims to history, names, ideas, symbols, and territory of Macedonia, a part of Greece. As a result considerable tension in relations between Greece and FYROM was observed, with Greece denying the recognition of FYROM under a name in which the term Macedonia is not accompanied by a geographical or other identifier.

of Greece as a modern, advancing country, full of development potential. This image contradicted the pre-existing negative stereotypes of the country. The spirit of enthusiasm and the ability to employ the EU fora to promote Greece's national interests resulted in Greece being very involved in EU initiatives towards the Balkans. In this regard, Greece played a major role in launching the Stability and Association Process for the Balkans, and then dynamically supported Croatia's EU membership bid.

Following Romania's and Bulgaria's accession to the EU, Greece started to share a territorial border with another EU member state for the first time since joining the EC/EU. This produced a number of feedbacks that have had a positive impact on Greece's role in the EU, including the perception of that role by others. Greek governments used this opportunity in a two-fold way. First, Greece sought to employ the EU to pursue its foreign policy objectives in the wider Black Sea area. Second, Greece followed a quite aggressive investment strategy in Bulgaria and Romania, taking advantage of the opportunities related to the existence of the Single Market. Given its level of economic development and at that time relatively high growth rates, for a short-while Greece was considered a regional leader and a hub for investment in south-eastern Europe.

The sovereign debt crisis put a dramatic halt to the prospects of Greece securing its role as a regional hub in south-eastern Europe, instead turning Greece into a case study in failed convergence, a fake promise of modernization, and 'a warning about the perils of Europeanization without deeper transformation' (Bechev, 2012: 6). With the onset of the sovereign debt crisis, given the degree of financial and political dependence of Greece on its Eurozone partners, Greece's position in the otherwise fundamental for the EU's future debates on economic governance and on the ways of addressing the crisis in the 'euro area' became at least uncomfortable, not to say constrained. Today, although a member of the Eurogroup, Greece finds itself unable to enrich the discussion on Europe's future and on the ways out of the crisis. Although claims at the domestic level about the direction and shape of the European integration process are made sporadically, they do not have any greater influence on the broader European debate, which is dominated by Germany.

To summarize thus far, there has been a tendency in the literature to consider Greece's membership of the EC/EU through the lens of democracy and its consolidation. Simultaneously, several observers (Verney, 1987; Ioakimides, 2000; Spanou, 2000) have described Greece's role in the EC/EU as oscillating between claims of exceptionalism and a self-imposed constraint. This stance towards the EC/EU was an outcome of specific developments on the Greek political scene in the post-1974 period, and especially in the 1980s: in the 1980s a structural imbalance between the rule of law and democracy was consolidated, thus affecting the powers of the state and corroding the virtues of democracy in Greece. A debilitating status quo emerged consistent with the Greek state being weak (Featherstone, 2012) and increasingly fragile to manipulation, demagogy, and abuse by specific groups of interest deliberately freeriding on democracy, and its mechanisms and principles. Although exhibiting all characteristics of democracy, the political system that emerged in Greece post-1974 prompts broader questions about the nature of contemporary (parliamentary) democracies. It also makes it imperative to reconsider the argument of the consolidating impact of EU membership on democracy in Greece, and in the remaining countries of Southern Europe.

The sovereign debt crisis in Greece is a direct result of the dysfunctional state-society relationship that consolidated in the 1980s and henceforth led to an exponential growth of the state, followed by the emergence of powerful groups of interest, such as trade unions and members of the ruling party, against which the state has proved powerless. Since misconceptions about how the economy works, the desired role of the state in the economy, sustainable growth models, entrepreneurship, and many others are widespread throughout Greek society, Greek voters have always been extremely vulnerable to political manipulation. The crisis has made the vulnerability even more acute, as it increases the stakes of political competition and makes it worthwhile for various radical political actors on the Greek political scene to resort to legitimate mechanisms of democracy to pursue their particular agendas. Discourses play a fundamental role in this regard. It follows that even if the notion of democracy occupies a marginal position in the Greek domestic discourse on the crisis, it is still worthwhile examining the meanings attached to it in the Greek political discourse.

Ideas of democracy in Greek parliamentary discourses on the crisis

To examine ideas of democracy and the various meanings attached to it in the Greek political debate on the crisis requires insight into the recent developments in the Greek political scene. Against this background, ideas of democracy entailed in respective discourses can be discussed.

Mapping the Greek political scene

Several typologies of the evolution of the Greek party system exist in the literature (Vernardakis, 2012; Pappas, 2003). Essentially, the development of the Greek party system can be divided into three stages. These include: (1) The stage of a predominant-party system (from 1952 to 1963) characterized by the presence of strong, unified right-wing parties having a coherent programme, capable leadership, and thus capable of producing strong governments. (2) The stage of polarized pluralism (between 1963 and 1981) consistent with proliferation of anti-system parties, an emerging opposition not only vis-à-vis the right-wing party but also against other major groupings, and an increasing competition (between the centre-right ND and the socialist PASOK) for the political middle ground. (3) The stage of a two-party system (since 1981) dominated by ND and PASOK (Pappas, 2003: 104–108). In 2007, and then in 2009, on the eve of the crisis, the Greek political scene was divided roughly into two camps with the remaining political groupings filling in the gaps in the political scene rather than having viable claims to power (see Table 1 for details). The elections of 6 May 2012 and 17 June 2012 brought about a new picture of the political scene in Greece, which can be characterized as fragmented, marred by deep cleavages among former colleagues, and vulnerable to extreme approaches.

Table 1: Elections to the Greek Parliament: 2007–2012								
	16 September 2007		4 October 2009		6 May 2012		17 June 2012	
	% of votes	no. of seats	% of votes	no. of seats	% of votes	no. of seats	% of votes	no. of seats
New Democracy	41.84	152	33.49	91	18.85	108	29.66	129
PASOK	38.10	102	43.94	160	13.18	41	12.28	33
KKE	8.15	22	7.53	21	8.48	26	4.50	12
LAOS	3.80	10	5.52	15				
SYRIZA	5.04	14	4.59	13	16.78	52	26.89	71
Democratic Left					6.1	19	6.26	17
Independent Greeks					10.62	33	7.51	20
Golden Dawn					6.97	21	6.92	18
Source: The Hellenic Parliament, Elections Results, available at: www.hellenicparliament.gr/en/Vouli-ton-Ellinon/To-Politevma/Ekloges/Eklogika-apotelesmata-New/#Per-13								

In view of the result of a ballot held on 6 May 2012, 31 political parties/groups were admitted by the Greek Supreme Court to participate in the elections. According to opinion polls, only 13 of them were considered capable of winning a seat in the Parliament. These political groups included ND, PASOK, and leftist/communist parties/groups such as the Coalition of the Radical Left (SYRIZA), the Communist Party (KKE), the Democratic Left (DIMAR), and the Ecogreens. Other parties that sought entry to Parliament included new political parties formed by former members of PASOK, namely the Social Agreement and the Civilians' Chariot, as well as groups formed by former members of ND, namely the Democratic Coalition and the Independent Greeks. Other parties seeking entry to Parliament included the Popular Orthodox Rally (LAOS) that was clinging to national and/or Christian sentiments, the nationalist Golden Dawn (GD), and the liberal and reformist party Drassi. The elections of 6 May 2012 led to inconclusive results. Commentators hailed the end of the two-party system in Greece, thus suggesting that old values and systems of power have been renounced by the voters, that a paradigmatic shift has taken place, and that the eve of a new political era in Greece has arrived. None of the parties that won seats in Parliament succeeded in forming either a majority government or a stable coalition.

As a result of the gridlock, an interim government was formed under the leadership of Panagiotis Pikramenos. The objective of that government was to prepare a new round of elections. Given the deep cleavages running throughout the society, aggravated by uncertainty caused by the possibility of Greece leaving the Eurozone, the outcome of the elections scheduled for 17 June 2012 was by no means certain. However, as a result of the ballot vote, ND marginally outpaced SYRIZA. Following difficult negotiations, a three-party coalition government, comprising ND, PASOK, and DIMAR, was formed under the premiership of ND's leader, Antonis Samaras. Given the precarious foundations of the coalition government, the prospects for the government seemed grim. However, the Prime Minister succeeded not only in turning the tide of negative attitudes towards Greece across Europe, but also in maintaining a fragile stability within the government. At the beginning of 2013 both PASOK and DIMAR were committed to long-term stability of the government, each of them for different reasons. DIMAR withdrew from the government in June 2013.

The greatest challenge to the government's stability stems from the key opposition party, SYRIZA. In January 2013, opinion polls suggested that popular support for PASOK had declined to a mere 8% and support for SYRIZA had increased to 28.5% (Public Issue, 2013a). In this context, SYRIZA started questioning the legitimacy of the government. In the same period as a scandal involving some PASOK members and related to the 'Lagarde list'[4] was revealed, SYRIZA launched direct political attacks against PASOK with the aim of destabilizing the coalition government. Essentially, given the political vacuum associated with PASOK's demise, SYRIZA seeks to turn itself into a key centre-left party openly voicing claims to a majority SYRIZA government. The greatest balancing force against the impact of SYRIZA on the Greek political scene stems from the KKE. Paradoxically, by denouncing the possibility of cooperation with SYRIZA and by exercising open critique towards it, the KKE, the orthodox communist party, shields Greece from falling into the radical leftism of SYRIZA.

Overall, the Greek political scene is far from stable, and the stakes remain extremely high in the political power game. It is against this backdrop that discourses on the crisis in Greece employed by the key actors on the Greek political scene should be read and ideas of democracy entailed therein conceptualized.

Extracting ideas of democracy from the political discourses on the crisis

The major dividing line in the Greek political scene and the major thread of the political debate is defined by the political parties' stance towards the two MoUs signed between Greece and its creditors. Ideas of democracy are employed on the margins of this debate. The pro-MoU camp consists of political actors that support the MoUs, conceiving them as instrumental in avoiding Greece's insolvency, securing its membership of the Eurozone and the EU, and hence giving Greece some prospects for the future. The anti-MoU camp consists of parties that, for a great number of competing reasons, renounce the MoUs, calling either for their unilateral rejection or for their vaguely defined but thorough renegotiation.

Significant migration between the two camps has taken place since 2010. Initially, the pro-MoU camp included only the socialist PASOK. Following the establishment of the interim government of Lucas Papademos in November 2011, by means of their participation in the government, ND, and LAOS, expressed their conditional support for the second bail-out package agreed in principle at the end of October 2011 (for details, see Visvizi, 2012e). In addition, following the 17 June 2012 elections, DIMAR joined the pro-MoU camp by virtue of its support for and membership of the coalition government of Samaras. As far as the anti-MoU camp is concerned, it includes a mix of right-wing and left-wing parties or

---

4 The Greek version of the 'Falciani list' containing the names of owners of deposits in the Swiss bank HSBC (see http://www.presseurop.eu/en/content/article/2575781-billion-euro-whistle-blower).

groupings, such as SYRIZA, the KKE, Independent Greeks, and Golden Dawn. Each of these political actors opposes the MoUs for ideologically different reasons. Therefore, the possibility of them forming a uniform anti-MoU bloc in the Greek Parliament is unlikely in the foreseeable future. Prior to the 17 June elections, SYRIZA proposed joining forces with the KKE and DIMAR to form a coalition government after the elections. Both the KKE and DIMAR rejected the proposal. SYRIZA made another attempt at consolidating the anti-MoU block by 'suggesting that they would accept the support of Independent Greeks in a confidence vote if there was a possibility of forming an anti-memorandum government after the elections' (Malkoutzis, 2012: 9). Given the ideological and programmatic differences inherent in the anti-MoU camp, the odds of turning it into a consistent and cohesive power block remain low. Overall, differences in approaches towards both MoUs persist in both camps, and these differences have been reflected in discourses employed by the diversity of actors on the Greek political scene. The following subsections offer an analytical review of these debates, focusing on the ideas of democracy entailed in discursive interventions by ND, PASOK, DIMAR, Independent Greeks, SYRIZA, the KKE, and the Golden Dawn, respectively.

Ideas of democracy in discourses employed by ND

ND joined the interim government of Papademos[5] in November 2011 driven by the recognition that the broad policy-framework, but not the specific policy-mix, envisaged in the MoU of May 2010 and for that matter also in the MoU of March 2012 constituted the only way towards economic recovery. In this context, for ND, the implementation of the reform programme along with the debt-restructuring schemes is consistent with Greece remaining in the Eurozone as well as with upholding Greece's European vocation. Particularly the MoU of March 2012 is seen in terms of an opportunity to pursue modernization of the Greek economy and breaking with Greece's past. The past is characterized in terms of high consumption, negligible manufacturing, and the prevalence of etatism, bureaucracy, politicking, paralysis, and a lack of democracy (Samaras, 2012b). In the ND's discourse the

---

5   The interim government led by Papademos, former Vice-President of the ECB, was sworn in Athens in November 2011. Due to its provisional nature and, even if approved by the Greek Parliament, contested democratic legitimation, it was endowed with a limited mandate. Its purpose was threefold: to ensure that the 6th tranche of the EU/IMF rescue package was disbursed; to negotiate the details of the voluntary bond exchange programme with private creditors along with provisions for Greek bank recapitalization scheme; and to pave the way to parliamentary elections, at that time tentatively scheduled for 19 February 2012.

MoUs are presented as the only solution to Greece's economic problems, geopolitical challenges, and its acute political isolation:

Greece finds itself in the centre of a region that displays an ever growing geopolitical instability. There are several, small and big countries, members and nonmembers of the EU, that see the necessity of stabilization in Greece ... Greece that until now was isolated can from this point onwards find supporters (Samaras, 2012b).

The MoU is seen as a tool to guarantee Greece's presence in the Eurozone and to avoid the return to the drachma. In this view, the MoU and its policies are considered fundamental for the process of stabilization of Greece, its economy, and its democratic system (Samaras, 2012b). The process of changes and reforms is supposed to mean constitutional and paradigmatic changes in both the society and the economy in view of Greece becoming a modern democracy, rather than 'a greenhouse for the emergence of extremisms' and political battle stage (Samaras, 2012b). Democracy is defined as:

the possibility of the majority to govern, the possibility for the minority to supervise and to become a majority; enforcement of laws; respect of the state towards the citizens and respect of the citizens for their duties/responsibilities. In brief, (democracy means) respect of all for the public good and for the rules related to democratic legitimation (Samaras, 2012a).

In discursive interventions by the ND's leader, a very clear link is established between democracy and the rule of law as well as its efficient enforcement; between democracy and the renouncement of illegal activities; and between democracy and lack of acceptance for violence and extreme positions, whether right or left. Samaras (2013b) asked: 'Is there a democracy that accepts [illegal activities related to violence and illegal trade]?' Following a terrorist attack at the central offices of ND in early January 2013, Samaras said: 'You cannot shoot democracy' (Samaras, 2013a).

There is an explicit understanding in ND's narrative that democracy is challenged in times of crisis, whereby the major challenges originate in rising unemployment and dramatic deterioration of living standards. These correlated phenomena undermine social cohesion and foster social exclusion. As such, not only do they fuel the emergence of radical and extreme political movements, including both the extreme right and the extreme left, but also make the society extremely vulnerable to discourses employed by the extreme political groupings (Samaras, 2012c). These very sober statements about democracy are entrenched in a broader conceptual context in which the power of democracy to face the challenges is underlined and a belief in democratic mechanisms is emphasized. In this sense, democracy is ascribed the role of a leverage to pave the way out of the crisis.

Ideas of democracy in discourses employed by PASOK

The socialist government of PASOK negotiated the first MoU with the Troika of Greece's creditors in May 2010. George Papandreou, at that time leader of PASOK and prime minister, presented it as the only way of rescuing the country: 'We know that times are difficult and painful ... but this is an effort to stop the country heading for the abyss' (Papandreou, 2010). In Papandreou's view, the crisis in Greece was a result of the speculative pressures of the markets, rather than of structural weaknesses inherent in the Greek economy. Therefore, as he frequently argued, to overcome the crisis required cooperation both at the EU level and within the framework of global governance. Europe, as an inherently democratic project – that 'rejected war and imperialism' and that 'exports peace as well as social and democratic values' (Papandreou, 2011b) – had a special role to play in this regard:

> *Today, Greece is at the centre of a wider speculative game which even has the euro as its target ... Our country is being treated as the weak link in the Eurozone. ... This crisis should unite us to build a stronger Europe, a Europe that offers an answer to common hopes of our citizens. [As Europeans] we support common principles, we share interests and objectives, and we solve the differences that we may have by means of democratic procedures. If today's Europe represents a project for peace, then at the same time it serves as an example of how to address the challenges of the globalized economy* (Papandreou, 2011b).

The notion of democracy acquired a new twist on the occasion of the announcement of a (failed) national referendum in late October 2011. Irrespective of the well-founded criticisms that Papandreou's idea of referendum evoked in Greece, the then Prime Minister repeatedly argued that the attempted referendum was an act of democracy and patriotism (Papandreou, 2011a). Given the fact that – as argued elsewhere – the proposed referendum constituted an escape strategy for Papandreou in an effort to save his political future and to legitimize policies that his government had pursued since late 2009 (Visvizi, 2012c), the honesty behind the referral to democracy and patriotism needs to be questioned.[6]

Quite a different view of democracy emerges from discursive interventions of Evangelos Venizelos, leader of PASOK since November 2011, following the forced resignation of Papandreou. Exerting critique of ND, Venizelos portrayed democracy as a political system that in times of crisis should foster pluralism, open up the space for political cooperation, and reject unhealthy political ambitions and unfounded claims to power. In this context, Venizelos argued that 'democracy is not a democracy of opinion polls' (Venizelos, 2012b), thus attempts at claims to power derived from therein are unfounded. Rather, as he implied, in democracies the division of power is an outcome of evolution that can bring change at any moment, whereby the interest of the nation, and not of the opinion polls, should serve as the main logic behind such evolution (Venizelos, 2012b). In Venizelos' view, democracy should serve as a front against extreme political positions, as a political tool employed to defend human rights. It is imperative, he argued, that democracy resists extreme positions that aim at violation of human rights:

> *[W]hen democracy turns into a democracy of extreme positions, gradually things lead to extremisms. Therefore, it is imperative that we resist with our political voice. Resisting desperation, discontent, confusion, and [extreme] arguments* (Venizelos, 2012a).

In his often very emotional and ethically laden speeches, Venizelos sought to embed the Greek predicament in a wider context of Europe/EU and global economic governance. He stressed the role of the socialist parties across Europe to bring politics and values to the debate on the crisis in the Eurozone, as opposed to the prevailing tendency to abhor politics and to employ technocrats to deal with the crisis. In the same vein, he touched on the strings of social justice and the economically weak strata of society, suggesting that Europe should change its current ways of addressing the crisis by means of rescuing its democracy. In this context, Europe/EU was presented through the lens of its fundamental values such as democracy, social solidarity, and social justice at the service of Europe's

---

6   In other words, if Papandreou was driven by an honest attempt to engage the Greek people in a discussion concerning the ways of handling the crisis, he should have called a referendum more than one year earlier, i.e. in April 2010, when the initial EUR 110 billion financial assistance programme was negotiated with the Troika of Greece's creditors. Reverting to popular support once a range of harsh fiscal austerity measures had already been taken and the country had fallen in deep recession was simply an attempt to escape the political consequences of his policies.

people and societies. The so-defined Europe constituted the only viable option for Greece's future (Venizelos, 2012a):

> *It is obviously very important for us, European socialists, to realize that we have a political and ethical duty to propose a way out of the crisis, a way that takes into account fiscal discipline and the financial dimension, and first and foremost the human dimension [of the crisis]. We deal not only with the markets, but also with societies, with people, with the unemployed, with pensioners, with youth that have hopes for their lives. ... Europe ought to, in my view, change itself, so that we can impose relationships of global governance, if we don't want democracy to fail* (Venizelos, 2012b).

Ideas of democracy in discourses employed by DIMAR

DIMAR was formed in 2010 by SYRIZA members that were dissatisfied with SYRIZA's increasingly anti-Europe stance. Essentially pro-EU and supporting Greece's membership in the Eurozone, DIMAR criticizes SYRIZA for its 'obsession for the denouncement of the loan agreement that would mean bankruptcy and a rift with the Eurozone' (Kouvelis, 2012b). DIMAR adopts a moderate approach to the MoUs. It opts for 'gradual disengagement from the memorandum ... via a strong renegotiation [of its provisions] as well as its firm focus on Greece remaining in the Eurozone' (Kouvelis, 2012b). The renegotiation of the MoUs would be consistent with softening certain elements of the economic adjustment programme outlined therein, such as the provisions concerning social protection, and labour issues: 'Our objective is to change policies in Europe in view of their focus on the real economy and upgrading of common policies targeting the debt crisis' (Kouvelis, 2012a).

Questions of democracy in discourses employed by DIMAR are linked predominantly with questions of racism and xenophobia, and as such they serve as an open critique of Golden Dawn. While racism and xenophobia are seen as the greatest challenges to democracy, they are associated with the inability of the state and of democracy itself to protect the citizens. As Kouvelis argues, unprotected citizens become vulnerable to radical ultra-right ideas. Therefore, DIMAR calls for the establishment of a democratic caucus that would aim at targeting these inherently undemocratic phenomena:

A citizen unprotected by the state and by democracy feels humiliated and becomes vulnerable to the temptation of ultra-right extremism, particularly when it arrives disguised as a protector, whereby the only thing that it is interested in is to spread racial hatred and hatred towards democracy (Kouvelis, 2012c). *The key issue is to mobilize all forces around a democratic caucus as a means of addressing the phenomenon of racism and primarily to address the undemocratic practices of those who seek to spread fascist ideas across the Greek society* (Kouvelis, 2012a).

Ideas of democracy in discourses employed by Independent Greeks

For the Independent Greeks, a party formed by an outspoken ND outcast, namely Panos Kammenos, the MoUs constitute a violation of Greece's sovereignty. Independent Greeks, the party, see themselves as a predominantly anti-memorandum movement that seeks to address all Greeks. According to their founding declaration, Independent Greeks demands the abolition of the memorandum and refuses to accept what it describes as 'an illicit debt created by loansharking interest rates' (Kammenos, 2012c). For the Independent Greeks party, the MoUs render Greece a powerless province in a 'federalist' Europe. Further, Europe is at times referred to as a 'Fourth Reich' dominated by Germany (Kammenos, 2012b). Independent Greeks expresses the view that the MoU 'seriously affects democracy' in Greece. Representatives of the party argue that the parliaments of countries where similar fiscal adjustment programmes are implemented have been turned into the 'servants of the demands of the Troikas and the creditors'. This constitutes a breach of the principles of the people's power, i.e. democracy itself (Marias, 2012). With regard to the state of democracy in Greece, Kammenos insisted that direct democracy should be applied at the level of adoption of government decisions: 'A "popular veto" has to be introduced to the decisions of Parliament. Citizens have the right not only to choose but also to deselect MPs when their actions harm the the society' (Kammenos, 2012a).

In December 2012, during the first conference of the Independent Greeks party, Kammenos called for the formation of a patriotic democratic caucus to govern the country. He emphasized that patriotism constitutes an ideological foundation and common sense, and therefore the establishment of a patriotic democratic caucus would save the country from the catastrophe brought about to the society by neo-liberal practices (Kammenos, 2012a).

Overall, one could argue that in the discourse developed by Independent Greeks in view of the crisis and the ways of addressing it, a very clear link has been established between the notions of Europe/EU and democracy. That is, Independent Greeks argues that a federalist Europe dominated by Germany imposes unfair solutions to countries challenged with illicit debts, thus breaching those countries' sovereignty. By depriving the national parliaments of the opportunity to make an impact on the design of the memoranda and loan agreements, and by limiting their power in view of shaping domestic policies, the EU/Europe and the memoranda constitute a violation of the basic principles of democracy.

Ideas of democracy in discourses employed by SYRIZA

The Coalition of the Radical Left (SYRIZA), which is made up of 16 ideologically diverse left-wing parties, includes social democrats, radical ecologists, radical socialists, Trotskyists, and even anarchists. Since 2010, SYRIZA has been against the MoUs. The MoUs – as recurrently stated – reflect the (abusive) power of the markets, undermine people's dignity and solidarity, and lead to a 'humanitarian crisis' (Tsipras, 2012b). Depending on the circumstances, SYRIZA has repeatedly called either for unilateral renouncement of the MoUs or for their renegotiation. The alternative 'solutions' to the crisis voiced by SYRIZA included assurance 'that minimum wages were increased, unemployment benefits extended and the public sector expanded' (Tsipras, 2012c). Clearly, SYRIZA is ignorant of the threat and the consequences of Greece leaving the Eurozone. On several occasions, SYRIZA implied that EU leaders were bluffing when they suggested the possibility of 'Grexit' (Greek euro exit) and that Europe would keep Greece in the Eurozone no matter what (Tsipras, 2012b; Lafazanis, 2012): 'They [the Europeans] can't kick us out. The memorandum is not part of the Eurozone institutional framework. It is a political choice that has been delegitimized by popular vote' (Lafazanis, 2012).

The concept of democracy is generously employed in very frequent discursive interventions of SYRIZA and its representatives. Given the mode by means of which the Greek Parliament is 'forced' to approve the provisions of the MoUs, the MoUs are considered undemocratic and anti-democratic (Chountis, 2012). Chountis (2012) asks: 'Is it democracy, when Greece is governed by the Troika, some representatives of the IMF and the Commission, whereby Greek ministers are considered/treated as their subordinates? In his New Year's speech, SYRIZA's leader Alexis Tsipras stated: 'it is our responsibility to turn the year 2013 into a year where democracy will win the memorandum and the markets and this will be a year of a return to dignity and solidarity' (Tsipras, 2013b). The concept of democracy is captured in a number of catchy phrases employed frequently by SYRIZA's leader. For example, 'the memorandum and insolvency' are confronted with 'the rejection of the memorandum and [return to] democracy', whereby 'intervention and kleptocracy' are confronted with 'justice and democracy' (Tsipras, 2013a). This colourful rhetoric abounding with references to democracy definitely adds to SYRIZA's popularity. Thus, the main opponent of the MoU, SYRIZA, successfully capitalizes on economic recession in Greece and the social discontent that it causes – as reflected in successive opinion polls – thereby legitimizing its claims to power.

In summary, it should be noted that in contrast to the dominant SYRIZA's discourse at home, when SYRIZA's leader speaks to foreign media he likes to present SYRIZA as a fairly moderate pro-European party, that 'respects the ordinary European taxpayer who is asked to shoulder loans to countries in distress, including Greece' (Tsipras, 2012a). SYRIZA is presented as a member of a broader European movement that fosters popular struggles and resistance movements as a means of defending democracy, equality, freedom, and solidarity, which are the most important values of the European political tradition:

Europe needs a new plan to deepen European integration. Such a plan must challenge neoliberalism and lead European economies back to recovery. ... it is the only plan that can restore the European vision of social justice, peace and solidarity. This plan will succeed only if popular struggles radically change the balance of forces. ... They keep democracy, equality, freedom and solidarity, [i.e.] the most important values of European political tradition, alive (Tsipras, 2012a).

However, it remains an open question as to how ideas of democracy can be reconciled with the call for popular (possibly violent) struggles aimed at radically changing the status quo in Europe.

Ideas of democracy in discourses employed by the KKE

Greece's oldest political party, the KKE, was founded in 1918 and historically has played a major role in the Greek left. Today, the KKE adheres to doctrinaire Marxist-Leninist communism. The KKE remains anti-EU and opposed to Greece's membership of the Eurozone. It supports the notion of 'complete disengagement' from the European Union, and wants to abandon the euro in favour of Greece's previous currency, the drachma. For the KKE, the crisis in the Eurozone and in Greece represents a crisis of capitalism, whereby the capitalistic system 'cannot address the crisis with the same ease as it could in the past' (Papariga, 2012a). As regards the MoUs, the KKE promotes 'rejection of the memoranda and bail-out agreements, unilateral cancellation of debt, [and] withdrawal from the EU' (Papariga, 2012b). In July 2012, Papariga argued that the EU is a 'perpetual Memorandum' and that 'either with the euro or with another currency – such as a 'Geuro' or drachma – the course to the bankruptcy of the people is inevitable so long as the path of capitalistic growth continues' (Papariga, 2012c). Unsurprisingly, in this discursive framework, questions of democracy translate into the doctrinaire notions of popular worker's power and ownership of the means of production as the only way 'to fulfil their contemporary needs' (Papariga, 2012a). The concept of democracy per se does not fit in the rhetoric resembling speeches of Soviet rulers from the 1950s and 1960s. The following quote depicts neatly the KKE's position on these issues:

> *[T]he abolition of the memorandum, in combination with the unilateral cancellation of the debt and the disengagement from the EU, [serves as a link] in the chain for the development of an aggressive, robust movement which will struggle to defend the interests of the workers, the self-employed and poor farmers. For the KKE such a struggle must be linked to the prospect of a more general political overthrow. The question of people's power must be promoted as the only real way out of the crisis in favour of the people* (KKE, 2012).

Ideas of democracy in discourses employed by Golden Dawn

Golden Dawn (GD) is a social alliance that made a spectacular entry into the Greek Parliament following the elections of May and June 2012. Frequently referred to as a 'neo-fascist' and 'ultra-right' grouping, it attracted considerable attention from foreign media. Due to its frequently provocative statements and actions, GD is subjected to criticisms in the Greek political scene too. Clearly, several opinions on Golden Dawn lack proper balance and perspective. Several intolerable statements and actions have been associated with GD. Notably, however, the specific agenda of GD and its sudden electoral success expose not only the lack of expertise but also of political experience of the majority of GD's parliamentarians. Due to the characteristics of GD, and the image that it acquired, GD is de facto contained in the Greek Parliament.

GD's official stance towards the MoUs has been defined in terms of a unilateral renouncement of the MoUs and cancellation of Greece's debt (Golden Dawn, 2012). The memoranda are considered as a catastrophe for the Greek economy, whereby the possibility of Greece leaving the Eurozone is claimed a bluff (Michaloliakos, 2012). However, even if GD declares itself as anti-MoU, it is unable to influence effectively the MoU debate. Indeed, although GD has a clearly defined position on the MoUs, its parliamentarians rarely address relevant topics directly. On several occasions, GD members admitted to their ignorance of matters of economy, thus justifying their tendency to avoid direct referrals to the MoUs. Clearly, the main focus of GD's political activity is directed elsewhere, namely to issues of illegal migration and the well-being of Greeks challenged by various hardships brought about by the crisis. In this context, questions of democracy are absent in GD's discursive interventions on the Greek political scene.

Conclusions

As highlighted in the discussion in the above sections, questions of democracy and democratic consolidation have always played significant roles in discourses framing Greece's membership of the EC/EU. Given the fact that following its entry into the EC a perverse political system – consistent with the corrosion of democratic values, principles, and mechanisms – emerged in Greece, the thesis of the consolidating impact of EC/EU membership on democracy needs to be revisited. Since the crisis in the Eurozone revived the debate on the state of democracy in the EU, whereby the EU/IMF interventions in the EU member states have been discussed in context of their impact on democracy, the notion of democracy in Greece has returned to the surface of scholarly and political debates in Europe and beyond.

Questions of democracy and democratic order remain salient in contemporary Greece. Their centrality stems from two sources. On the one hand, it is possible to establish a direct link between the sovereign debt crisis and the persistent structural imbalance between the rule of law and democracy. With its roots in the populist policies of Andreas Papandreou in the 1980s, this imbalance manifests itself through a structure of vested interests that not only paralyse the state apparatus but also hamper the possibility of reforming the public sector and pursuing a reformist agenda in the Greek economy. On the other hand, as the Troika of Greece's creditors is preoccupied with fiscal consolidation targets agreed in 2010, Samaras' government remains hostage to the politically driven commitments of previous governments. As efforts at restoring growth in Greece are blocked in this way, some very serious questions of democracy and its functioning arise too.

Although the question of the state of democracy defines the mainstream political debates across Europe today, in the Greek political discourses framing the crisis – overshadowed by the largely constructed notion of tax evasion – the concept of democracy, similarly as the issue of structural reforms, occupies a marginal position. In other words, in the conceptual and discursive framework employed at the Greek domestic level, notably in stark contrast to a discourse on the Greek crisis abroad, ideas of democracy remain largely implicit. However, it is possible to discern basic ideas about democracy and basic meanings attached to it by the key actors involved with the Greek political scene.

Overall, the concept of democracy has been linked with a number of issues and phenomena, whereby calls for the establishment of a democratic caucus to defend democracy on the eve of the crisis are common across the spectrum of the Greek political scene. As explained in this chapter, ideas of democracy are absent in narratives employed by the KKE and GD. Whereas, unsurprisingly, the KKE exchanges the notion of democracy for the doctrinaire concept of 'workers' rights', GD is preoccupied with other issues. As regards the democratic caucus, the radical-left SYRIZA calls for popular struggles to defend democracy, equality, freedom, and solidarity, and to overturn the established systems of power. The left-wing DIMAR, in the name of democracy, seeks to fight racism and xenophobia. The socialist PASOK wants to employ democracy and its mechanisms to promote social justice, equality, and a return to values and politics (as contrasted to technocratic approaches) across Europe. The centre-right ND links democracy with progress, change, the rule of law, and a reform drive. Lastly, for the Independent Greeks party, democracy and patriotism are correlated. In this view, democracy has further connotations with sovereignty and dignity.

A distinctive feature of the political discourse on the crisis in view of the ideas of democracy that it entails is reflected in the fact that frequently the concept of democracy tends to be linked with the founding values of the EU, such as sovereignty, equality, and solidarity. This is particularly visible in narratives employed by PASOK and SYRIZA. The connection between the founding principles of the EU and democracy can be detected in narratives employed by other actors too. In this sense, one could argue that the notions democracy and Europe/EU have largely converged in discourses framing the crisis. Serving as a backdrop of the political debate on the crisis, rather than constituting its essence, they provide a powerful context, against which claims about the crisis and the ways of addressing it are made, as is apparent in narratives employed by ND, PASOK, SYRIZA, DIMAR, and Independent Greeks.

Essentially, ideas of democracy that transpire through discursive interventions of the key actors engaged with the Greek political scene suggest an overstretched and internally incoherent understanding of democracy. In other words, the meanings attached to it range from modernization, change, and the rule of law, through social justice, equality, and solidarity, followed by human rights, to political mobilization and popular struggle aimed at (possibly forceful) abolishment of the established balance of power. In addition to being linked with concepts such as patriotism and sovereignty, democracy is also associated with resistance to violence and the fight against racism and xenophobia. There is a very clear understanding, expressed by the leaders of ND and PASOK, that democracy is challenged by social and political phenomena resulting from the economic crisis. There is an equally important realization, apparent in the narratives of ND and DIMAR that the society is increasingly vulnerable to political manipulation, which in itself constitutes another threat to democracy.

The diversity of frequently incoherent meanings attached to democracy in the political narratives employed by some political actors in the Greek political scene suggest that in some cases the concept of democracy is employed instrumentally as a means of political competition. Apart from sober and eloquent conceptualizations of democracy recognizing its shortcomings and its role in triggering the crisis in Greece, the political discourse is not devoid of attempts at abusing the concept of democracy. Capitalizing on people's pain, fear, desperation, and hopes for the future, some political actors establish a link either between democracy, popular (violent) struggle, and social justice, or between democracy, dignity, sovereignty and resistance to liberal policies. Undeniably, the basic principles of democracy are challenged by the economic crisis that unfolds in Greece. The crisis situation forces the key actors on the Greek political scene to uphold the salient questions of what democracy is and what is its purpose. In this view, given the fact that the sovereign debt crisis has been said to be the result of a corrosion of democratic values underpinning the Greek political system, the crisis may create an opportunity to rejuvenate democracy and the mechanisms that underpin it.

References

Primary sources
Bernard, S.L. (2012), 'S&P Lifts Rating on Greece to 18-Month High', *The Wall Street Journal*, 18 December 2012.
Chountis, M. (2012), 'Υπάρχει ακόμα Δημοκρατία στην Ελλάδα;' [Is there still democracy in Greece?], Speech at the European Parliament, 15 February 2012, http://www.europarl.gr/view/el/press-release/meps/meps-2012/February/february54.html
Golden Dawn (2012), 'Πολιτικές Θέσεις: Για την Χρυσή Αυγή του Ελληνισμού' [Political positions: For the Golden Dawn of Hellenism], Golden Dawn web portal, http://www.xryshaygh.com/index.php/kinima/thesis
Habermas, J. (2011), 'Euro-Krise Rettet die Würde der Demokratie', *Frankfurter Allgemeine Zeitung*, 4 November 2011.
IOBE (2013), 'The Greek Economy 04/12', *Quarterly Report*, Vol. 70, January 2013, Foundation for Economic & Industrial Research (IOBE), Athens.

Kammenos, P. (2012a), 'Π. Καμμένος: Αποτυχημένο το μεταπολιτευτικό μοντέλο' [The model of the past failed], *Naftemporiki*, 21 December 2012, http://www.naftemporiki.gr/story/352767

Kammenos, P. (2012b), 'Conservative rebel shakes up Greek politics', quoted in H. Papachristou, *Reuters*, 5 May 2012, http://www.reuters.com/article/2012/05/05/us-greece-kammenos-idUSBRE8440ED20120505

Kammenos, P. (2012c), 'Independent MP announces new party', *Athens News*, 24 February 2012, http://www.athensnews.gr/portal/8/53573

KKE (2012), Draft Law of the KKE for the abolition of the Memoranda – Loan Agreement, 17 July 2012, KKE web portal, http://inter.kke.gr/News/news2012/2012-07-17-programmatikes

Kouvelis, F. (2012a), 'Εισηγητική ομιλία του προέδρου της ΔΗΜΑΡ, Φώτη Κουβέλη, στη συνάντηση με αντιπροσωπεία δημοσιογράφων από χώρες της ευρωζώνης' [Introductory Speech by DIMAR's leader, Fotis Kouvelis, at the meeting of the representatives of journalists from the Eurozone], 12 December 2012, DIMAR web portal, http://www.dimokratikiaristera.gr/epikairotita/katalogos-deltion-graf-typou/4367-eisigitiki-omilia-tou-proedrou-tis-dimar-foti-kouveli-sti-synantisi-me-antiprosopeia-dimosiografon-apo-xores-tis-evrozonis

Kouvelis, F. (2012b), *Athens News Agency*, 11 May 2012, Issue No. 4068, http://www.hri.org/news/greek/ana/2012/12-05-11.ana.html#10

Kouvelis, F. (2012c), 'Ομιλία του Φώτη Κουβέλη στην κεντρική προεκλογική συγκέντρωση της Δημοκρατικής Αριστεράς στην Αθήνα' [Speech by Fotis Kouvelis during the main pre-election event of DIMAR in Athens], 29 April 2012, DIMAR web portal, htttp://www.dimokratikiaristera.gr/epikairotita/omilies-diloseis/3183-omilia-tou-foti-kouveli-stin-kentriki-proeklogiki-sygkentrosi-tis-dimokratikis-aristeras-stin-athina

Lafazanis, P. (2012), quoted in H. Smith (2012), 'Austerity will send Greece to hell, warns Alexis Tsipras', *The Guardian*, 17 May 2012, http://www.guardian.co.uk/world/2012/may/17/austerity-will-send-greece-to-hell-alexis-tsipras

Marias, N. (2012), 'Ν. Μαριάς: Το μνημόνιο βλάπτει σοβαρά τη δημοκρατία' [The memorandum harms democracy], *Naftemporiki*, 16 October 2012, http://www.naftemporiki.gr/news/cstory.asp?id=2244972

Mazower, M. (2012), 'Democracy itself is at stake in southern Europe', *Financial Times*, 3 October 2012.

Michaloliakos, N.G. (2012), 'Σταθερή στη θέση της η Χρυσή Αυγή: ΟΧΙ στο Μνημόνιο της υποταγής' [Golden Dawn maintains its stance: NO to the memorandum of subordination], speech by the GD's leader, Nikos Michaloliakos, at the Greek Parliament, 25 October 2012, http://www.xryshaygh.com/index.php/gengramateas/view/statherh-sth-thesh-ths-h-chrush-augh-ochi-sto-mnhmonio-ths-upotaghs-arthro

Papandreou, G. (2010), televised TV appeal, quoted in H. Smith (2010), 'Greece's Papandreou makes TV appeal for unity over financial crisis', *The Guardian*, 2 February 2010, http://www.guardian.co.uk/world/2010/feb/02/papandreou-tv-appeal-financial-crisis

Papandreou, G. (2011a), 'Παπανδρέου: Δημοψήφισμα για τη νέα σύμβαση' [Papandreou: Referendum for the new bailout], *Ta Nea*, 31 October 2011, http://www.tanea.gr/ellada/article/?aid=4669231

Papandreou, G. (2011b), 'Ομιλία Πρωθυπουργού Γιώργου Α. Παπανδρέου για την ημέρα της γερμανικής βιομηχανίας στο Βερολίνο' [speech by the Greek Prime

Minister, G. Papandreou at the Day of the German Industry in Berlin], 27 September 2011, http://government.gov.gr/2011/09/27/20322/

Papariga, A. (2012a), 'Ομιλία της ΓΓ της ΚΕ του ΚΚΕ Αλέκας Παπαρήγα στη 14η Διεθνή Συνάντηση Κομμουνιστικών και Εργατικών Κομμάτων' [Speech by the General Secretary of the KKE, A. Papariga, at the 14th International Congress of Communist and Workers' Parties], KKE web portal, http://www.kke.gr/diethnh/omilia_ths_gg_ths_ke_toy_kke_alekas_paparhga_sth_14h_diethnh_synanthsh_kommoynistikon_kai_ergatikon_kommaton

Papariga, A. (2012b), quoted in P. Bitsika (2012), 'Βουλή: Πρόταση νόμου από το ΚΚΕ για κατάργηση του μνημονίου' [The Parliament: Proposal of Law on the renouncement of the memorandum], To Vima, 13 July 2012, http://www.tovima.gr/politics/article/?aid=466682

Papariga, A. (2012c), 'The EU is a "perpetual Memorandum"', Athens-Macedonian (AMNA) News Agency, http://www.amna.gr/english/articleview.php?id=542

Public Issue (2013a), *Political Barometer* No. 116, January 2013, Kathimerini/SKAI, 10 January 2013.

Public Issue (2013b), *Political Barometer* No. 123, September 2013, Kathimerini/SKAI, 12 September 2013.

Samaras, A. (2012a), 'Τι σημαίνει Δημοκρατία;' [What does 'democracy' stand for?], *Real News*, 30 December 2012, http://www.inews.gr/268/samaras-ti-simainei-dimokratia.htm

Samaras, A. (2012b), 'Ομιλία του Πρωθυπουργού Αντώνη Σαμαρά στη Βουλή για το Πολυνομοσχέδιο του Υπουργείου Οικονομικών' [Speech by Prime Minister A. Samaras to Parliament on a draft law of the Ministry of Economics], Press Office of the Prime Minister, 7 November 2012, http://www.primeminister.gov.gr/2012/11/07/9818

Samaras, A. (2012c), 'Die griechische Demokratie steht vor ihrer größten Harausforderung' [The Greek democracy faces its greatest challenge], *Handelsblatt*, 5 October 2012.

Samaras, A. (2013a), 'Τη δημοκρατία δεν μπορείς να την πυροβολήσεις' [You cannot shoot democracy], *To Vima*, 14 January 2013, http://www.tovima.gr/politics/article/?aid=492991

Samaras, A. (2013b), 'Καμία χαλάρωση γιατί υπάρχει κίνδυνος να ξανακυλήσουμε' [No relaxation because the danger of collapse is not gone], A. Samaras in an interview with A. Ravanos, *To Vima*, 13 January 2013, http://www.tovima.gr/politics/article/?aid

Sen, A. (2012), 'The Crisis of European Democracy', *The New York Times*, 22 May 2012.

The Hellenic Parliament (2012), Elections Results, www.hellenicparliament.gr/en/Vouliton-Ellinon/To-Politevma/Ekloges/Eklogika-apotelesmata-New/#Per-13

Tsinisizelis, M. (2008), 'Greece in the European Union: A political/institutional balance sheet', in Ministry of Press and Mass Media (2008), *About Greece*, Hellenic Republic, Athens, pp. 145–158, http://video.minpress.gr/wwwminpress/aboutgreece/aboutgreece_greece_eu.pdf

Tsipras, A. (2012a), 'The Greek message for Angela Merkel', *The Guardian/Comment is Free*, 8 October 2012, http://www.guardian.co.uk/commentisfree/2012/oct/08/greek-message-for-angela-merkel

Tsipras, A. (2012b), 'I will keep Greece in the eurozone', *Opinion, Financial Times*, 12 June 2012, http://www.ft.com/intl/cms/s/0/4c44a296-b3b3-11e1-a3db-00144feabdc0.html #axzz2I4fNFcH7

Tsipras, A. (2012c), quoted in H. Smith (2012), 'Golden Dawn threatens hospital raids against immigrants in Greece', http://www.guardian.co.uk/world/2012/jun/12/golden-dawn-hospital-immigrants-greece

Tsipras, A. (2013a), 'Speech to the SYRIZA Parliamentary Club', 8 January 2013, SYRIZA web portal.

Tsipras, A. (2013b), The New Year's Appeal, SYRIZA web portal, http://www.syriza.gr/

Venizelos, E. (2012a), 'Ομιλία Ευ. Βενιζέλου στι Λαμια' [Speech by E. Venizelos at Lamia], 21 April 2012, http://www.pasok.gr/portal/resource/contentObject/id/381775e6-0bbe-4f76-97c8-0ceb52134c3a

Venizelos, E. (2012b), 'Ομιλία Ευ. Βενιζέλου στη συζήτηση επί του σ/ν του Υπουργείου Οικονομικών "Ρυθμίσεις συνταξιοδοτικού περιεχομένου και άλλες επείγουσες ρυθμίσεις εφαρμογής του Μνημονίου (ν. 4046/12)"', [Speech by E. Venizelos on the occasion of the parliamentary debate on law no. 4046/12 (i.e. the MoUII)], http://www.minfin.gr/portal/el/resource/contentObject/id/c2390b6c-f0a4-4e76-9fd8-6fe2d40703e3

Literature

Alesina, A., Favero, C. and Giavazzi, F. (2012), *The Output Effect of Fiscal Consolidations*, NBER Working Paper No. 18336, August 2012.

Bechev, D. (2012), *The Periphery of the Periphery: The Western Balkans and the Euro Crisis*, Policy Brief 60, European Council on Foreign Relations (ECFR), August 2012.

Blanchard, O. and Leigh, D. (2013), *Growth Forecast Errors and Fiscal Multipliers*, IMF Working Paper, WP/13/1, Washington, DC: International Monetary Fund.

Diamandouros, N. (2012), 'Politics, culture, and the state: Background to the Greek crisis', in O. Anastasakis and D. Singh (eds.) *Reforming Greece: Sisyphean Task or Herculean Challenge?*, Oxford: South East European Studies at Oxford (SEESOX), European Studies Centre, St. Antony's College, University of Oxford, pp. 9–19.

Featherstone, K. (2012), 'The Greek sovereign debt crisis and EMU: A failing state in a skewed regime', *Journal of Common Market Studies*, Vol. 49, No. 2, pp. 193–237.

Ioakimides, P. (2000), 'The Europeanisation of Greece's foreign policy: Progress and problems', in A. Mitsos and E. Mossialos (eds.), *Contemporary Greece and Europe*, Aldershot: Ashgate, pp. 359–372.

Malkoutzis, N. (2012), 'Greece's painful political transition: Analysis of the upcoming national elections', *International Policy Analysis*, Friedrich Ebert Stiftung, May 2012.

Mitsos, A. (2000), 'Maximising contribution to the European integration process as a prerequisite for the maximisation of gains', in A. Mitsos and E. Mossialos (eds.), *Contemporary Greece and Europe*, Aldershot: Ashgate, pp. 53–92.

Pappas, D. (2003), 'The transformation of the Greek party system since 1951', *West European Politics*, Vol. 26, No. 2, pp. 90–114.

Spanou, C. (2000), 'Greece: A truncated pyramid?', in H. Kassim, B.G. Peters and V. Wright (eds.), *The National Co-ordination of EU Policy*, Oxford: Oxford University Press, pp. 161–181.

Subacchi, P. and Pickford, S. (2012), 'The Euro on the brink: 'Multiple' crises and complex solutions', *Nomura Foundation Research Paper*, No. 7, January 2012, Nomura Foundation.

Valinakis, Y. (2012), *Greece's European Policy Making*, GreeSE Paper No. 63, Hellenic Observatory Papers on Greece and Southeast Europe, London: LSE.

Vernardakis, X. (2012), *From Mass Parties to Cartel Parties: The Evolution of the Structure of Political Parties in Greece through Changes in their Statutes and Systems of Financing*, The Legal Regulation of Political Parties Working Paper No. 27, June 2012, Leiden University.

Verney, S. (1987), 'Greece and the European Community', in K. Featherstone and D.K. Katsoudas (eds.) *Political Change in Greece: Before and After the Colonels*, London: Croom Helm, pp. 253-270.

Visvizi, A. (2012a), 'The crisis in Greece and the EU-IMF rescue package: Determinants and pitfalls', *Acta Oeconomica* Vol. 62, No. 1, pp. 15–39.

Visvizi, A. (2012b), 'The crisis in Greece & the EU economic governance: lessons & observations', in E. Latoszek, I.E. Kotowska, A.Z. Nowak, A. Stępniak, (eds), *European Integration Process in the New Regional and Global Settings*, Warsaw: University of Warsaw Press, pp. 183–204.

Visvizi, A. (2012c), 'The crisis in Greece, democracy and the EU', *Carnegie Ethics Online*, 10 December 2012, http://www.carnegiecouncil.org/publications/ethics_online/0076.html

Visvizi, A. (2012d), 'The Eurozone crisis in perspective: Causes & implications', in A. Visvizi and T. Stępniewski (eds.), *The Eurozone Crisis: Implications for Central and Eastern Europe*, Yearbook of the Institute of Central-East Europe, Vol. 10, No. 5, pp. 13–32.

Visvizi, A. (2012e) 'Greece: Between bailout and default', EurActiv.com, 7 February 2012, http://www.euractiv.com/countries/greece-bailout-default-analysis-510641

Visvizi, A. (2013) 'Addressing the crisis in Greece: The role of fiscal policy', in B. Farkas (ed.), *The Aftermath of the Global Crisis in the European Union*, Newcastle upon Tyne: Cambridge Scholars Publishing, pp. 211–240.

Going further peripheral?
Portugal, democracy, and the crisis

Cláudia Toriz Ramos

> *Government will strive for a cosmopolitan society free from peripheral temptations, those that more than three decades of democracy have not been able to withdraw completely and which became evident in economic stagnation, emigration ... and crescent marginalisation with relation to the centres of prosperity and progress of the globalised world.* (Governo de Portugal, 2011: 9)

Taking ideas on democracy from the 'periphery' of the European Union (EU) as the core of the discussion, this chapter addresses the Portuguese case and outlines the debate on national democracy at a time of crisis.

Portuguese transition to democracy in the 20th century was peripheral to Europe in the sense that it occurred later in time than the core democratisation in the 'old' continent (but in line with other southern countries in Europe such as Greece or Spain). The process was generated from within by a military coup d'état and revolution in 1974, but found a steady external pillar in accession to the European Communities (EC) in 1986, especially because at the time and after colonialism the material basis of Portuguese independence had to be reinvented.

Portugal put forward its application in 1977 and ever since has made a transition to patterns of living more akin with central Europe models in terms of tertiarisation of the economy, in the framework of common market, urbanisation, a boom in infrastructures, and in education and the development of welfare state functions. With the Economic and Monetary Union (EMU), came a further step into deep integration, yet the option of deepening integration has been strongly supported by national governments backed by national parties.

Within the panoply of enlargement, standard outcomes for new members are an expected effect of consolidation of democracy for those states that joined the Communities/Union while lagging behind core Europe from a political point of view. That was also the case for Portugal. In this chapter I argue that an effect of democratic consolidation happened as a result of membership, but I also argue that the deepening of integration as patterned by EMU is fostering political adaptations that at least challenge conventional national representative democracy.

Accordingly, internal political discourses on the crisis and its relation to Europeanization are analysed in order to outline internal ideas on impacts of recent events on national democracy. The empirical research for this chapter was concentrated on content analysis of political elites' discourses in institutional contexts: the parliament, the government, the presidency of the republic, and political parties. Public opinion data were only marginally considered as counterparts to political agents' utterances.

The chapter starts with a contextualisation of Portuguese integration in the European Union and therefore of Europeanization in the framework of enlargement. Then, the specific effects of the crisis on Portuguese national democracy are discussed, along the lines of conditionality, governmental agency, policymaking, and system impacts. The core elements of the final discussion are whether democracy is undermined by the crisis and whether the peripheral characteristic of this member state is accentuated by it.

Portugal: the context

To say that Portugal is peripheral implies the existence of a centre (Santos, 1985; Vasconcelos, 2000). The idea of the periphery applied to economic, cultural, social, and political patterns stems from analyses of regionalism that consider vast geographical areas (above the nation-state level) and their dynamic core areas (centre-periphery). At least since industrialisation, the 'core' of Europe has been founded on an axis running from the British Isles to northern Italy. Major dynamic centres have emerged along this line and exerted a 'power of attraction' upon peripheral areas. The geopolitical position of Portugal is western and southern in relation to Europe, maritime in relation to the continent, and northern in relation to the southern hemisphere. In narratives of Portuguese identity the 'Atlantic' position often emerges as both a geopolitical set of opportunities and a symbol of outwardness, sometimes presented in opposition to more continental appeals coming from core Europe: such as the narratives of the 15th and 16th centuries discoveries, the traditional British alliance, and NATO membership (Rato, 2001; Vasconcelos, 2000). Another characteristic amounting to the peripheral nature of the country is its combined geographical and human dimension (a territory of c. 92,000 km^2

and currently c.10.5 million inhabitants), which historically was often a reason for seeking for external opportunities in order to provide for comfortable living conditions for the population through trade, colonisation, and emigration, scaling being clearly a necessity, in terms of opportunity seeking (FFMS, 2012; INE, 2012).

Why was Portugal a candidate for membership of the European Communities? The reasons deserve some discussion. Further, the EU is a major political shaper of the states it integrates (cf. Featherstone and Radaelli, 2003; Graziano and Vink, 2008). Candidate states either are already fully-fledged democracies, in which case the political effect of Europeanization is eventually negligible, if not negative, or they are undergoing processes of consolidation, and in this case the EU's input may be a major contribution to internal political order. Market economy is also a main marker of the EU's criteria for enlargement. In general, countries aiming at accession recognise potential overall economic benefit from joining the broad communitarian market and, at least in some cases, with respect to further economic integration (namely EMU). However, wealthier economies may be less interested in accession than countries experiencing economic strain, notably for the structural support for adaptation ranging from funding to guidelines (Cameron, 2004). Experience accumulated to date shows that there is a very close relation between economic integration and political integration, the former being a major driver of further sovereignty shares. By touching the socio-economic basis of states' internal organisation, economic integration may lead to redesigning the polity, and therefore also democracy, in a multilevel framework (Schmidt, 2006).

At the end of the imperial cycle and decolonisation (1974), Portugal had to redefine its aims and priorities: the choice was in favour of Western Europe, as prestigious neighbour, and mirror and marker of 'civilisation', welfare, and democracy. Thus, together with Spain, Portugal became a member of the European Communities in 1986, after a relatively lengthy negotiation process (Assembleia da República, 2001; Vasconcelos and Seabra, 2000). At the time, Portugal was a recent and therefore fragile democracy aiming to overcome both the political shortcomings of 48 years of dictatorship and the frenzy of the revolution of 1974 (Maxwell, 1997; Rosas, 1999; Schmitter, 1999). The application to become a member of the European Communities (dating from 1977) was by then seen as a pillar of the economic and political reconstruction of the country within the western European pattern (Vallera, 2000; Vasconcelos, 2000). The proposal was indirectly backed by c.75% of the electors, i.e. the voters for the three parties supporting European integration ever since then, and opposition to it remaining only with the communist and extreme left-wing parties (Ramos and Vila Maior, 2011: 177–188).

Integrating the European Communities before European treaty amendments had been passed meant less economic and political integration than today. The 'common market' was seen first and foremost as an economic space. 'Europe', a more general concept, was perceived as western Europe, democratic Europe, wealthy Europe, and a grouping of open societies and dynamic cultures, all in all, appealing markers at least for that part of the population that aimed at living in accordance with western European patterns (cf. Pinto and Teixeira, 2005; Royo, 2005). Thus, for Portugal, European integration has meant further external support for steady evolution into democracy and a market economy. A boom has occurred in trade, infrastructures, education, science, and urbanisation, in line with the profile of the projects developed under EU funding (Martins, 2000; Mota, 2000). Nevertheless, accession dossiers on fisheries and agriculture were at the time criticised and continue to be the target of criticism due to their alleged failure to meet actual circumstances and the effective needs of both sectors in Portugal (cf. Pinto and Teixeira, 2005; Pinto, 2000; Vila Maior and Ramos, 2012).

The pillars of the Portuguese democratic regime were defined in the Constitution of 1976. In 1982, and already aiming at European integration, some amendments were made in order to erase both the traits of economic socialism and the political remnants of the revolution, notably the Council of the Revolution, a transitional military structure and type of trusteeship council to the democratic regime (Silva and Miranda, 2007; Vilaça, 2000). Still, it should be noted that while the democratic regime of the 1970s was by then the result of recent transition and needed external support for consolidation, the same does not hold true for the state, as the existence of the country as independent political state is remote, dating back to the post-feudal origins of western realms, the embryos of the modern state. European integration had no relation at all with independence struggles (Vasconcelos, 2000).

Despite the fact that the revolution brought with it a sudden burst of political participation, by opening political issues to public debate, European politics were never (nor are they at present) a major subject in the public sphere, the decisive role remaining with the agents of representative democracy (Freire, Magalhães and Lobo, 2007; Magone, 2005; Moury and Sousa, 2010). Portuguese awakening to political participation in the aftermath of the revolution was mostly channelled by political parties, some of which had played a role in resisting the dictatorship (Jalali, 2007). Civil society organisations with a specific interest in political participation – such as trade unions, business associations, and consumers associations – also emerged, but in the long run they did not take the lead with or ahead of the parties. This may have been due to a long tradition of neutralisation of political participation as carefully built throughout the 'Estado Novo' and in line with the fundamentals of the dictatorship (Freire, Magalhães and Lobo, 2007; Freire and Viegas, 2010; Santos, 1990).

At present, the main political parties are still the same as those in existence at the time of the 1975 elections, with the exception of the Left Bloc (Bloco de Esquerda, hereafter referred to as BE), which resulted from the merger of several left-wing smaller parties and tendencies. The Democratic and Social Centre – People's Party (Centro Democrático e Social – Partido Popular, CDS-PP) gathers Christian Democrats, Conservatives, and on issues concerning economics, even some Liberals. The Social Democratic Party (Partido Social Democrata-PSD) is the major right of centre party and moved from its original social democrat standpoints into options in line with the European Parliament (EP) People's Party, of which it is a member, together with the Democratic and Social Centre Party (Centro Democrático e Social, CDS). Left of centre is occupied by the Socialist Party (Partido Socialista, PS), which is aligned with European democratic socialism and is a member of the Group of the Progressive Alliance of Socialists & Democrats in the EP. The Communist Party (Partido Comunista Português, PCP) is a 'conservative' communist party. Together with the BE, it is a member of the EP's Confederal Group of the European United Left – Nordic Green Left. In Portugal, it runs for elections in coalition with the Green Party (Partido os Verdes) (cf. Jalali, 2007; Lisi, 2011). With regard to EU politics, the CDS, PSD, and PS are pro-integration parties, whereas the PCP and the BE tend to be Euro-sceptical (cf. Ramos and Vila Maior, 2011).

In summary, the recent 'European story' of Portugal is one of optimism about Europe and willingness to converge – into better quality of life and into better politics. The questions made conspicuous by the crisis concern whether the process will continue, whether it will continue at a slower pace, or whether Portuguese integration is at risk and Portugal is drifting farther into the periphery. The latter is also a question of the design of enlargements by the Communities/EU and on the conceptions of integration at the core of European integration dynamics.

The crisis and democracy: the problem and the methodology of the research

At the core of the research are ideas of democracy in a 'peripheral' country in the context of crisis. It was asserted above that the Communities were a relevant external condition in the construction of Portuguese democracy from the 1970s. However, at present, some impacts of integration may be hindering rather than fostering democratic practices at the national level. Ideas on democracy in the national political discourse are therefore scrutinised in order to check whether they reflect such a process.

From the conceptual point of view and for the purposes of this research, it is necessary to define democracy. Literature on the threshold of democracy states its basilar conditions, thus drawing the layout of an electoral democracy (cf. Dahl, 1998; Almond and Verba, 1963). However, western democracies are expected to be well above the threshold and therefore their evaluation is guided by a set of other criteria more in line with current quality of democracies assessments (e.g. Diamond and Morlino, 2004; Landman, 2008; *The Economist*, 2012). Issues such as basic freedoms and rights associated with fair electoral processes and pluralism emerge, but also the functioning of government and underlying political participation and culture. For the Portuguese case, the Index of Democracy 2011 (*The Economist*, 2012) signals a decline, the result of poorer assessment of the 'Functioning of government' and of 'Political participation', in the context of the European Union and International Monetary Fund financial assistance agreement. From the point of view of democratic legitimacy, this means that questions are raised not only at the level of output legitimacy, with reference to the capacity of a government to produce 'good' policies, but also at the input and throughput levels, as they cover responsiveness, transparency, and accountability of actions of government (Bekkers and Edwards, 2007).

Therefore, with reference to the literature and preliminary information from exploratory data, the Portuguese political discourse was analysed in an attempt to identify reactions to (1) the adoption of a strict conditionality agreement; (2) the agents involved in core governance; (3) the adoption of policies the matrix of which was not internally generated; and (4) the party system impacts of the process.[1]

---

1 The research concentrated on utterances of politicians (members of parliament, the Prime Minister (PM) and ministers, the President of the Republic (PR), and other agents of state institutions). Media and public opinion discourse was not the focus of the research, although it was marginally used to complement specific aspects of the analysis. Sources are listed at the end of the chapter, with the references. All URLs were consulted at the end of 2012. Parliamentary debates are identified in the text by the acronym of the proceedings (DAR) and issue date. Quotations have been translated from Portuguese into English.

Portuguese political discourse on the crisis

In recent years the political discourse in Portugal has been dominated by the crisis. The crisis became the first and gradually almost single issue from which every other political option derived.

However, the effects of the crisis were neither initially particularly evident (2007–2008), nor were its impacts expected to open such a crevasse in Portuguese financial, economic, social, and political tissues. The previous political cycle continued and the elections in 2009 confirmed the leadership of the Socialist Party, albeit without a parliamentary majority (CNE, n.d.a). Being a second mandate, the guidelines for governance were very much the same as they had been for the previous years, still within the trend of European integration running ever since accession, but with the strong input of convergence measures as defined for EMU (cf. Governo de Portugal, 2009; República Portuguesa, 2010a). However, difficulties regarding EU issues soon started to emerge, notably the debate on the budgetary deficit and the need to control it by adopting specific measures under 'stability and growth pacts' (internally known as PEC, Programa/Plano de Estabilidade e Crescimento) in line with EU guidelines and negotiated with the EU institutions as a means to face budget imbalance but leading to severe austerity – PEC I, PEC II, PEC III (República Portuguesa, 2010b, 2010c, 2011), and PEC IV (DAR, 24 March 2011). It was the fourth of these plans (i.e. fourth within a period of one year) that culminated in the political crisis: rejected in Parliament by the opposition (DAR, 24 March 2011), it led to the PM's resignation and the call for early elections by the President of the Republic in April 2011 (Presidência da República, 2011b). It was therefore a PM that had already resigned, and despite his previous resistance, who led the call for external intervention by the EU and the IMF in order to avoid the state's financial bankruptcy. The result was a tripartite conditionality agreement (dated 17 May 2011) between the Portuguese Republic, the European Union (European Commission and European Central Bank), and the International Monetary Fund (IMF), thereafter known internally as the 'troika agreement', the official versions of which are written in English (IMF-Governo de Portugal, 2011; EU-Governo de Portugal, 2011).

Subsequent elections, held on 6 June 2011, were therefore strongly conditioned by the inevitability of the agreement's fulfilment. Thus, its guidelines were explicitly integrated in the electoral programme of the right of centre PSD (2011) and the CDS (2011), while the left of centre PS did not mention it explicitly, despite being inevitably compromised by its fulfilment because it had been signed by the PS Prime Minister Socrates, who was once again running for the elections. The agreement was only rejected by parties farther to the left, namely the PCP (2011) and the BE (Bloco de Esquerda 2011). The PSD won the elections (with 108 of the 230 seats in Parliament) and formed a coalition government with the CDS (24 seats) in order to guarantee the support of a stable majority in Parliament (CNE, n.d.b). Since then, internal major political debates have focused on key issues of the financial and economic recovery of the country. The following analysis therefore follows closely the national political agenda since mid-2011, albeit not exhaustively.

National democracy and the conditionality agreement

Since May 2011, Portugal has been living under the conditionality agreements and their follow-up (Governo de Portugal, 2013). The strict necessity to abide by the terms of the agreements became imperative for the government but was accepted also by the main opposition party (the Socialist Party). However, more extreme party standpoints since the beginning of the recession and its growth as a result of austerity have meanwhile led to fairly generalised debates on the agreement, its feasibility, and the eventual necessity of renegotiation. From Parliament (in the many debates on European politics), to commentators in the media, organised civil society interests (cf. CES, 2012b), and to relevant political personalities,[2] many have raised doubts as to the benefits and feasibility of the terms of the memorandum. Even the government has at times not managed to avoid some internal tensions, due to divisive standpoints on the issue inside the coalition, which have then leaked to the media (Bastos and Galrão, 2012). However, the topic not only raises the issue of pragmatic feasibility and success but also calls for the debate on declining sovereignty, the feature identified in the Index of Democracy (*The Economist*, 2012) as crescent external dependency undermining government autonomy.

However, the impacts of conditionality upon sovereignty are internally acknowledged, even by members of the government and its supporting majority. Expressions such as 'loss of financial sovereignty' are used in official discourses. The PM stated in Parliament that 'a country does not lose sovereignty by adopting shared rules with other countries; it loses sovereignty whenever it does not have the

---

2 Individuals such as Mário Soares (*Expresso*, 2012), a former PM and PR, and a leading figure of the accession process, Freitas do Amaral (RTP, 2012a), former minister and PR candidate, and also a strong supporter of European integration, and Adriano Moreira (RTP, 2013), a leading political scientist and former leader of CDS, have put forward in the media serious criticisms of present political options.

sufficient material means for subsisting' (DAR, 13 April 2012: 9). Similarly, in his New Year speech for 2013, the President of the Republic affirmed: 'We must bring state budget into a balanced standpoint and we must reduce external debt. Until we do it, our financial independence will always be limited' (Presidência da República, 2013).

Thus, only utmost necessity provides a rational for the adoption and implementation of the agreements. From the point of view of the government, as expressed both in the PSD's electoral programme and in the government's programme (Governo de Portugal, 2011; PSD, 2011) it is an exceptional situation and one that calls for exceptional measures. The underlying reasons are not only the international crisis but also a major structural imbalance dating back to the origins of Portuguese democracy and which the crisis made unbearable and thus urgent to correct (Governo de Portugal, 2011; PSD, 2011). The previous government was and still is very often blamed for having worsened the problem by increasing the deficit and public debt. When presenting his government programme at the Assembly of the Republic, the PM stated: 'We can no longer choose between solving short-term and long-term problems. ... We now have to cope with both' (DAR, 30 June 2011, p. 11). A similar idea was put forward by the PR in his official 'Communication on financial assistance' in May 2011 (Presidência da República, 2011a).

The Socialist Party stood for a different diagnosis, despite its convergence in supporting the agreement. Its manifesto for the 2011 election emphasised the international crisis as the major reason for the debt crisis and was not explicit in mentioning the memorandum, although it adopted the political objectives contained within it (PS, 2011).

Governmental agents' rhetoric on the crisis, notably the PM, is blunter than had been the discourse of the previous Prime Minister and government. The explanation put forward provides a narrative of the genesis of the crisis that throws responsibilities upon the national community as a whole: the state, but also the people, are said to have expended beyond their 'possibilities' (Governo de Portugal, 2011; PSD, 2011) what creates a sort of collective *guilt*, because an ill-governed democracy is the responsibility of its citizens. To 'redeem' from wrongdoing, the country is thus invited to indulge in *sacrifice* (a word largely used in official discourses), identified with the immediate measures for budget balance recovery and forthcoming structural reforms: 'lack of competitiveness is the responsibility of the states that entered the euro but were not able to correct it' (DAR, 17 December 2011: 34). These measures are presented as carrying a European imprint:

> Macroeconomic adjustment is a grounded bet in the deepening of European integration and in particular in the single currency. This option is a national desideratum. As Europe was central for the transition into democracy, it will now be central in the transition into a more robust economy. (Governo de Portugal, 2011: 22)

The enthusiasm with the deepening integration dates back as far as when the PM was motivated to state in Parliament: 'We can thus introduce formal rules that will truly limit the *arbitrium* of each government' (DAR, 17 December 2011: 13). This was stated as a sequence of the December 2011 European Council meeting and in the context of the debate on the steps taken towards the adoption of the Treaty on Stability Coordination and Governance (TSCG). The same option for deeper economic integration is also expressed by the Socialist Party, although along with claims that different (but underspecified) measures are required, both from the EU and from the national government, for fulfilling a true economic union (DAR, 17 December 2011). By contrast, and on the same occasion, the Communist Party claimed that there was an ongoing process of *sovereignty extortion* (DAR, 17 December 2011: 18). The BE considered that the path chosen for fighting the crisis was creating 'burnt land for democracy' (DAR, 17 December 2011: 23). These arguments have since been repeated many times.

Opposition parties see the external representation of Portugal in the European Council as feeble and biased by asymmetrical intergovernmental negotiation (DAR, 17 December 2011). Their views are also echoed in public opinion, notably in the emergent negative image of a dominant Germany, many times personified in the Chancellor (Cara Chanceler Merkel, n.d.[3]; GMF, 2013). By contrast, the government and the supporting parties try to convey an image of successful negotiation and make efforts to detach the Portuguese case from the Greek case (DAR, 13 April 2012, 26 June 2012, 12 July 2012, 5 October 2012, 15 December 2012). Some flexibility of the government towards public opinion tendencies has been shown, as in the case of the recent debate on the single social tax (Taxa Social Única, TSU) for enterprises, a measure that created strong popular rejection and which the government then withdrew, thus making a case for its autonomous decision capacity, unlike the 'no option' narrative so often put forward (Governo de Portugal, 2012a; DAR, 22 September 2012; 5 October 2012).

The fact that the conditionality agreements touch structural pillars of the socio-economic organisation of the Portuguese state soon led to difficulties with the legal

---

[3] An open letter to the German Chancellor published online and in the media, at the time of her visit to Portugal in 2012, which registered 4226 subscriptions.

pillar of the system: the Constitution. Because some of the measures adopted for the 2012 budget in order to overcome the deficit might have had constitutional implications, the judgement of the Constitutional Court was asked for and some of the decisions for the forthcoming years had to be altered because they breached the constitutional principle of equality (CRP, n.d., Art. 13). However, under Article 282, No. 4 of the Portuguese Constitution, the Court also ruled favourably an exception for the year 2012, given the emergence created by the crisis (Tribunal Constitucional, 2012). The problem may continue to increase, since the fulfilment of some structural changes (as addressed below) may imply constitutional amendments, i.e. changes at the level of the polity.

Governmentalisation and technocratic drift in national governance?

The hypothesis of the governmentalisation and technocratic drift of national governance aims at revealing the ways in which conditionality translates into national decision-making and policy designing. From the point of view of democracy, this is also a question of legitimacy. Unlike recent changes in the composition of governments in other southern European countries (e.g. Italy, and Greece before 2012 general elections), the Portuguese Government's implementation of the troika agreement is the direct result of democratic elections held on 6 June 2011 (CNE, n.d.b) and from the outset has thus had a strong legitimacy to execute it.

However, governance in modern democracies has become more and more dependent on mutual communication between the political institutions and the citizens, promoting both responsiveness and accountability (i.e. taking into consideration the input, the throughput, and the output sides of legitimacy). The PM himself affirmed in Parliament that:

> *no reform will last in a country imposed simply by the force of ballots. It is decisive for those who received the votes that every day they regain trust and legitimacy so that they can execute their mandates.* (DAR, 1 July 2011: 22)

However, bottom-up processes of policymaking may be hindered in the context of conditionality, given the rigidity of the agreements. A closer look at the agents and processes involved is therefore relevant for the debate on democratic legitimacy.

One of the instruments for top-down governance is the claim that the issues being ruled are fairly technical and intricate in nature. In the context of European integration, and particularly EMU, the argument may find some room. A close look into the government's structure and composition (cf. Presidência do

Conselho de Ministros, 2011) yields evidence of the concentration of 'strategic' functions in the State Minister and Minister for Finance. This is emphasised in political discourse, since the Minister for Finance, Vítor Gaspar, has been the focus of much debate, not only for his competences but also for his decisions and background. Being an academician, and a former European Central Bank (ECB) Head of Economic Studies and Head of the Office of Economic Advisers at the European Commission (cf. Governo de Portugal, 2012a), he very much fits the profile of an EU technocrat. He has earned a reputation for being a tough executer of the troika agreement and at the same time a strict follower of a monetarist policy for combating the crisis (cf. his own writings cited in Butin et al., 2010; Gaspar, Smets and Vestin, 2011). He is often presented as a follower of the German Chancellor, and of the German Finance Minister's standpoints on crisis recovery. Although quite unknown internally until his appointment to office, Gaspar has acquired a reputation of being rigorous but has also been the target of severe criticism (e.g. Público, 2012; RTP, 2012b). Internal debates convey the idea that his role in government is so relevant that it outweighs the Prime Minister's role (DAR, 5 October 2012), a relatively young politician with a relatively short curriculum in major politics and in EU politics (cf. Governo de Portugal, 2012b). Although the government rejects this view, the opposition has very often emphasised it, an argument that has been propagated through public opinion formation mechanisms (DAR, 11 November 2011; 26 June 2012; 5 October 2012). Externally, there are signs that Gaspar has a good reputation (*Financial Times*, 2012).

The relations between the national government and the national parliament fall under the regular mechanism of internal democratic control and the scrutiny of the EU institutions, but for the government holding a majority and the Socialist Party standing for the agreement the process is fairly smooth, as described in the section below headed 'Europeanization, party system and pluralism'.

How the government establishes connections with external political entities is also a major question. Not only is the Minister for Finance in regular contact with the Council of Ministers (e.g. Council of Ministers, 2012) – this is also the case for other ministers, but Ecofin and the Eurogroup eventually became more relevant than ever – but also, and foremost, regular assessment of Portuguese progress under the troika agreement is undertaken by EU and IMF delegates (Governo de Portugal, 2013). The visits have had a certain amount of impact internally, especially at the beginning of the external intervention, when the media broadcasted press conferences with the IMF/ECB/EC delegates and questions would be put as if their role was of political decision-makers instead of a technical one (e.g. Público, 2011). Furthermore, forthcoming budget control mechanisms, such as those established in the TSCG, will foster the mechanisms of top-down supervision by the European Commission. The treaty was ratified in Parliament on 13 April 2012 and the prevailing view was that it would foster European economic integration, which is seen as beneficial for the country (DAR, 14 April 2012). However, the PCP and the BE strongly opposed it on the grounds of interference in national affairs.

From the point of view of bottom-up mechanisms measured by means of electoral and subsequent support, the government benefited from a comfortable majority and fairly strong upholding for the changes to be introduced. However, popular support has been falling rapidly, in pace with increased austerity and as doubts on the steps ahead become major (e.g. Eurosondagem, 2012; Magalhães, n.d.). In addition, surveys have highlighted that the Portuguese people's level of trust in EU institutions is higher than its trust in the Portuguese government and parliament (cf. European Commission, 2012; GMF, 2012). For the interpretation of this data, proximity to the national institutions as opposed to distance to the EU institutions should be considered, as proximity eventually results in more informed opinions on measures taken. However, it apparently reproduces the idea conveyed by the majority in government and parliament that virtue lies in the EU institutions rather than at home

Policies

In this section, I present an overview of the adoption of policies, of which the matrices were not internally generated but were made binding by conditionality requirements and of the support and/or opposition they are able to mobilise.

Measures to overcome the budgetary deficit have an immediate impact on the yearly state budget prepared by the government and presented to Parliament. Although harsh, the 2012 budget gained much acquiescence and did not give rise to substantial disagreement, either in Parliament (the PS, the main opposition party, abstained rather than vote against the proposed budget) (DAR, 11 November 2011) or at civil society level (cf. European Commission, 2012; GMF, 2012). However, due to worse results than expected throughout the year 2012, the 2013 budget discussion raised much more concern and many objections. Both budgets implied increased state revenues, mainly by means of taxation (which was substantially increased in 2013) and a diminution of state expenditure. The balance between both parts achieved for 2013 (c.80% versus c.20%) has been the reason for strong arguments, and has been at the root of growing anti-governmental demonstrations and strikes (e.g. CGTP-IN, 2012; Movimento 'Que se lixe a troika', 2012).

However, budget imbalance control is one of the primary targets of both memoranda of understanding; indeed, the perspective of raising taxes and cutting down expenses has been there from the beginning (cf. DAR, 30 June 2011). Eventually, the consequences of the process were not initially as evident in public opinion, and increased recession in association with the government's difficulty in speeding up structural reforms of the state apparatus itself (thus cutting expenditure) put an increased burden upon the revenue side. The tax increase was 'enormous', as the Minister for Finance himself stated in parliament (cf. Negócios, 2012).

Budget debates and the whole problem of the external debt consequently bring to the fore the debate and the necessity for measures concerning economic growth, i.e. the structural dimension ultimately underpinning the crisis and therefore its possible solutions. Structural measures of a liberal and monetarist imprint were included in the troika agreement and in the PSD electoral programme. Change was a keyword with the CDS being more cautious and eventually more attentive to the virtually disruptive effects of major structural change (CDS, 2011; PSD, 2011). However, currently, changes are addressed as structural adjustments, which seems rather euphemistic for the dimension of the alterations underway. The measures include a reduction in state functions (which opened the debate on the social functions of the state, notably health and education, and indirectly the debate on fundamental rights), privatisation of remaining public and semi-public enterprises, and more flexible labour laws, all in all a programme said to be designed for increasing competitiveness, attracting foreign investment, and thus managing to fuel economic growth (Governo de Portugal, 2011; Assembleia da República, 2010, 2011). Some of these measures are already under way, while others have just been started.

Hence, the structural problems of the Portuguese economy are now being widely debated: excessive weight of the public sector, excessive tertiarisation, lack of competitiveness, labour costs, investment, unemployment and youth unemployment, a need to reinforce the internal production of tradeablegoods, and the return to agriculture and industry (cf. DAR, 5 July 2012, 12 July 2012; Governo de Portugal, 2012c, 2012d). Apparently, many of the problems were tolerable until the convergence efforts for living under EMU started. Since then, and with increased intensity under the international crisis, the situation has become unbearable within the patterns of monetary union. Internal debates now focus a lot on the malign effects of European economic integration upon a peripheral country, notably the excessive expansion of trade and services, the excessive investment in the infrastructures and building sectors, and the decline of agriculture. Criticisms also come from people who have been in government (DAR, 12 July 2012, 5 October 2012).

The social implications of major reforms ahead are also a reason for concern. The PM announced from the outset that the Portuguese would have to impoverish. The immediate impact of austerity was recession and rising unemployment. Shrinking the public sector will bring further unemployment. Labour costs are being cut and labour standards lowered through changes in labour law (DAR, 3 September 2011, 12 May 2012). Free health and education services are increasingly put into question. Initially, in January 2012, the government managed to sign an agreement with both the representatives of employers and workers through the Portuguese Economic and Social Council (CES, 2012a) but more recent measures have raised harsh criticism from the same Council regarding the macroeconomic dimensions of the government proposals, notably for the 2013 budget (CES, 2012b).

Utterances expressing doubts about the survival of the 'European social model' (DAR, 5 October 2012), and expressions such as 'social violence' (BE on the 2012 budget) and 'social unsustainability' (Presidência da República, 2013) are now coming to the fore and even dividing the coalition: the CDS-PP being of a more conservative and thus less liberal profile, and the PSD itself, crafted as a willing-to-be social democratic party, made its way to the right of centre but has never been so close to liberal patterns as at present (Bastos and Galrão, 2012). The apparent exception to the ideological toolkit is the 'enormous' raise in taxes, which is nevertheless targeting workers even more than enterprises or profits, and thereby creating recession (DAR, 27 October 2012, 31 October 2012).

In a country of scarce liberal tradition with a long history of state dependency, the whole plan is raising major concerns and growing opposition. Whereas electoral support in 2011 was a vote for deficit reduction and expenditure cuts, the extent and depth of the measures to be taken are now shaking Portuguese society quite profoundly: −3.5% GDP and 15.8% unemployment rate in the third quarter of 2012 (INE, 2012). Although there was some non-partisan mobilisation against austerity almost from the beginning – some of it had started in 2011 with youth demonstrations connected to transnational movements (Geração à rasca, n.d.), along with some trade-unionism mobilisation (CGTP-IN, 2012) – the government sailed through calm waters up until September 2012, when, in preparing the 2013 budget, the PM put forward the proposal for creating the TSU (single social tax), as a way of lowering the fiscal burden upon enterprises by transferring a substantial part of it to the workers. Thereafter, tides of protest erupted (cf. *Jornal de Notícias*, 2012) to the point that the government had to give up the proposal and decide on alternative measures for raising income taxes (cf. DAR, 13 October 2012, 27 October 2012, 31 October 2012). The PR, among others, has highlighted the potential disruptive effect of the austerity measures on internal social cohesion and the need to maintain it while finding a way back to economic growth (Presidência da República, 2013).

However, frequently in parliament, the media, and informal civil society debates, the above-mentioned measures (e.g. prioritising debt service, raising taxes, privatisations, and reduced labour costs) are interpreted as part of a domination strategy of the European centre (identified with Germany, as mentioned above) over peripheral (southern) economies (DAR, 12 July 2012, 5 October 2012, 13 October 2012). The ideological dimension of the best choices for the EU and its member states is therefore a core debate, as addressed below.

Europeanization, party system, and pluralism

> *We must be aware that the financial assistance programme was supported by parties representing 90% of the members of parliament and that elections occurred only a year and a half ago. The country would not tolerate a serious political crisis along with the financial, economic, and social crisis in which it lives.* (Presidência da República, 2013)

The above quote is part of the President of the Republic's New Year address made in 2013. The Portuguese political system endows the President with relevant control powers, since he can dismiss the PM and either appoint a new PM or call for elections (CRP, n.d., Art. 133). In the quote, the PR is therefore making it clear that he is not going to endorse a political crisis (despite some criticisms as to the political options of the current government expressed in the same discourse). In line with previous discourses, he called for internal unity and cohesion and for close cooperation between the parties that supported the memorandum of agreement with the IMF/ECB/EC (i.e. between the parties in government and the main party in the opposition).

In Parliament, where democratic pluralism should be more obvious, the Socialist Party, the main party in opposition, seems to have been caught by the circumstances of the crisis. Bearing a strong responsibility over government options ever since 1986, for being in office several times and especially from 2005 to 2011, the party initially had no option but to embark on the 'there is no alternative' discourse associated with austerity measures. In fact, and despite rhetorical utterances trying to place the party as standing in the opposition, the results of its voting in parliament do not portray fierce opposition: the PS abstained, rather than vote against the 2012 budget approval (DAR, 12 November 2011), and abstained from voting on the censure motions to the government in June and October (DAR, 26 June 2012, 6 October 2012). At present, the PS is being challenged by the government to take part in structural reforms, notably the redesigning of the 'welfare state', eventually with a view to the possible need to amend the Constitution. Whereas left-wing parties firmly stand against austerity and changes in the welfare state, unconditional opposition is far more difficult for the Socialist Party to support, given the contradiction between such standpoints and the party's upholding of the conditionality agreement, where most of the reforms are inscribed. Furthermore, given that social concerns and social policies are part of the matrix of European democratic socialism or social democracy, the situation is awkward and hard to sustain before the electorate.

However, the 'merger' at the centre is a problem that is potentially traceable among other European socialist and social democratic parties gathering in the EP's Party of European Socialists. The monetarist imprint of the EU (and particularly EMU policies) is grounded in treaties and is therefore not an option, also at the national level. Clearly, conditionality agreements, where national capacity for negotiating is undermined by necessity, are being designed in accordance with the same pattern. According to the TSCG, the inscription of the 'golden rule' of the structural deficit limit under constitutional or para-constitutional format is an extension of this rigidity to national core legal instruments. It is sometimes argued that something that is a specific political option (as opposed to other possible options) becomes a sort of technical 'must' (DAR, 13 April 2012). Such a fact undermines political and party pluralism.

From the point of view of the parties, the process abovementioned may in the long run further increase the tendency to a merger at the centre, and eventually lead to redesigning the European political spectrum. In Portugal, remaining social democrats in the PSD, some socialists, some Christian democrats, and even some conservatives share some common opinions in their criticisms of the government's political options (as mentioned above), but this 'group' does not have the consistency of an organised political movement and even less of a party formation process. However, the dividing line may be reinforced between pro- and anti-integration standpoints. The circumstances of the crisis may induce political radicalisation, both on the left and on the right, as 'alternative' programmes to the mainstream EU options. This tendency was present in the most recent election in

Greece (*Athens News*, 2012); it may emerge in Portugal too, underpinned by the Communist Party and the new left BE, but for the time being popular support is not expressive (cf. above-mentioned surveys). Discontent and lack of trust in party politics (cf. European Commission, 2012) may also reinforce non-partisan movements and citizen initiatives, thus enforcing alternative mechanisms to conventional representative democracy.

Hence, Europeanization of party politics, stemming from top-down policies of a supranational level in which pluralism seems to be overwhelmed by bureaucracy, technocracy, and intergovernmental negotiation may be diminishing political options, rather than enlarging them.

Conclusions

The outstanding conclusion is that conditionality undermines national independence and free decision, for reasons of financial dependency and inherent conditions. Although the political guidelines are agreed with the national authorities, they are established externally and the negotiation is inevitably asymmetrical. In the Portuguese case, there is not a problem of formal legitimacy, since the government implementing the measures was the result of general elections and the programme put forward was very much in line with the external agreements. Parties are divided along a line of support versus opposition to the agreement, with parties standing for it being strongly in favour of enhanced economic European integration, even at the expense of limiting national autonomy. The same does not hold true for parties opposing the agreement; on the contrary, their claims are in favour of fostering national sovereignty and autonomous decisions. Given the institutional structure of the EU, the picture is very much one in which the responsibility for political decisions is national, but the overarching options and the design occur elsewhere. It should also be added that despite the change in scale, general orientations of the macroeconomic adjustments agreed with the EU and IMF meet former objectives defined for EMU and laid in the several PECs established in close connection with the EU authorities. From this point of view, current change is not an immediate result of the crisis, but rather the deepening of previous orientations defined in the context of monetary integration, the implementation of which did not work out as expected, on the sole responsibility of the states. The strength and centripetal effect of the process becomes evident, for example in the fact that it clashes with the national constitution and its underlying ideological pattern.

Governmentalisation is a consequence of the above-mentioned process. Top-down measures defined at the EU level then reach the national government and parliament with scarce room for manoeuvre. The technical nature of the core macroeconomic measures associated with economic and monetary integration limits the debate and paves the way for experts and technocrats in a very top-down manner. Besides, under conditionality agreements external agents do have a say in national affairs and this is visible also in the public sphere. Bottom-up mechanisms do not seem to be so intense, but the harshness of the measures under way may push citizens' resilience too far, thus inviting contestation, which has already emerged. Seen from afar, these are standard problems of two-step representative systems and their limits.

The set of policies designed to overcome excessive external debt and budget imbalance is in the first stage the result of financial emergency, but the second stage goes much deeper and draws an entire programme for redesigning the macroeconomic structure of the national economy, according to the guidelines set for EMU at the EU level. From this point of view, it is part of a strong process of Europeanization, for which the financial fragility created a major opportunity. The pattern, leading to a strong reduction of the role of the state, to the lowering of social rights, or to increased liberalisation of the economy, may collide with the Portuguese political regime profile, as designed in the aftermath of the revolution and fixed in the Constitution.

Therefore, the whole process of external intervention also carries an ideological dimension, which should resonate at the level of parliamentary debate. Oddly enough, or perhaps not, parties backing European integration are strongly pushed into a unanimous centre, and left with scarce room for manoeuvre, as is especially evident in the case of the Socialist Party, whose commitment with social and redistributive policies is expected to be major compared to parties on the right. Pluralism is therefore undermined by integration, eventually because the political structure of EU institutions and decision-making is also scarcely competitive, pending dominant intergovernmental arrangements and their technocratic backup.

Does the process increase the peripheral situation of Portugal with reference to core Europe? The political debates resonate with awareness of the peripheral condition of Portugal. However, the government and the underpinning parties present their political action in face of the crisis as an effort to meet EU central patterns, while opponents address it as the result and reinforcement of a structural situation of dependency in relation to the same centre. Whether convergence will occur depends on the success or failure of the ongoing political orientations. Given that strong instruments of Europeanization are at work, in the guise of conditionality, the process seems more centripetal than centrifugal. The effects may be different at political and economic levels: increased centralisation in the case of political levels, which does not mean an increase in democracy but the contrary, and a peripheral existence in the case of economic levels, resulting from the shortcomings of the national economy and, eventually, from the complementary but asymmetric nature of economic interests, as put forward in the framework of the European Union.

References

Primary sources

Assembleia da República (2010), Lei n.ª 3-A/2010. Grandes Opções do Plano para 2010-2013, in *Diário da República*, 1.º série — N. 82 — 28 de Abril de 2010.

Assembleia da República (2011), Lei n.ª 64-A/2011. Grandes opções do Plano para 2012-2015, in *Diário da República*, 1.º série, 1ª suplemento — N. 250 — 30 de Dezembro de 2011.

Athens News (2012), Elections 2012, in *Athens News*, http://www.athensnews.gr/content/55344

Bastos, I. and Galrão, M. (2012), O ano em que o XIX Governo tremeu mas não caiu, in *Económico*, http://mobile.economico.pt/noticias/o-ano-em-que-o-xix-governo-tremeu-mas-nao-caiu_159126.html

Bloco de Esquerda (BE) (2011), Mudar de Futuro. Pelo Emprego e pela Justiça Fiscal, http://www.esquerda.net/sites/default/files/compromisso_eleitoral_0.pdf

Cara Chanceler Merkel (n.d.), blog, http://carachancelermerkel.blogspot.pt/p/blog-page_3739.html

CDS (Centro Democrático e Social) (2011), Este é o Momento. Manifesto Eleitoral 2011. Por ti. Por todos. Portugal, http://www.cdsleiria.org/artigos/media/docs/307.pdf

CES (Conselho Económico e Social) (2012a), Parecer sobre a Proposta de Orçamento do Estado para 2013, http://www.ces.pt/download/1239/Parecer%20sobre%20a%20Proposta_de_OE%202013.pdf

CES (Conselho Económico e Social) (2012b), Compromisso para o Crescimento, Competitividade e Emprego, http://www.ces.pt/download/1022/Compromisso_Assinaturas_versao_final_18Jan2012.pdf

CGTP-IN (2012), CGTP-IN convoca Greve Geral para 14 de Novembro de 2012, http://www.cgtp.pt/trabalho/accao-reivindicativa/5539-cgtp-in-convoca-greve-geral-para-14-de-novembro-de-2012

CNE (Comissão Nacional de Eleições) (n.d.a), Eleições legislativas 2009, http://eleicoes.cne.pt/raster/index.cfm?dia=27&mes=09&ano=2009&eleicao=ar

CNE (Comissão Nacional de Eleições) (n.d.b), Eleições legislativas 2011, http://eleicoes.cne.pt/raster/index.cfm?dia=05&mes=06&ano=2011&eleicao=ar

Council of Ministers (2012), Council recommendation with a view to bringing an end to the situation of an excessive government deficit in Portugal. Brussels, 2 October 2012,

(OR. en) 14238/12 ECOFI 804 UEM 284, http://eurozone.europa.eu/media/826340/council_recommendation_pt_09.10.12.pdf

CRP (Constituição da República Portuguesa) (n.d.), Constitution of the Portuguese Republic Seventh Revision (2005), http://www.parlamento.pt/Legislacao/Documents/Constitution7thRev2010EN.pdf [English translation]

DAR (Diário da Assembleia da República) (n.d.), Diário da Assembleia da República. I Série, http://debates.parlamento.pt/catalog.aspx?cid=r3.dar

EU-Portugal (2011), Attachment 1: Portugal – Memorandum of Understanding on Specific Economic Policy Conditionality, http://www.portugal.gov.pt/media/371369/mou_20110517.pdf

European Commission (2012), Standard Eurobarometer 78, Brussels: European Commission, http://ec.europa.eu/public_opinion/archives/eb/eb78/eb78_anx_en.pdf

Eurosondagem (2012), Barómetro Eurosondagem, http://www.eurosondagem.pt/inform/barometro.htmsurveys

Expresso (2012), Mário Soares diz que PS deve romper com a troika, *Expresso*, 8 May 2012.

FFMS (Fundaçao Francisco Manuel dos Santos) (2012), *Fundaçao*, Pordata, http://www.ffms.pt/Pordata/home/12

Atkins, A., Fray, K., Carnie, K. and Nevitt, C. (2012), Ranking Europe's finance ministers, *Financial Times*, http://www.ft.com/intl/cms/s/0/617b5920-3324-11e2-aabc-00144feabdc0.html#axzz2KJ8CuqUQ

Geração à rasca (n.d.), website, http://www.geracaoarasca.info/

GMF (German Marshall Fund of the United States) (2012), Transatlantic Trends 2012. Country profiles: Portugal, http://trends.gmfus.org/transatlantic-trends/country-profiles-2/portugal/

Governo de Portugal (2009), Programa do XVIII Governo Constitucional, http://www.portugal.gov.pt/media/468569/gc18.pdf

Governo de Portugal (2011), Programa do XIX Governo Constitucional, http://www.portugal.gov.pt/media/130538/programa_gc19.pdf

Governo de Portugal (2012a), Vítor Gaspar. Ministro de Estado. Ministro das Finanças, http://www.portugal.gov.pt/pt/os-ministerios/ministerio-das-financas/conheca-equipa/ministro/vitor-gaspar.aspx

Governo de Portugal (2012b), Pedro Passos Coelho. Primeiro-Ministro, http://www.portugal.gov.pt/pt/o-governo/primeiro-ministro/pedro-passos-coelho.aspx

Governo de Portugal (2012c), Discurso do Primeiro-Ministro no workshop sobre reformas estruturais, 21 January 2012, http://www.portugal.gov.pt/media/428284/20120121_pm_reformas_estruturais.pdf

Governo de Portugal (2012d), Discurso do Primeiro-Ministro no seminário European Ideas Network Centro Jean Monnet – 31 de maio de 2012, http://www.portugal.gov.pt/media/613282/20120531_pm_ue.pdf

Governo de Portugal (2012e), Declaração ao País – 7 setembro 2012, http://www.portugal.gov.pt/pt/o-governo/intervencoes-primeiro-ministro/20120907-pm-declaracao.aspx

Governo de Portugal (2013), Memorandos, http://www.portugal.gov.pt/pt/os-ministerios/primeiro-ministro/secretario-de-estado-adjunto-do-primeiro-ministro/documentos-oficiais/memorandos.aspx

IMF-Portugal (2011), Attachment 1: Portugal—Memorandum of Economic and Financial Policies, http://www.portugal.gov.pt/media/371354/mefp_20110517.pdf

INE (Instituto Nacional de Estatística) (2012), website, http://www.ine.pt/xportal/xmain?xpid=INE&xpgid=ine_main

Jornal de Notícias (2012), Manifestações do 15 de Setembro, Indignação contra a austeridade leva centenas de milhares de portugueses para a rua http://www.jn.pt/Dossies/dossie.aspx?dossier=Manifesta%E7%F5es%20do%2015%20de%20Setembro

Magalhães, P. (n.d.), Margens de erro, blog, http://margensdeerro.blogspot.pt/

Movimento 'Que se lixe a troika' (2012), blog,

Negócios (2012), 'Enorme' aumento de impostos sem fim à vista, 3 October 2012 http://www.jornaldenegocios.pt/economia/detalhe/quotenormequot_aumento_de_impostos_sem_fim_agrave_vista.html

PCP (2011), Compromisso Eleitoral do PCP, http://www.cdu.pt/2011/compromisso-eleitoral-do-pcp-por-uma-pol%C3%ADtica-patri%C3%B3tica-e-de-esquerda

Presidência da República (2011a), Comunicação ao País do Presidente da República sobre a assistência financeira a Portugal, 6 May 2011, http://www.presidencia.pt/?idc=22&idi=53433

Presidência da República (2011b), Decreto do Presidente da República n.ª 44-A/2011, in *Diário da República*, 1.° série, n. 69, 7 de Abril de 2011.

Presidência da República (2013), Mensagem de Ano Novo do Presidente da República. 1 January 2013, http://www.presidencia.pt/?idc=22&idi=70860

Presidência do Conselho de Ministros (2011), Decreto-Lei n.ª 86-A/2011, in *Diário da República*, 1.° série, n. 132, 12 de Julho de 2011.

PS (2011), Programa Eleitoral. 2011-2015, http://www.ps.pt/media/eleicoes2011/Programa-Eleitoral-PS-2011-2015.pdf

PSD (2011), Mudar Portugal: Recuperar a credibilidade e desenvolver Portugal. Programa Eleitoral, http://www.psd.pt/archive/doc/PROGRAMA_ELEITORAL_PSD_2011_0.pdf

Público (2011), Presidente do BPI pede fim das conferências de imprensa da *troika*. 17 November 2011, http://www.publico.pt/economia/noticia/presidente-do-bpi-pede-fim-das-conferencias-de-imprensa-da-troika-1521353

Público (2012), Sondagem: Maioria dos portugueses quer Vítor Gaspar fora do Governo, 13 October 2012, http://www.publico.pt/politica/noticia/maioria-dos-portugueses-nao-cre-que-o-governo-acabe-a-legislatura-1567195

República Portuguesa (2010a), Grandes Opções do Plano. 2010-2013, Ministério das Finanças e da Administração Pública, http://www.parlamento.pt/OrcamentoEstado/Documents/gop/GOP_2010-2013_VF.pdf

República Portuguesa (2010b), Programa de Estabilidade e Crescimento. 2010-2013, http://www.parlamento.pt/OrcamentoEstado/Documents/pec/PEC2010_2013.pdf

República Portuguesa (2010c), Programa de Estabilidade e Crescimento. 2010-2013, http://www.parlamento.pt/OrcamentoEstado/Documents/pec/PEC2010_2013_18mar2010_VFA.PDF

República Portuguesa (2011), Programa de Estabilidade e Crescimento. 2011-2014, http://www.parlamento.pt/OrcamentoEstado/Documents/pec/21032011PEC2011_2014.pdf

RTP (2012a), Freitas do Amaral diz que receita da troika não é boa, 6 September 2012, http://www.rtp.pt/noticias/index.php?article=584859&layout=122&tm=9&visual=61

RTP (2012b), Sondagem indica que Vítor Gaspar é considerado o ministro com melhor desempenho, 5 June 2012, http://www.rtp.pt/noticias/index.php?article=560102&tm=9&layout=122&visual=61

RTP (2013), Entrevista a Adriano Moreira, 11 January 2013, http://www.rtp.pt/antena1/index.php?t=Entrevista-a-Adriano-Moreira.rtp&article=6025&visual=11&tm=16&headline=13

The Economist (2012), The Economist Intelligence Unit's Index of Democracy 2011, www.eiu.com

Tribunal Constitucional (2012), Acórdão do Tribunal Constitucional n.ª 353/2012, in *Diário da República*, 1.º série, n. 140, 20 de Julho de 2012.

Literature

Almond, G. and Verba, S. (1963), *The Civic Cuture. Political Attitudes and Democracy in Five Nations*, London: Sage.

Assembleia da República (2001), *Adesão de Portugal às Comunidades Europeias. História e Documentos*, Lisboa: Assembleia da República.

Bekkers, V. and Edwards, A. (2007), 'Legitimacy and democracy: A conceptual framework for assessing governance practices', in V. Bekkers, G. Dijkstra, A. Edwards, M. Fenger (eds.), *Governance and the Democratic Deficit*, Aldershot: Ashgate, pp. 35–60.

Butin, M. et al. (eds.) (2010), *The Euro: The First Decade*, Cambridge: Cambridge University Press.

Cameron, F. (ed.) (2004), *The Future of Europe: Integration and Enlargement*, London: Routledge.

Europeias, Lisboa: Instituto Diplomático, Ministério dos Negócios Estrangeiros.

Dahl, R. (1998), *On Democracy*, New Haven: Yale University Press.

Diamond, L. and Morlino, L. (2004), 'The quality of democracy: An overview', in *Journal of Democracy*, Vol. 15, No. 4, pp. 20–31.

Featherstone, K. and Radaelli, C. (eds.) (2003), *The Politics of Europeanization*, Oxford: Oxford University Press.

Freire, A., Magalhães, P. and Lobo, M. (2007), *Comportamento Eleitoral e Atitudes Políticas dos Portugueses: Eleições e Cultura Política*, Lisboa: ICS.

Gaspar, V., Smets, F. and Vestin, D. (2011), 'Inflation expectations, adaptive learning and optimal monetary policy', in B. Friedman and M. Woodford (eds.), *Handbook of Monetary Economics*, Vol. 3B, Amsterdam: Elsevier-North-Holland, pp. 1055–1095.

Graziano, P. and Vink, M. (eds.) (2008), *Europeanization: New Research Agendas*, Basingstoke: Palgrave Macmillan.

Jalali, C. (2007), *Partidos e Democracia em Portugal. 1974–2005*, Lisboa: ICS.

Landman, T. (2008), *Assessing the Quality of Democracy: An Overview of the International IDEA Framework*, Stockholm: IDEA.

Lisi, M. (2011), *Os Partidos Políticos em Portugal: Continuidade e Transformação*, Coimbra: Almedina.

Magone, J. (2005), 'As atitudes dos cidadãos da Europa do Sul para com a integração europeia: antes e depois da adesão (1974–2000)', in A. Pinto and N. Teixeira (eds.), *A Europa do Sul e a Construção da União Europeia: 1945-2000*, Lisboa: ICS, pp. 175–196.

Martins, V. (2000), 'Creating the internal market', in A. Vasconcelos and M.J. Seabra (eds.), *Portugal: A European Story*, Lisboa: IEEI-Principia, pp. 89–98.

Maxwell, K. (1997), *The Making of the Portuguese Democracy*, Cambridge: Cambridge University Press.

Mota, I. (2000), 'Application of structural funds', in A. Vasconcelos and M.J. Seabra (eds.), *Portugal. A European Story*. Lisboa: IEEI-Principia, pp. 131–152.

Moury, C. and Sousa, L. (2010), 'O posicionamento dos deputados e dos eleitores face à Europa: o caso de Portugal', in A. Freire and J. Viegas (eds.), *Representação Política. O Caso Português em Perspectiva Comparada*, Lisboa: Sextante, pp. 289–316.

Pinto, A. (2000), 'European integration of Portuguese agriculture', in A. Vasconcelos and M.J. Seabra, *Portugal. A European Story*, Lisboa: IEEI-Principia, pp. 153–163.

Pinto, A. and Teixeira, N. (eds.) (2005), *A Europa do Sul e a cconstrução da União Europeia: 1945–2000*, Lisboa: ICS.

Ramos, C. and Vila Maior, P. (2011), 'Ideas of Europe in Portuguese political discourse', in C. Ramos (ed.), *Ideas of Europe in National Political Discourse*, Bologna: Il Mulino, pp. 167–198.

Rato, V. (2001), 'A Aliança Atlântica e a Consolidação da Democracia' in J. Ferreira (ed.), *Política Externa e Política de Defesa do Portugal Democrático*, Lisboa: Ed. Colibri.

Rosas, F. (ed.) (1999), *Portugal e a Transição para a Democracia (1974–1976)*, Lisboa: Ed. Colibri.

Royo, S. (ed.) (2005), *Portugal, Espanha e a Integração Europeia: Um Balanço*, Lisboa: ICS.

Santos, B. (1985) 'Estado e sociedade na semiperiferia do sistema mundial: o caso português', in *Análise Social*, Vol. XXI, Nos. 3–5, pp. 869–901.

Santos, B. (1990), *O Estado e a Sociedade em Portugal (1974–1988)*, Porto: Ed. Afrontamento.

Schmidt, V. (2006), *Democracy in Europe: The EU and National Polities*, Oxford: Oxford University Press.

Schmitter, P. (1999), *Portugal: do Autoritarismo à Democracia*, Lisboa: ICS.

Silva, J. and Miranda, J. (2007), *Constituição da República Portuguesa*, 5th ed., Cascais: Principia.

Vallera, J. (2000), 'The negotiating process', in A. Vasconcelos and M.J. Seabra (eds.), *Portugal: A European Story*, Lisboa: IEEI-Principia, pp. 57–78.

Vasconcelos, A. (2000), 'Portugal: The European way', in A. Vasconcelos and M.J. Seabra (eds.), *Portugal. A European Story*, Lisboa: IEEI-Principia, pp. 11–38.

Vasconcelos, A. and Seabra, M.J. (eds.) (2000), *Portugal. A European Story*, Lisboa: IEEI-Principia.

Viegas, J. and Freire, A. (2010), *Representação Política: O Caso Português em Perspectiva Comparada*, Lisboa: Sextante Ed.

Vila Maior, P. and Ramos, C. (2012), 'Mapping European integration in Portuguese political science' In F. Bindi and K. Eliassen (eds.), *Analyzing European Union Politics*, Bologna: Il Mulino, pp. 435–464.

Vilaça, J.L. (2000), 'Portugal and European integration – negotiations and legal implications', in A. Vasconcelos and M.J. Seabra (eds.), *Portugal: A European Story*, Lisboa: IEEI-Principia, pp. 79–87.

EU membership and the question of Hungary's sovereignty: Ideas of the European Union before and following the crisis

Anna Molnár

This chapter examines standpoints of Hungarian political parties and public opinion on the European Union (EU) in the light of the economic, financial, and political crisis. A separate section on historical background sets the stage, and is followed by a section that focuses on the difficulties of the transition process to a functioning constitutional democracy and market economy using the conceptual framework provided by Dahrendorf (1990). Turning to Hungary's accession to the European Union, the chapter identifies, on the basis of sources that include opinion polls, documents, and speeches of Hungarian politicians and political parties, the stances of political parties on European integration. Last but not least, the chapter introduces the case of the debate between the Hungarian Government and the institutions of the European Union concerning the political situation and the quality of democracy in Hungary following the 2010 general elections.

The ongoing financial, economic, and political crisis has become the main element of the political debates and discourses among the Hungarian political parties. Due to the worsening economic and social situation and the decrease in trust in democracy in Hungary, Euro-scepticism is still on the rise, both within political parties and among the general public. On political level, hard Euro-scepticism is represented by the party Jobbik. The debate on the Hungarian political changes demonstrates clearly the standpoint of the ruling Hungarian government regarding the European Union, which can be defined as a soft Euro-scepticism based on national sovereignty. While the government sometimes uses a militant rhetoric, it has nevertheless supported the main elements of the deepening process of the EU. The Hungarian case also illustrates the creation of a European political space, in which domestic political affairs have become European ones, causing several heated debates among European politicians in different institutions of the EU. The chapter concludes that the idea of Hungary as semiperipheral or peripheral has gained ground after the country's accession to the EU.

The historical background

During the Cold War, Hungary did not have the possibility of creating normalised economic and political contacts with the European Economic Community (EEC) and its member states. In the 1980s the bipolar word started to disintegrate and Hungary introduced economic reforms and established more trade contacts with Western countries. In 1982 it became a member of the International Monetary Fund (IMF), fulfilling the part of a certain bridge between the two political and economic systems. After the Joint Declaration of Mutual Recognition between the Council for Mutual Economic Assistance (CMEA) and the European Communities (EC) in 1988, Hungary became in November of that year the first country of the CMEA to have a general agreement on commerce, trade, and co-operation with the EEC, abolishing different quantitative restrictions on Hungarian exports to the EEC (Tatham, 2009: 75). Another very important step from a centrally planned economy to a market economy was the introduction of a radical tax reform in 1987 (Council Decision, 1988).[1]

Between 1987 and 1990, following the formation of new political parties (e.g. Fidesz – the Alliance of Young Democrats) and the reformation of old political parties (e.g. Hungarian Social Democratic Party (HSDP)), Hungary's transition to liberal democracy, the so called regime change was completed. With the emendation of the constitution negotiated during the trilateral National Roundtable Talks of 1989 between the three sides (the Opposition Roundtable, the MSZMP (Hungarian Socialist Worker's Party – the communist party), and the "Third Side" (satellite organizations of the MSZMP)), political reforms were introduced in, for example, political pluralism, freedom of association, freedom of press, freedom of assembly, freedom of trade unions, and a democratic electoral system.

Alongside the introduction of liberal democratic institutions, Hungary strove to become an integral part of the Euro-Atlantic co-operation system. In 1990 the country became a member of the Council of Europe, in 1995 it entered the OECD, in 1996 the WTO, in 1999 it entered NATO, and in 2004 it became a member of

---

[1] Hungary was the first country among the former communist countries to introduce VAT (value added tax) and PIT (personal income tax) creating a special hybrid economic system between capitalism and communism.

the EU. Following the collapse of the communist regimes in Eastern Europe, the European Union was still not ready to realise the process of the eastern enlargement, but in 1989 the EU assistance project, the PHARE programme (Pologne, Hongrie – Aide à la Reconstruction Économique) was launched to help Eastern European political and economic reforms. The project was originally created to help the reconstruction of the economies of Hungary and Poland (Kormany.hu, n.d.a). Later, it became the main financial instrument for the pre-accession process of the Central and Eastern European countries.

The political and economic transition as well as the process of preparing for membership brought about the establishment of democratic political institutions. Within a short time, Hungary fulfilled the major political goals of the peaceful change of regime: political and human rights were expanded. As Timothy Garton Ash states, there was a process of '*refolution*' in Hungary:

Even in Poland and Hungary, what was happening could still hardly be described as revolution. It was in fact, a mixture of reform and revolution. At the time, I called it refolution. There was a strong essential element of change from above, led by an enlightened minority in the still ruling communist parties. But there was also a vital element of popular pressure from below. The story was that of an interaction between the two. The interaction was, however, largely mediated by negotiations between ruling and opposition elites. There were changes with revolutionary significance, a peaceful change of regime, without social pressure, but with the support of the society; that's why it was a 'Refolution'. (Ash, 1990: 14)

Following the collapse of the bipolar world, the potential EC/EU membership became the modernisation symbol of a possibly prosperous, democratic, and European Hungary. In the period of the collapse of the socialist state, the primary goal of the main Hungarian political parties was immediate accession to the European Union – a goal that was reflected in the slogan 'Back to Europe!' As Hungary had a special experience of liberalisation in economic and political fields (naturally only to a limited extent) in the 1980s, it was considered the country in the region of Central and Eastern Europe that was best prepared to join the EC/EU.

In 1989, Hungary had a very important role in the demolition of the Iron Curtain. The following was written in *Der Spiegel* 20 years later:

> There had been signs of Hungary's quiet departure from the camp of the Warsaw Pact states for years. But neither Hungary's allies nor the NATO countries took these signals seriously. Even in the summer of 1989, there still seemed to be too many factors standing in the way of a change in the post-war order. For one thing, Russian troops were still stationed in Hungary. The rest of the world was not truly convinced of the changes until August 19, 1989, when hundreds of East Germans, more or less unobstructed, slipped into the West through a rickety wooden gate near Sopron. It was the beginning of the end of East Germany. Roughly three weeks later, more than 10,000 East German citizens travelled to West Germany through Austria – legally, by this time.
>
> It was in Hungary where the first stone was removed from the Berlin Wall, then-German Chancellor Helmut Kohl reminded his fellow Germans when he spoke in Berlin on Oct. 4, 1990, the day after German reunification. And Hungary ... gave the regime of East German leader Erich Honecker the decisive push by opening the gates to the West for tens of thousands of East German refugees. (Mayr, 2009)

In 1990 the first freely elected Hungarian government soon declared its intention to join the European Communities. The first step of this long process, that is the Free Trade Agreement on Association between the European Communities and Hungary (Europe Agreement) was signed on 16 December 1991 and the association agreement came into force on 1 February 1994, and thus Hungary's preparations for her future EU accession had been started. The aim of the Europe Agreement was primarily the creation of a free trade area for industrial products, and secondarily the establishment of mutual preferences for agricultural products, the gradual liberalisation of the flow of capital, services, and labour, and the political dialogue.[2] This new commercial and trade framework created a market situation of hard competition for Hungarian business actors.

The difficulties of transition to constitutional democracy

In Hungary, just as in the case of other Central and Eastern European countries, the transition to liberal democracy implied the elimination of several burdens of its century-long political traditions. István Bibó, the famous Hungarian political thinker, called this 'the deformed political character of East-European countries'

---

[2] The history of Hungarian EU membership, http://eu.kormany.hu/the-history-of-hungarian-eu-membership

(Bibó, 1986: 226). Bibó referred to the lack of balance between desires and reality, emphasising that the nations in the region had become accustomed to posing unreasonable requirements, and that instead political activity was based on desires of possibilities that from time to time led to populism.

In 1990, Ralf Dahrendorf wrote that constitutional democracy is built in three stages. According to him the first stage is the drafting and establishment of a new constitution based on the basic values of fundamental rights, the rule of law, and separation of powers. He called this period 'the hour of the lawyers'. The second stage is the creation of a market economy (introducing antimonopolism, economic rivalry, and free competition). The last stage is the establishment of civil society (the building of substantial sources of power outside the state, a network of autonomous institutions and organizations that can not be eliminated by a monopolistic state or party authority). According to Dahrendorf, the first stage might last 6 months, the second 6 years, and the third 60 years (Dahrendorf, 1990: 86).

In the case of Hungary, the duration of the first two stages was not underestimated. The former Soviet-style Hungarian Constitution (Act XX of 1949), which was adopted by Parliament in 1949 and amended many times between 1949 and 1989, was based on the model of the 1936 Soviet Constitution (kormany.hu, nd). Although this constitution was changed fundamentally and radically during the symbolic year of 1989, its name remained 'Act XX of 1949', and this fact created space for a never-ending debate on the constitution among politicians and in the general public. In 1989, during the transition period, a fully new constitution was not elaborated but was just modified, due to the highly fragile and uncertain political situation in the country. One of the main factors of fragility was the fact that Soviet troops were still stationed in Hungary.

Regarding the second stage in the building of constitutional democracy, there were several steps in the creation of market economy, but the most important among them was the speedy privatisation process. In 1990 the State Privatization Agency was established and in 1990 the first Pre-Privatization Law (Act No. LXXIV of 1990) was adopted. It was followed in 1995 by the adoption of a new privatization law: Realisation of Entrepreneurial Property in State Ownership (Act XXXIX of 1995). In 1992, the proportion of private ownership in Hungary was 40%. In 1996, following the new legislation, it reached the level of 75% during the socialist-liberal governing coalition (1994–1998). In 2008 the proportion of private ownership was 90% (Pénzügminisztérium, 1997). In Hungarian society there is a widespread opinion that the rapid privatisation of the different sectors of the Hungarian economy was a basic condition to receive financial aid in order to avoid an even deeper financial crisis during the 1990s. Although this highly controversial process was successful, as it created the bases of the modern Hungarian economy, it is still the major element of political debates because of the high level of corruption accompanying the process (Mihályi, 2010, Vol. II: 142–191).

Péter Mihályi emphasises that the foreign currency revenues from privatisation were quite high in Hungary compared to similar countries. Between 1990 and 2007 the revenues (i.e. from combined HUF and foreign currency receipts) from privatisation amounted to EUR 12.5 billion. Mihályi underlined that it was a considerable sum, yet it was not a very large amount compared with the bailout (EUR 20 billion) received from the EU, IMF, and the World Bank in 2008 (Mihályi, 2010, Vol. II: 212). The most important result of the privatisation process was that it had created the basic conditions to develop a stable and efficient market economy in Hungary. However, the economic reforms during the transition period created serious social and economic problems, and the society had to face the new reality of uncertainty created by high levels of inflation and growing unemployment.

With regard to the third stage of the construction of constitutional democracy, there is still a question as to whether Dahrendorf has overestimated the required period (60 years) to create a real framework of civil society in post-communist countries. Following the transition period, in common with other countries in the region of Central and Eastern Europe, Hungary had to face numerous problems, such as:

- the lack of democratic traditions and market economy
- a political elite without democratic experiences
- weakness for interest representation at the EU level
- a weak civil society
- ethnic intolerance
- low turn-out at political elections
- a general political apathy
- lack of pragmatism
- reinforcement of populism
- a low GDP per capita (below one-third of the EU average before the EU accession)

As for Hungarian civil society, one illustration of its weakness is the proportion of membership in civil organisations. According to data published by the EU in its Eurobarometer surveys results in 2004, 55% of the respondents in EU27 were not a member of a civil organisation (compared to 49% in EU15 and 72% in EU10); however, the proportion of civil participation was much worse in Hungary, where 79% of the respondents did not belong to a civil organisation (Füzér, Gerő, and Sík, 2005: 14–15; Eurobarometer, 2004a: 146) Civil society, in filling of the space between the individuals and the state, potentially plays a central role in strengthening democratic institutions and promoting the creation of the conditions of a working system of checks and balances. According to Putnam, a high level of civic mindedness and civic participation in a society supports the working democracy, the functioning of society and facilitates economic exchange (Eurobarometer, 2004a: 143).

Hungary joins the EU

Hungary submitted its official application for EU membership in 1994, and accession negotiations started on 31 March 1998. In order to become part of the EU, as a European State (Article 49 of the EU Treaty), it had to fulfil the conditions known as the Copenhagen criteria:

- be a stable democracy
- have a working market economy
- adopt the common rules, standards, and policies that make up the body of EU law (*acquis communautaire*)

Given that the conditions had been fulfilled, Hungary became a member of the European Union on 1 May 2004. Not only did the internal factors have an important impact on the prolongation of the accession process. External factors, such as the reunification of Germany (the country most involved in the enlargement process) in 1990, the great extension of the *acquis communautaire* (for institutional reasons), the deepening process of integration (from the Treaty of Maastricht to the Treaty of Nice), the 1995 enlargement (to include Austria, Finland, and Sweden), the creation of the European Economic Area, the crisis of the area covered by the European Monetary System (EMS) (especially in Italy), and the economic recession of the Southern and Western European countries from the 1990s onwards all created more complex circumstances for the accession negotiations, in contrast to the Iberian enlargement. After the 1991 collapse of the Soviet Union there was no real risk involved in accelerating the accession process of Central and Eastern Europe. However, the Central and Eastern European countries were still in an economic and political transition process, with a low GDP per capita. Last but not least, the war in Yugoslavia, which was a real security challenge to the whole European Union and to its single member states, had to be taken into account.

Following the collapse of the communist regime, the image of Europe was determined by the economic and political expectations of the Hungarian citizens. In the referendum held on the issue of EU membership (2003), the turnout was 45.6%, and 83.76% of the voters said 'Yes'.[3] Thus, despite a relatively low level of participation, a high percentage of the Hungarian population voted in favour of the accession to the EU. According to Sükösd, the reason for the low turnout might have been the lack of genuine debate in the political sphere, as there had been no serious arguments for or against the accession of Hungary, and this had led to a staggeringly low level of interest in European issues. The communication campaign started abruptly, and rather late, which also contributed to the communication deficit (Sükösd, 2003). In 2005, a Hungarian poll was carried out to examine what Hungarians thought about the EU membership and its local consequences. The results were similar to other opinion polls of the period: 75% of the subjects were in favour of Hungarian membership, and 25% were against it (Kormány, 2006: 89).

According to Marján, the real challenge for all new members of the EU is hidden in the process of convergence to EU average income. Based on the experience of the Southern European countries, it could take several decades to be rid of the differences between the incomes. The process of convergence is even more difficult for the Central and Eastern European countries, partly because of a more handicapped start (until 1989 lack of experience in the functioning of market economy and democracy), partly because of the decreasing resources available in the EU (Marján, 2006).

Although the political democratisation and consolidation of the country was formally completed, in 2008 József Juhász and Péter Tálas, both of whom are experts on security policies, suggested that this process and the Europeanization of Hungary had only partially taken place, even at the institutional level, since corruption, lack of transparency, and unaccountability were still characteristic features of the Hungarian institutional culture. For Hungary, in common with the other countries in the region of Central and Eastern Europe, there was no alternative to accession, and this helped the country to move from the centre of European peripheries to the periphery of the European centre. Hungary missed the organic development of the integration process. The country had to make up for this within

---

3   Czech Republic: turnout 55.21%, 'Yes' vote 77.33%; Poland: turnout 58.85%, 'Yes' vote 77.45%; and Slovakia: turnout 52.15%, 'Yes' vote 92.46%.

14 years, and this has resulted in many traumatic experiences (Juhász and Tálas, 2008).

In Hungary the process of Europeanization is highly dependent on the question of national identity and in turn sovereignty is closely connected to some issues of the Treaty of Trianon,[4] which still has to be digested, discussed, and verbalised by Hungarian society. All stages of elaboration have to be experienced. The biggest problem is that the issue of losing territories with Hungarian population was a taboo subject, swept under the carpet during the communist era. The historian Ablonczy mentions the fact that the trauma caused by the Treaty of Trianon has not yet been digested by the nation (Ablonczy, 2010). In an interview, he said Hungarians are not yet over the 'mourning work'. He also pointed to the fact that the idea of revision has been overcome by history, and in uniting Europe in the 21st century politicians have the primary goal to mobilise all the vast human energies for positive goals, and in a civilised manner (Ablonczy, 2010).

Political parties' standpoint on the EU

Hungary's first free election campaign

During the first free election campaign in 1990 there was a common agreement among the political parties that the most important foreign policy goal was early membership of the EU for Hungary. There was only one anti-European political party: the communist Workers' Party, the smaller of the two successor parties to the Hungarian Socialist Workers' Party, which was an extra-parliamentary movement following the first free elections. Apart from this movement, all the mainstream parties formed during the period of peaceful transition in the period 1987–1989 were pro-European, but some differences can be identified in their political goals regarding EU membership and integration.

Left-wing parties

The Hungarian Social Democratic Party (HSDP) and the Hungarian Socialist Party (HSP, the main successor party to the Hungarian Socialist Workers' Party) emphasised concentration on *welfare issues, social democratic aspects,* and a *supra-*

---

[4] The Treaty of Trianon was a peace agreement signed in 1920 by Hungary and the Allied Powers, concluding World War I. Hungary lost two-thirds of her territory and half of her population (one-third of her ethnic-Hungarian population).

national federalist vision of integration. As a consequence of the 1990 electoral failure of the HSDP, the traditional social democratic party was not able to form a parliamentary party. Following the transitory period, from 1991 the socialist party (the larger of the two successor parties to the Hungarian Socialist Workers' Party) became the most important mainstream party, and by 1993 had transformed into a centre-left party of a 'social democrat' or 'social liberal' kind. As a testimony of its pro-European attitude, the HSP frequently called the attention of the Western European public and politicians to the very important role of Gyula Horn, the former Minister of Foreign Affairs, in the German unification (Navracsics, 1997: 10-11). The pro-EU left-wing actors (e.g. HSP and the Alliance of Free Democrats (AFD)), have considered the accession as an *anti-nationalistic* and *modernisation project*. These parties have emphasised the *economic advantages* of membership, and the *finalisation of the change of the regime*.

The liberals

The AFD and Fidesz (Alliance of Young Democrats), concentrated on the *neoliberal, capitalist approach* of the European economy based on *free-trade principles*. For the liberals, EU membership was the only way to *modernise* the country. After a short transitory period the two liberal parties sharing similar visions concerning the EU went in two different political directions: the AFD, in becoming an authentic social-liberal party, started to concentrate on the social democratic aspect of the EU, while Fidesz moved towards a more conservative interpretation of Europe, defining itself as a liberal conservative party (Navracsics, 1997: 12).

Conservative parties

Conservatives focused on the *political aspects* of European integration based on the *conception of a Europe of nations*. The Hungarian Democratic Forum (HDF), the Independent Smallholders' Party (ISP), and the Christian Democratic People's Party, defined Europe by its *cultural aspects*, emphasising that Hungary was an organic part of the West, but 'it was violently isolated from its natural environment for forty years' (Navracsics, 1997: 13). Thus, their political slogan was not 'the road to Europe', but *return to Europe*.

The European Parliament election campaigns in 2004 and 2009

EP elections, treaty processes, and EU presidencies are the occasions when EU issues increasingly emerge in the press and in national parliaments. Examination of the reasons for the low level of participation in the 2004 EP elections proved that political parties dealt with EU issues in a superficial and infrequent manner. At the same time, the interest in domestic affairs received priority from both voters and politicians. A 2004 Eurobarometer poll on the attitudes in the candidate countries showed that nearly two-thirds of the population wanted their country's campaign to focus on domestic issues, primarily on agriculture (Eurobarometer, 2004b). The least important question was the one of EU institutional reforms (Enyedi, 2006: 257–260).

Although Fidesz represented a soft version of Euro-scepticism, the party remained convinced of the need for accession. In the party campaigns for the 2004 European Parliamentary elections, Fidesz drafted a long document on their viewpoints concerning the EU, thus exhibiting more interest in the European issues than exhibited by any other party. By contrast, the most pro-EU AFD wasted hardly a word on the topic in their Liberal Charter. The socialist idea of a common list of Hungarian representatives (with all different parties included) was received as wholly unacceptable by all other parties (Enyedi, 2006: 254–256).

In the Hungarian campaign prior to the 2009 EP elections, the election programmes of the mainstream parties concentrated on domestic issues. They therefore formed part of a trend that characterised the majority of EU members. The campaign of the European People's Party contained more issues concerning market liberalisation, less environmental control, and stricter immigration policy, while the Party of European Socialists in their campaign focused rather on stricter environmental requirements, more serious labour regulations and a more liberal immigration policy. The fact that these campaign programmes were not available in the Hungarian language on the Hungarian parties' web pages shows a very important element of the communication deficit at the national level.

In the 2009 EP elections, voters in Hungary could choose from the programmes of eight different parties, and in Parliament the programmes of the four parliamentary parties were introduced (EUvonal, 2009). Hungary's Minister of Foreign Affairs Kinga Göncz, in her presentation of the Socialist Party's programme, emphasised that although the European campaign was dominated by domestic policy issues, it was important for potential EP members to focus on European matters too. In her view, the task of EP representatives was to help Hungary benefit from membership through the representation of Hungarian interests. The HSP

EP programme included the necessity of maintaining employment possibilities, the improvement of small and medium-sized enterprises (SMEs), crisis management based on solidarity, maintaining the achievements of a social Europe, the shaping of a liveable environment, the creation of cross-border health-care services, and the establishment of a minority-friendly Europe (HSP, 2009). As a consequence of the numerous Hungarian minorities living in the neighbouring countries, Hungary has always been interested in the accession of these countries.

The EP programme of Fidesz (Fidesz, 2009) was presented by Pál Schmidt, head of the party EP list. He underlined the necessity of Hungary's development being further supported by the EU through the Structural Funds. In addition, Schmidt emphasised the need to strengthen the public service function of the media in order to inform the public about the EP members' work. Further, he emphasised that the priority role of Hungary in the region had been lost and needed to be re-established (EUvonal, 2009).

István Szent-Iványi, in the name of the Liberal Party (AFD) (EUvonal, 2009) expressed the social message of the party centred on the termination of hatred. At the centre of the AFD political programme stood the four fundamental freedoms, namely the free movement of goods, capital, services, and persons, and, as a fifth freedom, the free movement of knowledge in the EU (AFD, 2009). Szent-Iványi stressed that only the AFD programme was in harmony with that of its own political EP party family (ELDR).

The person at the top of the MDF (Magyar Demokrata Fórum, Hungarian Democratic Forum) party-list, Lajos Bokros, claimed that in the EP the Hungarian representation should serve the interests of Hungary. According to him, the common agricultural policy was not sustainable because it did not serve global efficiency and solidarity. Besides these weaknesses, he mentioned ten further fields, among them the importance of environmental protection, the expansion of the labour market, and the further enlargement of the EU (EUvonal, 2009).

Several press publications dealt with the EU parliamentary elections. Political scientist Ádám Kégler stressed in his article that voters generally evaluate the work of their national governments in the run-up to elections, and thus mostly the opposition parties receive the majority of votes. The campaigns tend to focus on internal issues rather than genuine European problems (Kégler, 2004).

At the EP elections of 4–7 June 2009 the turnout in Hungary was 36.2%, which was a fall from 38.5% in the 2004 elections. Four of the participating eight parties gained over 5% of the votes. The elections resulted in a sweeping right-wing victory, with 75% of the total votes being won by the three rightist parties. The central right Fidesz-KDNP coalition won 56.37%, the MDF received 5.3%, while Jobbik (still not in Parliament) received 14.77%. At the same time, the governing Socialist Party received only 17.38% of the total votes. The other party of the governing coalition, the AFD, did not even receive enough votes to secure a place in the EP. Despite all this, it is worth noting that it was mostly the 'protest' votes that played a decisive role at the EP elections.

The 2009 European Parliamentary elections showed a relatively low level of interest in integration among Hungarians. The reason for the lack of participation might have been the low level of involvement of the society in the debate on the accession to the EU by the government and consequently a lack of information among the people about the EU's institutions and their operations.

Although the mainstream parties (including Fidesz) supported the reform process of EU institutions regarding the EU Constitutional Treaty (signed in 2004 and then rejected in 2005 by two referenda) and the Treaty of Lisbon that came into force in 2009, the lack of real debate about the future of the Union was also reflected in the mainly superficial but supportive speeches in Parliament concerning the EU Constitutional Treaty. It should be emphasised that Hungary had ratified the Constitutional Treaty and wanted to see it implemented. After the failure of the EU Constitution, Hungarian politicians of the mainstream political parties continued to support the idea of creating a new treaty containing the major elements of the EU Constitutional Treaty. It is worth mentioning that during the entire reform process of EU institutions, all parliamentary parties in Hungary were pro-European. Hungary was the first member state to ratify the Lisbon Treaty, and all parliamentary parties supported the Lisbon Treaty unanimously during the ratification process.

2010: changing political landscape and debate on the political changes

Since the general elections of 2010, the Hungarian political landscape has changed due to the high level of protest votes: Fidesz received a more than two-thirds majority in Parliament, the socialists lost their political support, Jobbik became the third main party in the country, the two more important parties of the transition period, namely the liberals (AFD) and the MDF disappeared, and last but not least the LMP (Lehet Más a Politika, 'Politics Can Be Different'), a new green and an anti-corruption party, entered Parliament.

The Fidesz-KDNP coalition received 53% of the votes and 68% of the seats in Parliament, which enabled it to pass the new Hungarian constitution even without the vote of the opposition and the significant involvement of the opposition in the political process. The new Hungarian constitution, approved by the centre-right government with a two-thirds majority on 18 April 2011, was signed into law on 25 April 2011. This date had a symbolic message for its religious content (Easter Monday). The Socialists (MSZP) and the new liberal and green party, LMP, boycotted the parliamentary debates and the vote. The extreme right party Jobbik voted against the new basic law, for different reasons. The new constitution came into force on 1 January 2012. It has several symbolic messages that has been widely criticised by Hungarian and international media. The political changes and the new constitution have also received critique from the Venice Commission for Democracy through Law of the Council of Europe, the EU institutions (European Parliament, European Commission), and the United States of America.

In 2012 the European Commission launched three infringement procedures against Hungary (the independence of its central bank law, the retirement age limit of judges and prosecutors, and the independence of the data protection authority). Following internal and external criticism (e.g. calling for a review of the European Parliament resolution of 10 March 2011 on media law in Hungary) (European Parliament, 2011) the laws (such as the Media Law, Act CLXXXV of 2010) were mostly modified. However, there was still widespread opinion that the centre-right government had a high level of concentration of power and control over the country's institutions and public life. The Venice Commission expressed the opinion that the process would have required 'the largest consensus possible within Hungarian society' (Venice Commission, 2011).

In contrast to the above-mentioned critique, the Transition report 2012 of the European Bank for Reconstruction and Development which describes the political situation following the general elections in April 2010 stated a different view on the political situation of the country pointing out the strong popular support of the ruling Fidesz coalition, in contrast to the one enjoyed by the previous ruling party (HSP). The European Bank for Reconstruction and Development (EBRD, n.d.:8) underlined that:

Hungary is committed to, and applying, the principles of multiparty democracy, pluralism and market economics in accordance with the conditions specified in Article 1 of the Agreement establishing the Bank. Hungary has achieved significant progress overall towards development of a functioning market economy and a multiparty democracy.

According to the critics of the constitutional framework the process was too fast, not transparent, and, as debated by the opposition parties and by EU institutions, considered by the left-wing opposition as a sign of deconsolidation of liberal democracy and a move from liberal democracy to centralised illiberal or partial democracy. There is reason to emphasise that the words 'liberal' and 'liberalism' have become used almost as swear words in the Hungarian society and in the political debate, due to the negative attitude in society towards the high level of liberalisation and privatisation of the Hungarian economy, and due to the negative public opinions about the most recent socialist-liberal governments.

The main reason for the crisis of liberalism is the decline in support for the political and economic transition, the decline in trust in the function of democracy, the high level of corruption among politicians (which surfaced during the socialist-liberal governments' period of office before the 2010 elections), and the worsening economic situation of Hungary. In 2011 the European Bank for Reconstruction and Development presented its document on transition economies (the Transition Report), which demonstrated a decline in public support for democracy and market economy in the countries that joined the EU (EBRD, 2011). The decrease in support for democracy was higher in the countries hit hard by the financial crisis (Krugman, 2011).

Hungary has been (and still it is) among the countries in Europe hardest hit by the international financial crisis since 2008, and is finding itself in a seemingly never-ending economic recession. The country has had economic problems since the beginnings of the 21st century. Due to Hungary's high budget deficit, the European Union's excessive deficit procedure has been in place against Hungary since its year of entry to the EU.

In recent years, in order to reduce the budget deficit, the Orbán government has elaborated the 'unorthodox economic and financial programme' by introducing the highest bank tax, special taxes on certain businesses, buying back energy and water companies, and using an anti-IMF campaign, which has been quite popular within Hungarian society, and not increasing personal income-taxes. That's why it was also important for the Hungarian Government to avoid new loans from the IMF, not to accept the austerity programme proposed by the IMF, and to maintain its economic sovereignty, at least on the surface.

Although in 2011 the Hungarian deficit was only slightly above the 3% threshold due to the new taxes introduced by the Orbán government, in 2012 the European Commission – using the tools of the 'six-pack' of EU fiscal rules – proposed the suspension of Hungary's Cohesion Fund support from 2013. In explaining its decision, the Commission stated that deficit reduction was caused by 'one-off revenues' due to the temporal taxes on banks, junk food (the 'chips tax'), and telecom firms, and in the view of the EC this was not sustainable. Olli Rehn said: 'Today's proposal should be seen as a strong incentive for Hungary to conduct sound fiscal policies and put in place the right macro-economic and fiscal conditions to ensure an efficient use of Cohesion Fund resources'. The Hungarian Government declared the EC's decision 'unfounded and unfair' and as 'using double standards' (Euractiv, 2012). Finally, in June 2013, Ecofin approved the European Commission's proposal to remove Hungary from the excessive deficit procedure.

Euro-scepticism

After the EU accession, the 'EUphoria' in Hungarian society was soon replaced by a feeling of disappointment ('EUphobia'). Hungarians think that this happened partly because the accession took place later than expected and partly because it did not fulfil the sometimes-exaggerated hopes (of convergence to the EU average), let alone the communication deficit regarding the accession. According to data gathered in 2004, the proportion of those who thought that EU membership would be advantageous for Hungary peaked in autumn 2002 with 76%, followed by consistent decline (Eurobarometer, 2004b). During the next one and a half years, as 'the requirements set and support offered by the Union became clear', the proportion of optimists decreased by 18 percentage points by spring 2004, 'when only 58% of Hungarian citizens professed to believe that EU membership would be advantageous for the country'. Among the new member states, Hungary still remained one of the three most optimistic countries regarding the advantages expected from EU membership (Eurobarometer, 2004b, 1: 4). To Hungary, membership represented an opportunity to catch up with the more developed European nations, because in 2004 the GNP per capita in six regions of Hungary was below 75% of the EU average, (38.25% – 60.47%), and only that of Central Hungary was 89.24% of the EU average.

From Table 1, it is evident that in most of Hungary's regions there has not been any economic convergence to more developed ones in recent years. Moreover, in the case of some Hungarian regions, a certain amount of divergence can be observed.

Table 1: GDP per capita (PPP), percentage of the EU average of NUTS[5] regions of Hungary

NUTS 2	2003	2004	2005	2006	2007	2008	2009
Central Hungary	99.9	101.2	103.3	105.1	102.9	105	109
Central Transdanubia	58.0	60.1	59.3	57.0	57	58	54
Western Transdanubia	67.7	65.9	62.6	63.2	61.5	62	60
Southern Transdanubia	45.6	45.0	43.7	42.6	42.7	44	45
Northern Hungary	40.6	41.9	41.5	40.3	40.1	40	40
Northern Great Plain	41.8	41.4	40.1	39.1	39.4	40	42
Southern Great Plain	43.6	44.1	42.8	41.9	41.8	43	43

Source: Eurostat: http://epp.eurostat.ec.europa.eu

The Eurobarometer of October 2006 already clearly showed Hungarian society's disappointment in the EU accession. Since the spring of that year, the support for EU (people who see EU membership as a good thing) membership had dropped by 10%, to 39%, probably due to the country's domestic political issues (such as elections, growing economic problems, and a general feeling of uncertainty) (Eurobarometer, 2006: Autumn: 6).

By 2007, the support for membership had further decreased, as is evident in the following Eurobarometer statistics. Although general support of the EU had never been as high as in 2007, that year showed the lowest level of support ever in Hungary's history: 57% of EU citizens thought that their country's membership was 'a good thing', and only 15% viewed the membership as wholly wrong. This indicated a 4% rise as compared to the previous Eurobarometer. Contrary to these findings, 40% of Hungarians did not consider the EU accession beneficial for their country, and only 37% claimed that it was 'a good thing'. Hungarians were among the most pessimistic citizens, both with regard to the issue of membership (ranked 25th place), and to the advantages of membership (27th place) (Eurobarometer, 2007: Spring: 15-16)

According to the data gathered for the Standard Eurobarometer of autumn 2008, Hungarian pessimism can be traced already in the answers to the first set of questions, as only 31% of the respondents evaluated membership positively, in contrast with the EU average of 53%. It is worth noting that in autumn 2004 the percentage of positive responses was still high, at 49%. While 60% of the EU average citi-

---

5   In the EU, regional statistics are based on a common classification of territorial units: the Nomenclature of Territorial Units for Statistics (NUTS). NUTS has three regional levels, each with minimum and maximum thresholds for the average population size of the regions.

zens claimed that the EU imposed its opinion on the member states, only 57% of Hungarians shared this view. At the same time, and in contrast to the EU average of 60%, only 47% of Hungarians thought that their country's opinion counted at the European level (Eurobarometer, 2008: Autumn: 31-32).

From Table 2, it is evident that in recent last years, support for EU membership has decreased significantly. In 2004, 49% of respondents considered membership a good thing, whereas by 2011 only 32% stated that this was the case. The proportion of those stating that membership was a bad thing rose from 10% to 22% between 2004 and 2011, with a further rise to 23% in 2009 at the peak of the financial crisis, followed by a fall to 15% in the year of the general elections (2010). In 2010, the proportion of respondents stating that EU membership was a 'good thing' was 38% as compared to 34% in 2009. The change in percentage might have reflected new hope for stronger representation of national interests on EU level. The proportion of respondents who thought that membership was 'neither good nor bad' also increased, from 36% to 44% over the same period.

Table 2: Responses (%) to questions starting 'Generally speaking, do you think that (your country's) membership of the European Community (Common Market) is ... ?' that were recorded during Eurobarometer surveys conducted between 2004 and 2011

Date	'A good thing'	'A bad thing'	'Neither good nor bad'	'Don't know'
10/2004	49	10	36	5
06/2005	42	12	43	3
10/2005	39	14	42	5
04/2006	49	10	38	3
09/2006	39	19	38	3
05/2007	37	17	43	3
10/2007	40	17	41	2
04/2008	32	21	43	4
10/2008	31	21	45	3
06/2009	32	23	41	4
11/2009	34	22	42	2
06/2010	38	15	45	2
05/2011	32	22	44	2

Source: Eurobarometer Interactive Search System, http://ec.europa.eu/public_opinion/cf/showtable.cfm?keyID=5&nationID=22,&startdate=2004.10&enddate=2011.05

According to the results of opinion polls conducted by Medián in 2004, 80% of the respondents supported the EU membership of Hungary. Although in 2011 the percentage had fallen to 68%, two-thirds of the population still supported Hungary's membership of the EU (Medián, 2012). In 2012, the results of an opinion poll conducted by Századvég showed that less than half (49%) of the respondents said that membership of the EU was beneficial for Hungary and 53% did not support further deepening of the European integration process (Origo, 2012).

Party attitudes

Post-accession factors have played some role in emphasising Euro-scepticism in Hungary following the accession to the EU. During the government of the second conservative coalition (1998–2002) only two small non-parliamentary parties took a hard Euro-sceptic line: the far right Hungarian Justice and Life and the Hungarian Workers' Party adopted a strong opposition to Hungary's EU membership. According to Taggart and Szczerbiak (2001), 'soft Euro-scepticism' was taken up by two parties in the then governing coalition, Fidesz and the Smallholders Party (the smaller partner). The leader of Fidesz, PM Viktor Orbán, increasingly accepted 'national interest' Euro-scepticism (Taggart and Szczerbiak, 2001).

Based on the results of the Dutch and French referenda on the Constitutional Treaty of the EU (2005), it became clear that there could also be critical attitudes towards specific issues of the EU in traditional democratic member states. Gradually, people in the new member states have begun to realise that such critical views do not mean opposition to the EU as a whole. Fidesz appeared to represent a soft Eurosceptic ('Eurorealistic') standpoint, whereby the party's opinions on the democratic basis of the European Union as well as the more critical statements regarding specific issues fell within the traditionally accepted attitudes in the EU.

During recent years, growing social and political disillusionment has emerged. Since the last general election of 2010, the Hungarian political discourse on EU issues has changed and in recent years Euro-scepticism has been on the rise. Semi-hard or sometimes hard Euro-scepticism is represented by the party Jobbik, 'The Movement for a Better Hungary' (i.e. by burning the EU flag and advising referendum on EU membership), whereas soft Euro-scepticism/Eurorealistic standpoints (based on national sovereignty and national interest) are held by the governing parties.

During the second conservative government, semi-hard or sometimes hard Euro-sceptic standpoints were still represented by Jobbik, while pro-European/ euro-optimist positions were more common among members of the Democratic

Coalition led by a highly criticised ex-socialist party leader and the LMP. According to a research carried out by the Hungarian Europe Society the Fidesz 'covers internal divisions', as the research indentified two wings in Fidesz: 'a less visible, Euro-constructive one and a noisier, Euro-pessimist one led by Viktor Orbán' (Európa Társaság, 2013: 4). At the national level, the MSZP carefully avoids taking a position in debates concerning the future of the EU. Only the LMP has a coherent federalist vision of the EU (in its 2010 electoral manifesto) (Európa Társaság, 2013: 4).

Although the Hungarian presidency of the EU Council between January and June 2011 provided a better opportunity to bring the EU and its institutions closer to Hungarians, Euro-scepticism still increased in Hungary. The debates regarding the Hungarian legal changes shadowed the results of the successful EU presidency, focusing on, for example, the Roma integration, economic recovery, and the enlargement process of the EU.

Whereas Fidesz represents a soft Euro-scepticism or 'Eurorealism', the party has not opposed the enlargement process or (after heated negotiations) the deepening of the economic governance of the Economic and Monetary Union (EMU) ('six-pack' governance package). During the Hungarian EU presidency, Hungary worked for a 'stronger Europe'. In his assessment of the results of the presidency, Viktor Orbán said that 'Hungary's EU presidency has successfully achieved its targets and contributed to strengthening the EU' (Fidesz, 2011).

However, during the anniversary of Hungary's 1848 revolution against Austrian Habsburg rule, the Hungarian prime minister accused the European Union of treating Hungary as a colony. He said that Hungarians would not live in accordance with the commands of foreign powers. Following the possibility of the suspension of EU funds (as a consequence of the ongoing excessive deficit procedure) for Hungary, he spoke about 'double standards', and said: 'We will not be a colony … Our rightful demand is to have the same standards apply to us, which apply to other (EU) countries' (BBC, 2012).

As a result of the 2010 parliamentary elections, Jobbik became the third main party in Hungary, with 17% of the votes. Its popularity is highly connected to the economic problems in Hungary (in 2010 the GDP was −6.3%, and the unemployment rate was above 11%), and to the disappointment in the process of democratisation and Europeanization due to the high level of corruption. The characteristic features of Jobbik's extreme rightist ideology are anti-democratic feelings, nationalism, chauvinism, and racism. They usually do not reject the application of radical methods in resolving social problems.

Although Jobbik is strongly Euro-sceptic, it considers itself rather Eurorealistic (a concept that many analysts equate with 'soft Euro-scepticism').[6] Jobbik, whose political standpoint floats between soft and hard Euro-scepticism, do not yet wish Hungary to leave the EU, but according to Gábor Vona they do not exclude this possibility either. In one of his interviews in September 2009, Vona claimed:

Several of our supporters have expressed the possibility of leaving the EU. Under certain circumstances I do not exclude this either, but first let us see what we can do within the Union. The Czechs, Poles, Slovaks, Irish, and Finns, among others, have benefited from the membership much more than us. Success can be brought about only by a more combatant attitude. (Teol, 2009)

Instead of the joint Euro-Atlantic political direction followed by the parliamentary parties since the change of political regime, Jobbik focuses its political objectives on turning to the East, which does not coincide with the traditional approach of 'third way' foreign policy. They explain that this is not simply because of seemingly obvious economic reasons, but due to the 'Eastern identity' of the Hungarians emphasised by the party. In the party's interviews and articles, Jobbik stresses opening up towards Moscow, the Arab world, and the Far East, and shows a somewhat anti-Israeli attitude and Euro-scepticism (Vona 2009).

The Jobbik, like extreme right nationalistic parties in general, represents a semi-hard Euro-sceptic standpoint in not supporting the further deepening of the European integration process. The party appears to see the integration as standing for a supranational political structure that aims at renewed suppression of small countries. In Hungary, the reason for growing Euro-scepticism is probably the lack of economic growth following the accession (2004) and the disillusionment with the process of democratisation and liberalisation.

---

6   Soft Euro-scepticism includes viewpoints against one of the policies of the EU. Those who express revulsion against the political or economic 'deepening' of the EU (e.g. objection against the introduction of the euro) are also counted among 'soft sceptics'. In short, those who belong to the soft wing of Euro-sceptics are not against the process of European integration, but have different opinions about particular measures. They attach primary importance to the vindication of national interests. By contrast, the representatives of the hard Euro-scepticism are entirely against the political and economic integration, and they stand against the EU membership of their own country. They generally express criticism against capitalism, liberalism, and socialism, considering these as power tools of the EU (Taggart and Szczerbiak 2001: 8).

Debate with the EP

The new Hungarian basic law (constitution) have attracted criticism from the institutions of the European Union. The European Commission has played an active role as guardian of the EU Treaties, for example by 'monitoring developments related to the Hungarian Constitutional system since 2011' and accusing Hungary of nonconformity with EU legislation during a plenary debate in the European Parliament on 17 April 2013 (Euractiv, 2013ab).

In May 2013 the European Parliament made public a draft version of the report on the state of fundamental rights in Hungary, prepared by the EP's Committee on Civil Liberties, Justice and Home Affairs (Tavares, 2013). The draft Tavares Report was criticised by the Hungarian Government, which said that it was based on false premises. The case of the Tavares Report demonstrates clearly the standpoint of the Hungarian Government regarding the European Union, which can be defined as Eurorealism and soft Euro-scepticism based on national sovereignty. The case also clearly demonstrates the creation of a European public space, as domestic political affairs have become European ones, causing several heated debates among European politicians in different institutions of the EU.

The draft Tavares Report concerns the process of lawmaking in the past three years (e.g. a new constitution and cardinal laws), and states that the content of the constitutional and legal changes in very short time frames are incompatible with the values defined in Article 2 of the Treaty on European Union (TEU), which states that the European Union is 'founded on the values of respect for human dignity, freedom, democracy, equality, the rule of law and respect for human rights, including the rights of persons belonging to minorities'(Council of the European Union, 2012: 21). The report emphasises that the lawmaking process harms the rule of law (Tavares, 2013). Its recommendations include the creation of new mechanisms (based on an Alarm Agenda, a three-way dialogue, and the creation of the Copenhagen high-level group) to follow the development of fundamental rights in all EU-member states, as also in Hungary. In the worst scenario, the outcome of this process (placing Hungary under guardianship) may be the suspension of Hungary's voting rights in the European Council (Article 7), as was proposed by MEP Guy Verhofstadt (liberal ALDE group) in April (European Parliament, 2013). The report *urges the Hungarian authorities to implement as swiftly as possible all the measures the European Commission as the guardian of the treaties deems necessary in order to fully comply with EU law, fully comply with the decisions of the Hungarian Constitutional Court and implement as swiftly as possible the following recommendations, in line with the recommendations of the Venice Commission, the Council of Europe and other international bodies for the protection of the rule of law and fundamental rights, with a view to fully complying with the rule of law and its key requirements on the constitutional setting, the system of checks and balances and the independence of the judiciary, as well as on strong safeguards for fundamental rights, including freedom of expression, the media and religion or belief, protection of minorities, action to combat discrimination, and the right to property.* (European Parliament, 2013: Para. 71)

According to Viktor Orbán, as stated in his speech during the debate in the EP plenary session in July 2013, the report was unfair to Hungary and the Hungarians, because it did not pay tribute to the efforts made to modernise the country, thus applying double standards against Hungary. In Orbán's opinion, the setting up of new mechanisms would go against the treaties and would be risky because it could lead to placing a member state of the EU under guardianship (Euractiv, 2013c).

Although the Tavares Report was adopted after the debate (with 370 supporters, 249 against, and 82 abstentions), Prime Minister Viktor Orbán did not accept the result, saying that 'the report seriously violated and restricted Hungary's independence and the freedom of its parliament' (Hirado, 2013). He considered that this could lead to a unilateral overriding of the treaties on the basis of which Hungary joined the European Union (Hirado, 2013). He expressed his opinion that the approval of the Tavares Report was merely a political attack by the European left-wing against the right-wing Hungarian Government. According to Orbán, the European left-wing could not accept the two-third majority in the Hungarian Parliament and the introduction of a banking tax and public utility fee cuts. The tone of the Hungarian prime minister's speech reflected the rhetoric of a warrior. He emphasised that Hungarians did not want to live in a Brussels-centred European empire, where countries at the peripheries were told what to do, thereby restricting their independence. He emphasised the concept of a Europe of free nations. For Orbán, the EP, as an 'an army of bureaucrats unable to resolve the crisis', went beyond its authority. He suggested that the European dispute would continue because the government would refuse to withdraw the bank tax and the public utility fee cut scheme (Politics, 2013).

On 5 July 2013 the Hungarian Parliament adopted a resolution – the Resolution on the Right of Hungary to Equal Treatment – in response to the EP decision, stating that the European Parliament harmed European values and was on a hazardous path. The resolution emphasises the Christian roots of the Hungarian state, the standing up for European values and against the communist dictatorship. Further, the resolution entails the historical role of Hungary during the period of the demolition of the Iron Curtain. It repeats some of the ideas mentioned in the previous speeches of Orbán, such as the denial of a European Union whereby the larger nations abuse their power and national sovereignty is violated. The resolution states that the Hungarian people 'have had enough of dictatorship after 40 years behind the iron curtain' (*Hungarian Spektrum*, 2013). At the same time, the resolution expresses Hungary's wish for dialogue with the European Union institutions, and readiness for reasonable compromises, as well as the expectation of respect and equal treatment of Hungary from the European Union's institutions. It also emphasises that the EP went beyond its authorities and against basic European values by passing the resolution based on the Tavares Report: 'The European Parliament made demands, introduced new procedures, and created institutions that violate Hungary's sovereignty as guaranteed in the fundamental treaty' (*Hungarian Spektrum*, 2013). Further, the text supports the idea that was apparent in the PM's speech about alleged business interests lying behind the political declarations, referring to the debate regarding the cost reduction of energy paid by families, which could 'hurt the interests of many European companies that for years have had windfall profits from their monopoly in Hungary' (*Hungarian Spektrum*, 2013), stating that:

> *it is unacceptable that the European Union tries to influence our homeland to further the interests of these companies. ... We call on the Hungarian government not to give in to the pressure of the European Union, not to let the nation's rights guaranteed in the fundamental treaty be violated, and to continue the policies that make the lives of the Hungarian people easier.* (*Hungarian Spektrum*, 2013)

The 'Eurorealism' or soft Euro-scepticism focusing on national sovereignty and national interests of Fidesz and its leader is represented in the resolution. As a charismatic politician, Viktor Orbán has a strong impact on the masses. It should be emphasised that, at the same time, the governing Fidesz's political attitude towards Brussels is still not opposed to the further deepening or enlargement process of the EU, but concentrates on fairly popular issues, such as blaming the EU for Hungary's problems or suggesting that there were business interests (e.g. multinational companies or banks) lying behind the Tavares Report and its approval; the standpoint can thus be considered Eurorealist. Fidesz's attitude regarding the EU's focus on the defence of Hungarian national interests is still very fluid, floating between pro-EU and Euro-sceptic standpoints, due to its wide range of social backgrounds and its rather vague ideological platform.

Conclusions

Accession to the EU resulted in serious trauma for Hungary, known as the 'post-accession crisis'. Under the influence of the change of the regime, there was, on the one hand, a social-structural crisis because the economic deficit was transformed into a social deficit during the process of crisis management, while on the other hand, the new democratic state had no time to develop fully, and thus remained weak. Speeded-up democratisation led to a serious social deficit, namely in terms of economic and social insecurity.

When Hungary's accession to the EU was achieved, the state was still weak. It was this fact that caused the trauma; the country was not ready for accession, from the point of view of either societal capacity or the state of development of the institutional structure. In addition, the onset of the 'accession and reform exhaustion' has resulted in the rise of populism (Ágh, 2008: 94–95). In 2010, the new governing coalition responded to these challenges by strengthening and centralising state capacities and by adopting a Gaullist-populist approach based on national sovereignty.

Following the last general election, the Hungarian political discourse on EU issues has been changed and in recent years Euro-scepticism has continued to rise. As a result of the social, economic, and political crisis, the peripheral position of Hungary has been strengthened following the country's accession to the EU. In the case of Hungary, the legitimacy of the EU depends on the velocity in closing up its position in relation to the developed member states. The financial and economic crisis resulted in slow, or from time to time blocked, economic convergence towards the centre of the EU. The public opinion regarding the future of the EU is highly connected to the economic efficiency of the European integration and the economic developments of its member states.

References

Primary Sources

Ablonczy, B. (2010), 'A "trianoni gyászmunkát" végre el kell végezni. Pozitív célok – nemzeti érzésből', http://tudomany.ma.hu/tart/cikk/h/0/71189/1/tudomany/Ablonczy_a_trianoni_gyaszmunkat_vegre_el_kell_vegezni

AFD (2009), 'Mit tesznek Önért a magyar liberálisok az Európai Parlamentben a következő öt évben? 2009', http://www.szdsz.hu/resources/userfiles/file/szdsz_eu_program.pdf

BBC (2012), 'Hungarian PM Viktor Orbán denounces EU's 'colonialism', 6 March 2012, http://www.bbc.co.uk/news/business-17394894

Council of the European Union (2012), Consolidated Versions of the Treaty on European Union and the Treaty on the Functioning of the European Union, http://register.consilium.europa.eu/pdf/en/08/st06/st06655-re07.en08.pdf

Eurobarometer (2004a), 'The social situation in the European Union', http://epp.eurostat.ec.europa.eu/cache/ITY_OFFPUB/KE-AG-04-001/EN/KE-AG-04-001-EN.PDF

Eurobarometer (2004b), 'Public opinion in the candidate countries', National Report, Executive summary, Hungary, http://ec.europa.eu/public_opinion/archives/eb/eb61/exec_hu.pdf

Eurobarometer (2006, Autumn), 'Standard Eurobarometer 66, Public opinion in the European Union', http://ec.europa.eu/public_opinion/archives/eb/eb66/eb66_highlights_en.pdf

Eurobarometer (2007, Spring), 'Standard Eurobarometer 67, Public opinion in the European Union', http://ec.europa.eu/public_opinion/archives/eb/eb67/eb_67_first_en.pdf

Eurobarometer (2008, Autumn), 'Standard Eurobarometer 70, Public opinion in the European Union', http://ec.europa.eu/public_opinion/archives/eb/eb70/eb70_first_en.pdf

Council Decision 88/595/EEC 21 November 1988, 'Agreement between the European Economic Community and the Hungarian People's Republic on trade and commercial and economic co-operation', [1988] OJ L327/1.

EBRD (2011), Transition Report: 'Crisis in Transition: The People's Perspective', http://www.ebrd.com/downloads/research/transition/tr11.pdf

EBRD (n.d.), Transition Report 2012, Document of the European Bank for Reconstruction and Development, 'Strategy for Hungary', as approved by the Board of Directors at its meeting on 11 October 2011, http://www.ebrd.com/downloads/country/strategy/hungary.pdf

Euractiv (2012), 'EU to cut Hungary's regional funds over deficit', 23 February 2012, http://www.euractiv.com/regional-policy/eu-cut-hungary-regional-funds-de-news-511049

Euractiv (2013a), 'Hungary and the Rule of Law – Statement of the European Commission in the Plenary Debate of the European Parliament', 17 April 2013, European Commission, SPEECH/13/324, http://europa.eu/rapid/press-release_SPEECH-13-324_en.htm?locale=en;

Euractive (2013b), 'Commission accuses Hungary of transgressions', 18 April 2013, http://www.euractiv.com/future-eu/commission-lists-hungary-transgr-news-519202

Euractiv (2013c), 'Viktor Orbán angry at EU's criticism of Hungary's democratic values', 3 July 2013, http://www.euractiv.com/video/viktor-orban-angry-eus-criticism-529065

Európa Társaság (2013), 'Where Does the PERC Index Stand? Or: From EU Destructives to Federalists: Relationship of the Hungarian Parties to the European Union', Executive Summary, http://www.europatarsasag.hu/images/2013Jan/PERC%20%20executive%20summary.pdf

European Parliament (2011), European Parliament resolution of 10 March 2011 on media law in Hungary, http://www.europarl.europa.eu/sides/getDoc.do?pubRef=-//EP//TEXT+TA+P7-TA-2011-0094+0+DOC+XML+V0//EN

European Parliament (2013), 'MEPs voice concerns over constitutional changes in Hungary', Justice and home affairs, 17 April 2013, http://www.europarl.europa.eu/news/en/headlines/content/20130416STO07356/html/MEPs-voice-concerns-over-constitutional-changes-in-Hungary

Euvonal (2009), 'Terítéken a pártok EP-programjai', 29 June 2009, http://www.euvonal.hu/index.php?op=hirek&id=5910

Fidesz (2009), 'Igen, Magyarország többre képes', http://static.fidesz.hu/download/yar/program2009_magyar.pdf

Fidesz (2011), 'EU stronger than at start of Hungarian presidency', 5 July 2011, (MTI-fidesz.hu), http://www.fidesz.hu/index.php?Cikk=165020

Hirado (2013), 'EP approves Tavares report on fundamental rights in Hungary', http://www.hirado.hu/Hirek/2013/07/03/19/EP_approves_Tavares_report_on_fundamental_rights_in.aspx

HSP (2009), 'Az MSZP EP delegáció vállalásai 15 pontban, célkitűzések az Európai parlamentben 2009-14 között', http://mszp.hu/public/downloads/pdf/mszpvallalasok_a_kovetkezo_ciklusra.pdf

Hungarian Spektrum (2013), 'Viktor Orbán's answer to the Tavares report', http://hungarianspectrum.wordpress.com/2013/07/04/viktor-orbans-answer-to-the-tavares-report/comment-page-1/

Kormany.hu (n.d.a.), 'The history of Hungarian EU membership', http://eu.kormany.hu/the-history-of-hungarian-eu-membership

Kormany.hu (n.d.b.), 'The Fundamental Law of Hungary', http://www.kormany.hu/download/4/c3/30000/THE%20FUNDAMENTAL%20LAW%20OF%20HUNGARY.pdf

Krugman, P. (2011), 'Depression and Democracy', The New York Times, 11 December 2011. http://www.nytimes.com/2011/12/12/opinion/krugman-depression-and-democracy.html?_r=0

Mayr, W. (2009), 'Hungary's Peaceful Revolution: Cutting the Fence and Changing History', 29 May 2009, http://www.spiegel.de/international/europe/hungary-s-peaceful-revolution-cutting-the-fence-and-changing-history-a-627632.html

Medián (2012), Egy szabadságharc frontvonalai: A közvélemény az IMF-tárgyalásokról és az EU-ról, 19 March 2012, http://www.median.hu/object.90dcfe43-2f4b-448d-adb4-6bb74fdf1129.ivy

Origo (2012), Századvég – kedvezőtlenül alakul Magyarország uniós tagságának a megítélése, 19 March 2012, http://www.origo.hu/itthon/20120131-szazadveg-kedvezotlenul-alakul-magyarorszag-unios-tagsaganak-a-megitelese.html

Politics (2013), 'EP approval of Tavares report European left-wing's scheme, Orbán says', 5 July 2013, http://www.politics.hu/20130705/ep-approval-of-tavares-report-european-left-wings-scheme-orban-says/

Tavares, R. (2013), 'Draft Report on the situation of fundamental rights: standards and practices in Hungary', European Parliament, Committee on Civil Liberties, Justice and Home Affairs, http://www.europarl.europa.eu/sides/getDoc.do?pubRef=-

%2F%2FEP%2F%2FNONSGML%2BCOMPARL%2BPE-508.211%2B02%2BDO
C%2BPDF%2BV0%2F%2FEN

Teol (2009), 'A Jobbik felszámolná a "poronty bizniszt"', 7 September 2009, http://www.teol.hu/tolna/kozelet/a-jobbik-felszamolna-a-poronty-bizniszt-255753

Venice Commission (2011), Strasbourg, 20 June 2011, Opinion no. 621 / 2011, CDL-AD(2011)016 Or. Engl. European Commission for Democracy through Law (Venice Commission) Opinion on the new Constitution of Hungary, Adopted by the Venice Commission at its 87th Plenary Session, Venice, 17–18 June 2011.

Vona, G. (2009), 'A Magyar Gárda nem adja fel', 3 February 2009, http://www.mno.hu/portal/606865?searchtext=Vona%20G%C3% A1bor; Kiskáté, 26 April 2009, http://jobbik.hu/rovatok/egyeb/kiskate; Rendhagyó interjú Vona Gáborral a Jobbikot ért vádakról, titkokról, hazugságokról 12 August 2009, barikád.hu http://barikad.hu/node/34279; Can Europe exist without Russia? http://www.jobbik.com/europe-news/3053.html

Literature

Ágh, A. (2008), 'Kitekintés a Kelet-Közép-Európai Konszolidációra', *Politikatudományi Szemle* [Review of Political Science], 2008/1, pp. 95–11.

Ash, T. G. (1990), *We the People: The Revolution of '89 Witnessed in Warsaw, Budapest, Berlin and Prague*, London: Granta Books.

Bibó, I. (1986), 'A kelet-európai kisállamok nyomorúsága', in I. Bibó, *Válogatott tanulmányok II (1945–49)*, Budapest: Magvetõ Kiadó, pp. 185–265.

Dahrendorf, R. (1990), *Reflections on the Revolution in Europe: In a Letter Intended to Have Been Sent to a Gentleman in Warsaw*, London: Chatto & Windus.

Enyedi, Z. (2006), 'Az európai pártrendszer hatása a kelet-európai és a magyar pártstratégiákra', in I. Hegedűs (ed.), *Magyarok bemenetele: Tagállamként a bővülő Európai Unióban*, Budapest: DKMKA, pp.155-180, http://www.personal.ceu.hu/departs/personal/Zsolt_Enyedi/magyar/hu2.pdf

Füzér, K., Gerő, M., Sik, E., Zongor, G., (2005), *A társadalmi tőke növekedésének lehetőségei fejlesztéspolitikai eszközökkel*, TÁRKI, http://www.socialnetwork.hu/cikkek/SikEsSokTarsToke06.htm

Juhász, J. and Tálas, P. (2008), 'A szélsőjobboldal, a jobboldali radikalizmus és a populizmus előretörésének okairól Kelet- és Közép-Európában' in *Európai Tükör*, No. 4, pp. 116–124.

Kégler, Á. (2004), 'Európai Parlamenti kampány: Hazabeszélnek', *Figyelő*, No. 15, pp. 20-21.

Kormány, A. (2006), 'Vélemények az EU tagságról és annak következményeiről', in *Európai Tükör*, No. 10, pp. 89–97.

Marján, A. (2006), 'Az EU-bővítés: vissza- és előretekintés', in *Európai Tükör*, No. 11, pp. 5–16.

Mihályi, P. (2010), *A magyar privatizáció enciklopédiája*, 2 Vols, Budapest: Pannon Egyetemi Könyvkiadó–MT A Közgazdaságtudományi Intézet.

Navracsics, T. (1997), 'A missing debate? Hungary and the European Union', *Sussex European Institute SEI Working Paper*, No. 21, Sussex European Institute http://www.sussex.ac.uk/sei/documents/wp21.pdf

Pénzügyminisztérium (1997), 'A gazdasági átalakulás számokban 1989–1997', Budapest: Pénzügyminisztérium.

Sükösd, M. (2003), 'Kommunikációs deficit Magyarország Európai Uniós csatlakozásának média-bemutásában: megoldási irányok és nyilvánosság-modellekok', in *Médiakutató*, pp. 73–83.

Taggart, P. and Szczerbiak, A. (2001), 'Parties, Positions and Europe: Euroscepticism in the EU Candidate States of Central and Eastern Europe', *Sussex European Institute Working Paper*, No. 46, Sussex European Institute, http://www.sussex.ac.uk/sei/documents/wp46.pdf

Tatham, A.F. (2009), *Enlargement of the European Union*, Austin: Kluwer Law International.

The EU membership yet to come?
Turkish civil society speaking in times of crises

Ülkü Doğanay, Özlem Erkmen, D. Beybin Kejanlıoğlu

Civil society organizations (CSOs) play an important role in transmitting social, cultural, and political ideas of Europe and the European Union (EU) mainly through decentralized political socialization. By the end of the 1990s the European Commission recognized CSOs as potential catalysts of change, a basis for administrative reform, and a source of legitimation (Warleigh, 2001: 622; Smismans, 2003: 478). As a result, the Commission acknowledged the CSO's capacity to foster a more participatory democracy within the candidates and developing countries. A well-functioning civil society is seen as vital for the candidate countries in order to draw them closer to the prospect of European integration. For this reason, since the approval of Turkey's candidacy for membership at the Helsinki Summit held in 1999, the EU has exerted considerable transformative power over Turkish civil society (İçduygu, 2011: 381; Smismans, 2003: 479; Ergun, 2010: 507). In addition, the EU's involvement has changed the nature of civil societal activity and has increased the CSOs' capacity to contribute to Turkey's democratic consolidation.

Parallel to the significance attributed to civil society by the EU, the CSOs have also played an important role in Turkey's involvement in the EU as agents of structural transformation. A number of renowned organizations have lobbied for Turkish accession in Brussels, forced the Turkish Government to adopt many reforms, and promoted a change in 'domestic affairs, in state-society relations and in the social, political and economic context of the EU-Turkey relationship' (İçduygu, 2011: 384). Nevertheless, despite the pro-EU attitude of many prominent civil society actors, the CSO's perception of Europe cannot always be considered on the basis of a pure relation of belonging. Diverse civil society actors are taking varying positions in the ongoing process of Europeanization and the question of Turkish membership of the EU. Euro-sceptic arguments have always been partially supported, but they became much more vociferous after 2006 with the decision by the EU to suspend the negotiations with Turkey. This incident created some tension in the relations and for some CSOs it resulted in a shift from pro-EU to Euro-sceptic tendencies.

Research conducted during the post-Helsinki period shows that the EU's image has faded considerably and that the belief in Turkey's membership and its benefits has gradually lost ground since 2006 (EB62, 2004; EB63.4, 2005; EB67, 2007; EB71, 2009; EB72, 2009; EB74, 2010; EB75a, 2011; EB75B, 2011; EB76, 2011; EB77, 2012; ATAUM, 2010; TÜİK, 2011). Albeit few in numbers, a common finding of the studies that problematize the civil society actors' perception of the EU is that wide-ranging competing views in terms of advantages and disadvantages of Turkey's EU membership dominate the discourses on the EU. For example, in her study based on in-depth interviews with the representatives of Turkish CSOs, Ayça Ergun reveals that the representatives of the CSOs put special emphasis on the role of the EU in the democratic consolidation of Turkey. A similar emphasis can be found in Şeyhmus Diken's (2006) research, which is based on interviews with the representatives of 48 CSOs. The EU is attributed the role of a criteria setter and standard provider, as well as a guardian of civil and political rights in Turkey. Nevertheless, the research also shows that partly due to the EU's reluctance regarding Turkey's membership, the EU is either criticized as being 'orientalist', 'non-coherent', 'unsteady', 'ambiguous', 'discriminatory', 'full of contradictions', and 'having potential for crises' or more radically it is seen as a threat to state sovereignty and integrity (Ergun, 2010: 516–520). Similarly, in their analysis of pro-EU and Euro-sceptic circles' arguments, Eylemer and Taş (2007: 573) conclude that business circles and some of the major CSOs known to be favourably disposed towards the EU voiced their resentment towards the EU decision to suspend partially the accession negotiations.

Research on EU-Turkey relations has tended to focus on how Turkish society conceives of the EU. However, there is a need for research on CSOs' views on the crises as critical moments in EU-Turkey relations and on the future of the EU. It may be claimed that the crisis periods in EU-Turkey relations as well the economic crisis that the Union is currently facing have caused a considerable decline in the belief in Turkey's membership and its benefits, and a decay in optimistic views about the future of the EU. In this respect, the evaluations of civil society actors on the economic crisis and its impact on the future of the EU and their expectations about EU-Turkey relations are worth studying.

This chapter studies how civil society actors that have been active in areas directly related to Turkey's harmonization process to the EU (such as human rights and democratization) perceive of (1) the EU as a democratic entity, (2) the EU's ongoing economic crisis, and (3) the future of the EU. For this purpose, 16 in-depth interviews were conducted with representatives of Turkish civil society organizations based in Istanbul, Ankara, and Izmir, in the period of September–December 2012.[1] The chosen organizations are all known for their commitment to democracy and human rights, as well as for their engagement in European matters. More information on the organizations is provided in the Appendix at the end of this chapter. The interviewees were expected to provide a panorama of Turkish civil society's positioning between pro- and anti-EU perspectives.

The chapter is structured in three parts. The first part provides a historical perspective and an overview of the critical junctures in EU-Turkey relations. The second part focuses on the ways in which the harmonization process to the EU has contributed to the development of civil society in Turkey and on the role of CSOs in this process. The third and final part presents an analysis of civil society's perceptions of the EU and European democracy, as well as their views of Turkey's EU bid and the EU's future.

Critical junctures in EU-Turkey relations

Turkey was one of the first countries to develop an association relationship with the European Communities (EC). In 1959 Ankara applied to become an associate member of the European Economic Community (EEC) and in 1963 the Ankara Agreement was signed. The association agreement aimed to bring Turkey into the Customs Union (CU) and eventually into the EEC. In 1974, Turkey's occupation of Cyprus caused serious problems in the relations. In 1978, the Turkish Government decided to freeze relations with the EC following the then Prime Minister Bülent Ecevit's decision to cancel a third round of tariff reductions. After the coup d'état in 1980, the relations between Turkey and the Communities broke down completely. In 1987, Turkey once again applied for full membership, and in December 1989 the Commission approved Turkey's ability for membership but postponed the evaluation of its application. In March 1995, the EU-Turkey Association Council

---

[1] See the Appendix for the full list. D. Beybin Kejanlıoğlu and Özlem Erkmen conducted interviews in İstanbul, while Ülkü Doğanay interviewed Avrupa Çalışmaları Ege Derneği (Aegean Association on European Studies, AÇED) in Izmir. The Türk Sanayici ve İşadamları Derneği (Turkish Industry & Business Association, TÜSİAD) interview took place in Brussels and was conducted by Ülkü Doğanay and Özlem Erkmen. We thank Burcu Ballıktaş for helping us by conducting and decoding the interviews in Ankara. Quotes in the text were translated from Turkish to English by the authors.

finalized the agreement on the CU. Wide-ranging constitutional reforms followed this agreement. A package negotiated by the Turkish Grand National Assembly (TGNA) in June and July 1995 brought the first comprehensive amendments to the 1982 constitution. At the Luxembourg summit in December 1997, accession negotiations were opened to all applicant countries except Turkey. Turkish authorities reacted with anger and argued that the decision was unjust and discriminatory. Consequently, Turkey refused to attend the March 1998 European Council meeting in Cardiff, where Turkey was not included in the group of Eastern European countries under consideration for accession in the near future.

The relations between the EU and Turkey gained an unexpectedly positive momentum in December 1999 when the EU Helsinki Council decided on Turkey's candidate status. Following the Council's decision to adopt Turkey's accession partnership in March 2001, the Turkish Parliament adopted the Turkish National Programme for the adoption of the acquis communautaire. Encouraged by the EU, the Turkish Government showed deliberate willpower in order to initiate legislative and constitutional reforms. Parallel to this, the pro-EU groups including the business circles, CSOs, and the academic community strengthened their position and increased their pressure on policymakers (Eylemer and Taş; 2007: 564).

Especially, the EU's decision to start negotiations with Turkey in 2002 was 'a long-awaited affirmation of Turkey's European vocation, a project whose roots date to the beginning of the Turkish Republic' (Kubicek, 2005: 361). This decision was considered by most political actors as the EU's acknowledgement of Turkey's ideal to become an essential part of the 'modern', 'contemporary', 'democratic', and 'prosperous' West, which constitutes a fundamental premise of Turkish modernization since the late 18th century (Doğanay, 2011: 264; Ahıska, 2003). New provisions in the areas of freedom of thought and expression, the fight against torture, democracy, freedom and security of the individual, freedom of association, and gender equality were adopted with nine harmonization packages between 2001 and 2004. Moreover, as of 2004, a total of 44 constitutional amendments had been adopted and 218 Articles of 53 different laws had been changed.[2]

---

2 For example, in August 2002 the Turkish Parliament decided to approve a package of 14 reforms, including the abolition of the death penalty, the authorization of broadcasts of different native languages and dialects, including Kurdish, the right to education in one's native language, and the rights of ownership of immovable property for the minorities. In May 2004, with the constitutional amendments that entered into force, new regulations on gender equality, freedom of the press, the status of international conventions, and the functioning of the judiciary were adopted (ABGM, 2008). For an evaluation of legislative and constitutional reforms pursued by Turkey en route to the EU, see Phillips (2004: 94–95) and Kubicek (2005: 365–366).

On 17 December 2004, when the Commission decided to start negotiations with Turkey, political and civil society actors in Turkey welcomed the decision in a festive atmosphere. The decision was considered a fundamental milestone in EU-Turkey relations in many circles, including the political elites[3] and the media[4]: 'Turkey was finally in Europe'. In October 2005, official entry talks began. A Eurobarometer survey from autumn 2004 showed that a considerable majority of the Turkish people (62%) believed that membership would be a 'good thing' for Turkey, while in spring 2005, 68% responded that becoming a member of the EU would benefit Turkey (EB62; EB63.4). Nevertheless, the positive atmosphere created by the Commission's decision of 17 December was short-lived. Turkey's signature of the Additional Protocol in July 2005 heralded a new crisis. Together with the protocol, Turkey agreed to extend its existing Customs Union with the EU to the new member states. As a result, the EU insisted that Turkey had to open its seaports and airports to Greek Cypriot vessels. The Turkish Government refused to move on this issue until the isolation of Northern Cyprus had ended. The crisis reached a peak in November 2006 when the Commission recommended partial suspension of membership negotiations with Turkey, due to lack of progress on the Cyprus issue. In December 2006, EU foreign ministers decided to follow the Commission's recommendations and suspended talks with Turkey on 8 of the 35 negotiating areas. This decision, which created deep frustration, is a milestone in EU-Turkey relations. It is not only considered by Euro-sceptics as evidence of the EU's intention of keeping Turkey out of the EU but also gives prominence to the arguments that the EU is unfair, discriminatory, and thus undemocratic within political[5] and media elites and business cir-

---

3   In the speeches delivered by the ruling Justice and Development Party (AKP) on 20 December 2004 at the Turkish National Assembly, deputies and members of the government saluted the European Commission's decision to start membership negotiations as an outcome of 'modernization efforts of more than hundred years', as 'a turning point in Turkey's EU adventure', as 'an irreversible juncture', and as 'a dream coming true' (Doğanay, 2011: 272–273). For an analysis of the Turkish parliamentary elite's attitudes towards the EU see Akşit et al. (2011) and MacLaren and Müftüler-Baç (2003). For an early study of Turkish elite perspectives on Turkey's membership of the EU, see MacLaren (2000).
4   Research by Kejanlıoğlu and Taş (2009) on the newspaper coverage of the EU summit in 2004 shows that 67% of the news and commentaries supported Turkey's EU membership.
5   In her analysis of Turkish parliamentarians' discourses on Europe, Doğanay shows that after the EU's decision to suspend negotiations with Turkey on eight chapters, expectations of achieving full membership faded, both within the ruling party and within the opposition parties. Doğanay concludes that 'as the optimism toward membership lessened in 2006, the reactions were rationalized by arguing that the EU «is not the only way». Moreover, the emotional attachment to Westernisation as a «desire» shifted towards a sense of disappointment and even anger vis-à-vis the probability that this desire would never be realized. At this point, reactionary-nationalist discourse based on the arguments that «the entire world is against Turkey» and «EU's demands constitute a threat against the national integrity» was shared by all parties' (Doğanay 2011: 291).

cles, as well as some civil society organizations known to be favourably disposed towards the EU (Ergun, 2010; Eylemer and Taş, 2007).

Consequently, the level of trust in the EU has declined in Turkey. According to the results of Eurobarometer surveys, the ratio of those stating that membership would be a 'good thing' gradually decreased within a period of five years, from 62% in autumn 2004 (EB62), to 52% in spring 2007 (EB67), and to 48% in spring 2009 (EB71). In autumn 2009, the overall image of the EU was positive for 46% of the Turkish population (EB72), while in 2010 the ratio was only 42% (EB74). In spring 2009, while those who thought that EU membership would be favourable for Turkey was 57% (EB71), the percentage decreased to 50% in autumn 2009 (EB72) and to 42% in autumn 2010 (EB74). In spring 2011, the Eurobarometer data showed that only 41% believed that EU membership would be a good thing, whereas 29% believed it would be a bad thing (EB75a).[6] Furthermore, a study published in 2010 by Ankara University European Research Centre found that 83.9% of the respondents thought that the EU was not credible and not treating Turkey fairly, and 32.8% of them believed that full EU membership would never be realized (ATAUM, 2010). Similarly, a survey conducted by the Turkish Statistical Institute (TÜİK), searching for the results of a potential referendum on Turkey's accession to the EU, showed that the support for accession decreased from 52.5% in 2010 to 44.8% in 2011. According to the survey results, only 35.3% of the population thought that Turkish EU membership would have positive effects on their lives (TÜİK, 2011).

A further development that has fostered Euro-sceptic circles' reservations about the EU since 2009 is the ongoing economic crisis in the EU, which has made it difficult for some countries in the Eurozone to refinance their government debt. Following the economic crisis, which mainly influences Southern Europe, the idea that the future of the EU and European democracy is at risk has gained support in

---

6 Akşit et al.'s (2011) survey questioning parliamentarians' perceptions and attitudes towards the EU, which was conducted as a part of the Turkish Elite Survey, showed that parliamentarians' perceptions differed from those reported in the results of the public opinion polls. The research revealed that, when asked if Turkey's membership of the EU would be 'a good thing', 98.4% of the parliamentarians stated that it would be a 'good thing'. When asked to evaluate whether Turkey would benefit from membership, a similar majority (96.8%) indicated that Turkey would benefit from eventual membership (2011: 399). Nevertheless, the study also reveals that despite the strong support for membership, the parliamentarians appear to have a low level of trust in the EU institutions (on a scale of 0–10, the level of trust in the European Commission of the parliamentarians was 5.04, the trust in the European Parliament was 4.33, and the trust in the EU Council was 4.82) (Akşit et al., 2011: 399–400). The authors interpret this low level of trust as an indicator of possible 'repercussions in the formulation of necessary legislation during the accession negotiations' (Akşit et al., 2011: 404).

Turkish public opinion.[7] Motivated by the relative recuperation of the Turkish economy, certain politicians, business circles, media professionals, and civil society actors speculate that staying out of the Eurozone would favour Turkey since the European economy is on the verge of collapse.[8] As a result, whereas Eurobarometer surveys in spring 2004 indicated that 48% of the public believed that membership would bring economic welfare to Turkey (EB62), the ratio decreased to 32% in spring 2009 (EB71) and slightly increased to 35% in autumn 2010 (EB74). By contrast, the ratio of those who answered 'economic prosperity' to the question 'What does EU mean to you personally' declined dramatically from 31% in spring 2011 (EB75b) to 13% in autumn 2011 (EB76). This ratio increased to 23% in 2012 (EB77). Eurobarometer surveys also show that Turkish public opinion considers its national government a more effective player in combating the economic crisis (46%) than the United States (20%) and the EU (9%) (EB77).[9] In addition, a recent research, conducted in 2012 by Türk-Alman Eğitim ve Bilimsel Araştırmalar Vakfı (TAVAK) (Turkish-German Foundation of Education and Scientific Research) showed that in terms of the Turkish economy, 78.4% of the Turkish population believed that Turkey does not need the EU (Milliyet, 2012; HaberTürk, 2012).[10]

As a last point, we should mention that in the second half of 2012 the EU-Turkey relations were at an impasse with the start of the Greek Cyprus Presidency. Even though the Turkish Government has decided to continue to cooperate with EU institutions other than the Greek Cyprus presidency, some facts and figures negatively influence the expectations of the Turkish people about a recovery in EU-Turkey relations in the short term: only 1 of the 13 chapters (25th, Science and Research) opened to negotiations in the accession process has been provisionally closed to date; 18 chapters have been frozen, due to vetoes by Cyprus, France, or the European Council as a whole, and with only 3 chapters remaining, no new chapters have been opened to negotiations since 2010 (Paul, 2011). Along with this standstill, the reactions of the Turkish Government and the ruling Justice and Development Party [Adalet ve Kalkınma Partisi (AKP)], to the latest Progress

---

7   For comments, columns, and discussions about the future of the EU, see for example Özel (2011), Küçükcan (2012), Yiğit (2012), and Yavuz (2012).
8   For sample coverage in the Turkish press of the discussion on a possible collapse of the EU or the Euro, see HaberTürk (2011), Haber Rüzgarı (2012), HaberArtı (2012).
9   Interestingly, the percentage for the USA is the highest in any of the countries covered by the EB77 survey.
10 We (the authors of this chapter) were unable to access the publication of this research, which found extensive coverage in the press. For news announcing the results see, for example, Milliyet (2012) and Haber Türk (2012).

Report (15th) can be interpreted as meaning that EU accession will not be part of the Turkish short-term agenda.[11] By contrast, progress reports show that Turkish democracy is far from reaching European standards in terms of the implementation of the reforms. The government's tendency to suppress opposition through the long-term custody and imprisonment of journalists, scholars, students, and even lawyers, as an extension of the relations of dominance among the executive, judiciary, and police powers, continues to keep Turkey away from European democracy.

Turkish civil society: a beneficiary and a driving force of Europeanization

The strong state tradition in Turkey has acted as a constraint to civil society for a long time. Especially after the 1980 coup, CSOs almost disappeared. However, the 1980s, under the Turgut Özal governments, were also marked by substantial economic liberalization. Drawing on support from the wave of liberalization, CSOs started to demand greater political liberalization and became more visible and vocal in the 1990s (Kubicek, 2005: 367). The development of civil society and CSOs' participation in democratic processes as socio-political actors were furthered with the accession and harmonization processes. It should be acknowledged that CSOs acted as catalysts and controllers in the process of making and implementing legal institutional regulations for harmonization with the EU. In other words, the process was a twofold operation: on the one hand, the EU, which considers the development of civil society an essential aspect of democratic consolidation, has contributed to the development of civil society in Turkey; on the other hand, CSOs' activities in support of the harmonization, especially the implementation of the reforms concerning human rights, women rights, and protection of the minorities, contributed to the consolidation of democracy, and to the success

---

11 Minister for European Union Affairs and Chief Negotiator Egemen Bağış evaluated the Turkey 2012 Progress Report as far from being a guide for Turkey but rather as a product of the efforts of individual bargaining (Today's Zaman, 2012a). Bağış also considered the report a complete disappointment for Turkey. He defined it as a film script that did not present an objective picture of Turkey and that nobody knew how it would eventually play out. Bağış blasted the EU by saying that the way the report was written actually served the interests of those people who do not want to see Turkey move along with further democratization efforts (Today's Zaman, 2012b). AKP politician Burhan Kuzu threw a copy of the recent EU Commission report on the floor during a live television interview, saying 'This is a report to be thrown in the trash. There is no trash can here, so I'm throwing it on the floor' (Ergin, 2012).

of the reforms to some extent. Below, in this section, we first focus on the way in which EU candidacy has altered the characteristics of civil society in Turkey. Thereafter, we turn to the role of the CSOs in Turkey's process of Europeanization.

The contribution of the EU candidacy process to the development of civil society in Turkey can be examined under some major headings. First, by its decisions made in Helsinki in 1999 and Copenhagen in 2002, the EU facilitated reforms concerning the freedom of association in the country. In 2002 and 2003, amendments to the law on associations were made as part of the second, fourth, and seventh harmonization packages, and in 2004 a new law on associations came into effect. The law on associations passed in 2004 reduced the possibility for state interference in the activities of associations. Limitations on the establishment of associations on the basis of race, ethnicity, religion, sect, region, or any other minority group were removed. In 2008, a new law on foundations relaxed the conditions for establishing a foundation and eased the regulatory framework for the selection of board members, the acquisition or sale of assets, fund raising from abroad, and co-operation with foreign foundations.[12] Additionally, the returns and compensations to the religious minority foundations (Greek and Armenian), whose properties had been seized in the 1960s, were permitted through a series of legal arrangements made in 2003, 2008, and 2011.[13]

Along with legislative changes, the EU has also contributed to the development of civil society in Turkey through direct financial assistance. The grants provided by the EU to CSO projects in Turkey have increased significantly following the Helsinki Summit, and especially since 2002. In total, 44 separate pre-accession assistance[14] funds were raised during the period 2002–2010 for 1124 projects operated by associations, foundations, unions, chambers, and cooperatives,[15] amoun-

---

12 Despite the progress, the 2011 Turkey Progress Report of the European Commission indicates that the CSOs continue 'to face closure cases plus disproportionate administrative checks and fines. Membership in associations continues to require a Turkish residency permit and foreign CSOs are subject to specific regulations. Legislative and bureaucratic obstacles impeding the financial sustainability of CSOs persist, e.g. with respect to the collection of domestic and international aid, to obtaining public benefit status for associations and tax exemptions for foundations, etc. The lack of simplified rules creates difficulties for small or medium-sized associations.' The report also highlights that especially in the south-east of Turkey 'Civil society organizations and human rights defenders often face prosecution and legal proceedings on charges of terrorist propaganda during demonstrations and protest meetings' (European Commission, 2011:27).
13 See Cengiz (2010a, 2010b) for further information on property seizure of the religious minority foundations and the consequent process.
14 Formerly referred to as the 'Pre-accession Financial Instrument for Turkey'.
15 As highlighted by İçduygu (2011), based on their legal status, the CSOs in Turkey can be examined

ting to more than EUR 104 million in total (ABGS, 2010).[16] The EU-Turkey Civil Society Dialogue[17], which aimed to foster the dialogue between civil society organizations in Turkey in different fields with their counterparts within the EU, was also established through EU funding.[18]

In addition to direct financial and legal benefits, the CSOs have also received training benefits from the EU. Assisting these organizations in institutionalization has been central; they have been involved in seminars, conferences, and training sessions. For example, the Civil Society Development Programme of the EU (CSDP) has organized continuous seminars in order to boost the capacity of the CSOs working at grass-root level, and hence to 'help establish a more balanced relationship between citizens and the state' (Göksel & Güneş, 2005: 66). Furthermore, direct exchange between civil society actors in Turkey and the EU's institutions, mainly through interactions, partnerships, and networking activities, has helped the CSOs to acquire 'skills and tools to conduct their activities in a "European" way' (Ergun, 2010: 508).

Lastly, it is also worth mentioning the 'enabling impact' of the EU, underlined by two civil society activists, Diba Nigar Göksel and Rana Birden Güneş. The membership prospect and cooperation with European actors have bolstered the prestige of CSOs as well as their ability to raise issues that could not have been raised easily before: 'Besides direct support ... NGOs from Turkey are taken quite seriously by the officials of EU member states as well as EC authorities ... being listened to as a credible voice in Europe has strengthened the standing of many NGOs on the domestic scene as well' (Göksel and Güneş 2005: 67).

The number of associations and foundations has grown remarkably since the Helsinki Summit: the total number of registered associations and foundations in-

---

under four categories: Associations – participatory or community organizations requiring a system of membership; Foundations – mainly established through an initial endowment; Cooperatives – commercial entities with active shareholders; and Professional organizations – establishments engaged in promoting the professional interests of their members.

16 A total of 169 associations and 294 foundations benefited from almost EUR 46 million of the whole amount.
17 As a result of the need for intercultural dialogue, in 2005 the EU developed a strategy to strengthen civil society dialogue amongst candidate countries and EU non-governmental organizations. Civil Society Dialogue (CSD) aims at leading to a better understanding of the values and policies of the EU amongst Turkish citizens. Within this framework, voluntary organizations such as associations, foundations, platforms, citizen initiatives, professional organizations, commercial and industrial chambers, cooperatives, and unions form the target groups of the civil society dialogue (EU Delegation, n.d.).
18 For instance, in 2007, especially two 'Instrument for Pre-accession Assistance (IPA)' projects amounting to EUR 11.7 million were dedicated to this issue (European Commission, n.d.).

creased from around 64,000 in 1998 to almost 97,000 in 2012.[19] More significantly, the EU's involvement has changed the nature of civil society's activities in Turkey. As Ergun (2010: 519) emphasizes, 'CSOs, which were previously based on the voluntary participation of members and supporters and funded by membership fees and modest donations ... [became] professionalized, issue-orientated and working on a project basis.' Concomitantly, civil society actors have become more active in shaping public opinion and in pushing the government to accomplish the legal and institutional reforms necessary for Turkey's democratic consolidation as well as its accession to the EU.

Moreover, by referring to statements and directives from the EU, the vast majority of the well-known CSOs became spokesmen for EU-related democratic reforms.[20] Especially, CSOs located in large urban centres, organizations related to big business and the private sector, and organizations run by liberal intellectuals became important actors, not only in promoting a pro-EU perspective but also in formulating certain concrete EU-related reforms. For instance, before the Copenhagen Summit, the İktisadi Kalkınma Vakfı (IKV) [Economic Development Foundation] started a broad-based movement of 175 civil society organizations called the 'Movement for Europe 2002', to push the government towards alignment with the EU and to provide collective support for Turkey's EU accession and reforms (Eylemer and Taş, 2007: 564). Similarly, ARI Hareketi (ARI) [ARI Movement], which promotes participatory democracy in Turkey, 'has also been very active in advocacy work to communicate the EU-related views of Turkish civil society to officials and public in both Turkey and Europe' (İçduygu, 2011: 386). In terms of advocating the necessary reforms, also noteworthy is the Women's Coalition's impact on decision-makers regarding reform of the Turkish Penal Code (Göksel & Güneş, 2005: 68). In addition, two prominent women's associations, Kadın Adayları Destekleme Derneği (KADER) [Association for Supporting and Training Women] and Türkiye Kadın Girişimciler Derneği (KAGİDER) [Women Entrepreneurs Association of Turkey] introduced a gender-sensitive approach to the pre-accession process (İçduygu, 2011: 387). Moreover, the Türk Sanayici ve

---

19 For more information on the number of CSOs and relevant graphics, see the webpage of İçişleri Bakanlığı Dernekler Dairesi Başkanlığı (Department of Associations of the Ministry of Foreign Affairs) at both http://www.dernekler.gov.tr/index.php?option=com_content&view=category&layout=blog&id=52&Itemid=12&lang=tr and http://www.dernekler.gov.tr/index.php?option=com_content&view=category&layout=blog&id=51&Itemid=66&lang=tr

20 Regardless of the EU's role in fostering CSOs in Turkey, for an evaluation of CSOs' limited capacity to adopt and implement EU values in their internal mechanisms and activities, see İçduygu (2011: 389–393). In addition, see Heper and Yıldırım (2011) for an evaluation of the development of civil society in Turkey and its limitations.

İşadamları Derneği (TÜSİAD) [Turkish Industry & Business Association] has not only accomplished lobbying activities before the EC and EU member states delegations since 1996, with its Brussels Representative Office, but also, through its reports, has influenced the legal and institutional reforms of the Turkish Government.

Nevertheless, although Turkish civil society generally holds its pro-EU perspective despite continuing crises with and within the EU, it cannot be argued that Turkey's perception of Europe can always be considered on the basis of a pure relation of belonging. The effort to be a part of Europe always embodies contradictions, as Ahıska (2003: 353) argues: 'The West has either been celebrated as a "model" to be followed or exorcized as a threat to "indigenous" national values.' In this respect, especially the ideas of the Euro-sceptic circles have gained further validity in periods of crisis. For example, the opposition of some European circles to the possibility of Turkey's EU membership on the grounds of its lack of 'Europeanness' increased the hesitancy of Euro-sceptics and cautious groups in Turkey, including the CSOs (Eylemer & Taş, 2007: 565). In response, the conditions peculiar to Turkey – the imperative to protect the national independence vis-à-vis the imperialist 'external powers', which had posed a threat against Turkey in the past and which potentially may pose a threat today, as well as the 'hidden agenda' of these powers – constitute, at the discursive level, the fundamental arguments of those who are agnostic about the sincerity of the EU.[21] Mainly, some strict, ideology-based CSOs, especially those holding nationalist and Islamist perspectives, are highly critical of Turkey's EU membership process. Beside this 'hard Euro-sceptic' position, reference can also be made to 'soft Euro-scepticism' generally internalized by the centre-left (Yılmaz, 2011). In addition, there are others who adopt a cautious perspective towards the EU, such as Müstakil Sanayici ve İşadamları Derneği (MÜSİAD) [Independent Industrialists and Businessmen Association], an 'Islamic-oriented business association' in Yankaya's (2009) terms.[22]

---

21 The conditions peculiar to Turkey are repeatedly addressed by political parties and civil society actors. Öniş (2007) defines this situation as a paradox of many established parties on both the left and right ends of the political spectrum. Accordingly, these parties 'can be characterized as «defensive nationalists» in the sense that they are broadly supportive of EU membership in principle but tend to be uncomfortable with key elements of EU conditionality. If membership could be accomplished without reforms, many of these parties would welcome the opportunity' (Öniş 2007: 247). For other analyses of the Euro-sceptic positions of Turkish political parties, elites and the general public, see Yılmaz (2011) and Bardakçı (2010).

22 As stated by Eylemer and Taş, (2007: 564), 'MÜSİAD expresses its position «beyond the dilemma of being totally against or totally for the EU membership» depending on the costs and benefits of EU membership for Turkey.'

Civil society's perceptions of the EU

Inspired by the EU's emphasis on civil society as a significant element of the European democratic culture, our study, the findings of which are presented in this chapter, investigated how the representatives of the CSOs in Turkey perceive (1) the limits of the European Union as a democratic entity; (2) the impact of the EU's ongoing economic crisis concerning the democratic values of Europe and the democratic procedures of the countries influenced by the crisis; and (3) the future of the EU and the EU-Turkey relations.

For the purpose of the study, in-depth interviews were held with the representatives of 16 CSOs based in Istanbul, Ankara, and Izmir. The CSOs were selected on the basis of several criteria. The first one was their engagement in European matters. Most of the organizations mentioned in the above short summary of the role of the CSOs in the harmonization process of Turkey to the EU were included in the research. Their interests in Turkey's accession process and/or their active role in the process constituted a second selection criterion. The following were selected on basis of the second criterion: the Dış Politika Enstitüsü (DPE) [Foreign Policy Institute], ARI, the Marmara Grubu Vakfı (MGV) [Marmara Group Foundation], Türkiye-Avrupa Vakfı (TAV) [Turkey-Europe Foundation], Türkiye Ekonomik ve Sosyal Etdüler Vakfı (TESEV) [Turkey Economic and Social Studies Foundation, and Avrupa Çalışmaları Ege Derneği] (AÇED) [Aegean Association on European Studies].

Because structural and legal reforms for harmonization mostly concerned human rights and democracy, commitment to these issues was a third selection criterion. On the basis of this criterion, the following were included in the research: the İnsan Hakları Derneği (İHD) [Human Rights Association], İnsan Hakları ve Mazlumlar İçin Dayanışma Derneği (MAZLUMDER) [Organization of Human Rights and Solidarity for Oppressed People], Türk Demokrasi Vakfı (TDV) [Turkish Democracy Foundation], Türkiye İnsan Hakları Vakfı (TİHV) [Human Rights Foundation of Turkey], Çağdaş Yaşamı Destekleme Derneği (ÇYDD) [Association for the Support of Contemporary Living], and Sosyal Demokrasi Vakfı (SODEV) [Social Democracy Foundation].

Furthermore, some organizations were added to the sample due to their ability to represent finance and business circles, namely TÜSİAD, KAGİDER, and the Türkiye Odalar ve Borsalar Birliği (TOBB) [Union of Chambers and Commodity Exchanges of Turkey]. The aforementioned three organizations also played an active role in Turkey's accession process through their Brussels offices. In addition, the Türkiye İşçi Sendikaları Konfederasyonu (TÜRK-İŞ) [Confederation of Turkish Trade Unions], representing labour, was included in the sample.

While, on balance, the study sample is pro-EU, due to the criterion of engagement in European matters, it also contains some organizations mostly known for their Euro-sceptic arguments, such as MAZLUMDER and TÜRK-İŞ. However, findings showed that it is almost impossible to make a strict classification of the interviewees according to their pro-EU and Euro-sceptic tendencies. It is common for formerly Euro-sceptic CSOs to embrace pro-EU arguments currently and/or for formerly pro-EU CSOs to become Euro-sceptic over time, or more interestingly, to show signs of both tendencies in their discourses simultaneously (see the Appendix for detailed information about these CSOs).

In-depth interviews with the representatives, who mainly held executive positions in the organizations (i.e. president, vice-president, secretary general, branch director, or head of EU department), were conducted between September and December 2012, using a semi-structured interview questionnaire. Subsequently, the interviewers transcribed the tape-recorded interviews, each of which had lasted 50–90 minutes.

Coexistence of contradicting definitions of Europe

According to the interviewees, the basic characteristics of Europe are the principles of the supremacy of law, freedom of expression,[23] respect for human rights, minority rights, gender equality,[24] multiculturalism, tolerance, secularism, and democracy that is shaped by these principles. The EU was identified as a 'peace project' (representatives of the MGV, TDV, TAV, and TÜSİAD), underpinned by the ideas of the Enlightenment (AÇED), created in the name of stability and cohabitation within multiculturalism (TDV), and as something that softens the 'aggressive and competitive nature of the nation state' (AÇED). By contrast, the need for economic convergence in the Union's early stages was not disregarded. The establishment of the Union was explained as a 'common response from European bourgeoisie to the internationalization of economy' (AÇED). The MGV representative identified the EU as a 'project of economic and social development', while the TOBB representative described it as a 'both political and economic project'. According to the TÜSİAD representative, 'the EU started as a site of materialization of the ideal of political peace through concrete economic integration, yet

---

23 For the İHD representative, freedom of expression was the keystone of the EU. The TESEV representative emphasized the core values and basic human rights.
24 The KAGİDER representative stated that the EU represented equality for men and women.

became a supranational regulatory agency of different interests.' Stability and welfare offered to member states were most often emphasized as the advantages of the EU.

The interviewees who displayed a pro-EU attitude or even described themselves as a 'fan of the EU' (MGV) described the EU as 'a story of success, a road to peace, ease and prosperity, which is followed worldwide' (AÇED), as 'admirable' (MGV), and a 'peak or climax of democracy' (ARI), and pointed to the power of the EU to transform or Europeanize its periphery (AÇED). Although almost all interviewees agreed on the fundamental values of the EU, they also supported varied Euro-sceptic arguments. Only one (MAZLUMDER) of 16 CSO representatives expressed clearly that her organization had an anti-EU perspective[25]; TÜRK-İŞ had a sceptical outlook until 2004,[26] while AÇED, DPE, İHD, KAGİDER, MGV, TDV, TESEV, TOBB, and TÜSİAD declared their pro-EU positions at different degrees.

Both the pro-EU and anti-EU discourses of CSO representatives seem eclectic. They used contradicting arguments in combination; the EU can sometimes be defined as something totally opposite of the values attributed to it. For example, the MAZLUMDER representative accused the EU of double standards and said that MAZLUMDER was staying away from it, just because they did not believe in its objectivity. However, unexpectedly, she added: 'I realize now that the Union has reached the most universal standards and values'.[27]

For those defining themselves as pro-Europeans, the eclectic discourse contains more remarkable contradictions. Even those who defined the EU as the 'peak of democracy' (ARI), claimed that the EU was 'insincere',[28] 'having double stan-

---

25 However, the MAZLUMDER representative, who defined her association as an EU opponent, said she could also think of EU membership as desirable.
26 After a change of executive team in 2004, TÜRK-İŞ conducted a survey among 3000 workers, 65% of whom thought the EU membership would have positive effects on working life in Turkey. However, the respondents' perception of the EU was not particularly positive, as they described the EU as being unfair towards Turkey.
27 It is the desire to be independent from EU interventions that keeps MAZLUMDER away from EU funds. For example, as they regard homosexuality as a product of disidentification policies, the representative was concerned about being forced to acknowledge homosexual rights. Similarly, KAGİDER and ARI representatives said that the EU has some priorities and provides financial support to projects concerning these areas. The ARI representative thought that the EU restricted the fields of activity by intervening in the scopes, methodologies, and outputs of the projects. He added that ARI wanted to act in its preferred areas, not in those proposed by the Union.
28 The AÇED representative stated: 'The fortress-Europe, while closing itself to outsiders, excludes its universal values in a sense. I find it insincere.'

dards',[29] and being 'prejudiced and unfair against Turks'[30]. The EU was criticized for being 'xenophobic',[31] due to its immigration and asylum law and visa policy (MAZLUMDER), and of 'having double standards' because of (1) its behaviour towards Turkey concerning Cyprus[32] and Armenian[33] issues; (2) the European Court of Human Rights' (ECHR) decision on Leyla Şahin case[34]; (3) 'Islamophobia'[35]; and (4) right-wing nationalism rising, especially with the economic crisis[36]. Other Euro-sceptic arguments were that the EU is an entity 'aiming for uniformity, purification, and disidentification' (MAZLUMDER); 'desecuritizing the outsiders and secluding itself', and also 'homogenizing, [and] exclusivist with its fortress Europe ideal' (AÇED).

However, such discrepancies in discourse are sometimes sourced from the reactions Turkey received from European countries at critical junctures, thus displaying the dynamic aspect of EU-Turkey relations. For example, the ARI representative said that the ARI had changed their pro-European attitude after the Lisbon

---

29 For the ARI representative, the EU was not a reliable entity. It contained many double standards, as any state or institution. The ÇYDD representative used the same description but in terms of the EU's non-intervention in the undemocratic affairs of the Justice and Development Party (AKP) government.

30 The MGV representative thought that the EU violated its own values, due to its prejudice against Turkey: 'While supporting and mentoring the other candidates, the EU leaves Turkey aside. This prejudice is inappropriate. There is no need to be jealous of Turks and Turkey. I call out especially to France.'

31 The MAZLUMDER representative stated: 'Minorities are scapegoats in some countries. Especially in countries facing crisis, migrants and foreigners are strongly repressed because people think that they are culpable of the inland unemployment.'

32 The ARI and TDV representatives claimed that the EU has failed in the Cypriot issue's management, and the TDV representative added that 'The EU has broken its word to Turkey on the Cypriot issue.'

33 The MAZLUMDER representative stated: 'The EU stresses the Armenian issue while it overlooks the Serbian problem. I find this very insincere.' The TDV representative claimed that the EU compels Turkey to acknowledge the 'Armenian problem' as a prerequisite to the accession, and that 'This kind of political criterion has never been asked of any of the candidates before.'

34 The Leyla Şahin versus Turkey case was litigated by a student challenging the Turkish law, which prohibits the wearing of headscarves in state buildings. The Court upheld Turkish law. The MAZLUMDER representative considered the ECHR's decision a violation of religious rights and as proof of the EU's double standards in terms of human rights.

35 The MAZLUMDER representative said: 'The EU fights against hostility towards Jews and does not interpret anti-Semitism within freedom of expression, but the burning of Quran in France, the releases of movies insulting Islam have been considered as a component of this freedom. Isn't it a paradox?'

36 The KAGİDER representative mentioned Germany, France, and Austria as nationalist countries standing against Turkey.

Treaty came into force, which had shown internal problems within the EU.[37] He questions why, given that European states would insist on being part of the EU if they did not get along with each other, given that they have differing views of Turkey's membership. Instead, they now preferred to think of it as 'a carrot for the democratization of Turkey'. Similarly, the ÇYDD representative emphasized their broken dreams about the EU and referred to the 'EU carrot'.[38] The TÜRK-İŞ representative related TÜRK-İŞ's recent disinterested stance towards the EU to the fact that the chapter concerning labour issues was among the last of the chapters to be considered.

There are also more reasonable assessments of the EU, differentiating basic values from its structure. For example, the TESEV representative stated, 'the EU clearly has, in its own right, democratic aspirations but there are problems within the EU and the way it's structured. There is the Parliament, which has always been the democratically elected body, but also you have the Council and the Commission that have powers over the democratically elected body in the EU. So, there is a conflict there.' By contrast, the TÜSİAD representative criticized the composition of the European Parliament, despite his perception of the EU as a most democratic structure.

Europe and 'Europeanness': the opposition between 'us' and 'them'

Concurrent with the negative features attributed to the European Union, some CSO representatives addressed the EU within the framework of nationalist discourses in terms of the opposition between 'them' and 'us'. Turkey and the Turkish people are positioned as victims in this oppositional relationship. The EU, as the villain, is criticized of being unfair to Turkey: 'Turkey, being geographically in the European continent' (MGV, TAV), or the idea of Turks being already Europeans or 'even better than Europeans' (MGV) is largely supported.

The same problem of eclecticism continues with regard to the perception of EU-Turkey relations. For example, the MGV representative considered Turkish people as Europeans:

---

37 See Risteska's (2010) assessment of the effects of the Lisbon Treaty on Accession Countries, including Turkey.
38 This expression refers to EU membership as a reward offered to Turkey in order to persuade and encourage the Turkish Government to adopt reforms.

Turkey is already European. We are as European as the people in the Balkans. Suleiman the Magnificent arrived in Europe in 1398. How many of the European states have existed over there ever since? I am going farther back. The Turkish presence in the Balkans and the Black Sea region goes back to the fourth century, to the Byzantine Empire. There are still many places called by Turkish names. Who named these places? How many Europeans have been in those regions ever since?

The MGV representative tried to strengthen her thesis that Turks are already Europeans, with the fact that the Ottoman Empire was founded in Rumelia: 'The main goal of the Turks is, and has always been, Europe. All geographical movements have aimed at Europe. None of them has been marched towards Asia.' However, she did not explain this relationship of belonging only in terms of geography. She also tried to relate Ottoman values to current European values: 'We believe in European values from the bottom of our hearts. The Ottoman Empire has been established on European values too: the freedom to mother tongue, the fair taxation system, etc. have been implemented for years'. Similarly, the TDV representative stated: 'Since its foundation, the Republic of Turkey has always followed similar ideals with the EU.' He pointed out that the Ottoman Empire had supported multiculturalism and that many ethnic groups had lived together as Ottoman citizens for ages. He found that the fundamental principle of 'peace at home and peace in the world' of the Turkish Republic had similarities with the values of the EU, which he described as a peace project. According to him, even today, 'Turkey has already reached so many European standards' and 'is a member of the EU in several ways'.[39] He underlined the fact that currently Turkey was the sixth largest economy in Europe and affirmed that it had served as a model for many EU members with some reforms (e.g. the pharmaceutical track and trace system).[40]

Even though some similarities are emphasized, the unfair manner of the EU emerges as the major source of Euro-scepticism. The MGV representative wished 'Europeans to be as loyal as us to European values and to apply them'. She stated that 'Being founded with European values does not necessarily mean being a good performer and implementing democracy.' Europeans are also criticized for

---

39 'Turkey is already a part of the EU in many ways. There are currently more than 3.5–4 million Turks living in Europe and hundreds of them are employers. In fact, this means a de facto membership of the Union.'

40 The interviewees largely emphasized the progress in Turkish economy and considered it is stronger than the European countries facing the crisis. The İHD representative was more suspicious about this optimistic picture, and reminded that the government maintains the IMF programme without the IMF and tries to sustain the economy with consecutive pay rises.

'seeing Turkish people as the only opponent' and all obstacles to Turkey's EU bid are explained by this idea: the major breaking point here is the EU membership of Cyprus (TDV). The TÜRK-İŞ representative raised a similar point and evaluated the membership of Cyprus as a decision showing the power of lobbying rather than the democratic aspirations of the EU.

In contrast to the general discourse, SODEV, TESEV, and TÜSİAD representatives spoke of mutual problems in the accession process. The SODEV representative blamed the Turkish Government for not being strongly attached and dedicated to the EU bid, and for losing public support and interest in the process. Similarly, the TAV representative stressed the lack of knowledge of European issues on part of the Turkish Government, and related the emotional reactions[41] to this ignorance. In common with the MGV and TDV representatives, the SODEV representative accepted that the EU had been founded on ideal values but he still emphasized the importance of how it was governed: 'Things go wrong sometimes, but there are CSOs, unions, and professional associations that can act collectively to overcome the problems. The EU should have a more social face.' The TÜSİAD representative blamed both sides for the suspension of the process: with regard to the EU, he referred to Sarkozy's anti-Turkish tendency, the Cyprus issue, and the communication deficit; and with regard to Turkey, he referred to Article 310 of the Penal Law that is criticized for limiting the freedom of expression, the AKP government's Balyoz and Ergenekon operations against secular and military forces,[42] and constraints on the freedom of the press. The TESEV representative[43] also underlined the present stalemate in EU-Turkey relations, and explained this with reference to the existence of internal problems on both sides: 'Europe is dealing with its own problems. There is lack of interest in Europe about Turkey, unfortunately. In Turkey, as a reflection of a lack of interest in Europe, Turkey's agenda is domestic, which is kind of understandable. So, the process will probably continue but at a very slow pace.'

---

41 See Footnote 3 for examples.
42 The Ergenekon investigation into the activities of Turkey's *derin devlet* (deep state) was launched in 2007, and the Balyoz investigation into an alleged secularist military coup plan dating back to 2003 started in 2010. A number of journalists, academics, retired generals, and/or military officers in active duty were detained, many of them were arrested within the two operations. The logic of the operations, the process of prosecution, and the trials are intensely discussed in Turkey. Some people embrace the operations as an opportunity for the country to struggle against the deep state and militarism, while others fiercely oppose the process, which they accept as an attempt to discredit and disable secularist opposition to the ruling Justice and Development Party.
43 It should be noted that the interviewed TESEV representative was British. Hence, his remarks could not be expected to reflect Turkish nationalist discourse.

The democratic problem as secondary among the obstacles to Turkey's accession

Most CSO representatives believed that 'Turkey will not be accepted no matter what it does' (TDV)[44] because of 'its negative image in the eyes of the EU' (MGV, TOBB).[45] The main obstacles to Turkey's accession are considered to be the existing agreement concerning the Customs Union, which empties the EU's economic argument for making Turkey a full member (AÇED, DPE); cultural differences (ÇYDD); the membership of Cyprus (TDV, TÜRK-İŞ); the stance of certain member states – namely Cyprus, France, Germany, and Austria –towards Turkey (TESEV, TÜRK-İŞ); population (ÇYDD); the Armenian issue (TDV); the geographical position of Turkey and its neighbours (MGV, AÇED); and PKK (Kurdistan Workers' Party) terrorism (AÇED, TDV). The representatives emphasized that these problems are not under Turkey's control, but have been provoked by actors against Turkey or by the Union itself.

The MGV representative thought that the decline in public support for EU membership was a result of a general feeling of being ostracized and pushed away from the Union. She said: 'Turkish people are very proud of themselves, no one should ever humiliate a whole nation.' This and the above statements prove that civil society actors in Turkey approach the EU membership issue in an emotional way. The TDV representative summarized the situation by saying 'We are already heartbroken.'

This discourse points out a nationalist tendency. It is also coherent with the fact that Turkey's lack of improvement in some fields[46] was considered either secondary or wholly disregarded by most of the interviewees (with the exception of İHD, TÜSİAD, and TESEV). For example, the TDV representative was quite optimistic about Turkey's position on human rights and democracy: 'Despite all the obstacles, Turkey's movement to modernization continues. By means of the reforms, [minority] foundations have taken their properties back, the minimum age to be elected has been set to 25, and outstanding progress in human rights has been achieved.' The TDV representative illustrated Turkey's improvement in human rights with the introduction under Turkish law of opportunities for education and broadcasting in languages other than Turkish. As other examples of evidence of the impro-

---

44 Similarly, the KAGİDER representative emphasized the Cypriot issue as a big obstacle that makes all achievements worthless in the eye of the EU.
45 The TOBB representative mentioned the negative image of Turkey in Europe but avoided enunciating any views about Turkey's possible membership of the EU.
46 For example, human rights, freedom of expression, minority rights, and judicial independence.

vements, he cited the increase in the number of newspapers and television stations (broadcasting in different languages), the existence of the parliamentary human rights commission of the Turkish Grand National Assembly, and the improvement in political participation possibilities for minority groups.

Instead of focusing on the socio-political origins of the problems in Turkey's democratization and accession processes, some interviewees seemed content with explaining the issue in terms of education and ignorance. For example, the MGV representative compared Turkey's literacy and graduation rates to EU member states,[47] and said: 'I don't believe that Turkey can contribute to the EU without producing knowledge individually and applying it. For this, first of all, Turkish people should be more educated.' CSOs supporting this argument (AÇED, MGV, SODEV, TDV, and ÇYDD) mostly organize conferences[48] and other educational initiatives and use EU funds for such activities.[49] The DPE representative thought that education was the only way to develop empathy and tolerance among people. In this respect, he assigned the role of mentoring to the EU.[50]

It may be said that Turkey's prominent civil society actors naively believe in 'education' and 'public enlightenment on European matters' for the resolution of accession problems in general. However, it would be a simplification to think that all civil society actors in Turkey are indifferent to the role of democracy problems in the accession process. Turkey's lack of democracy and human rights was partially mentioned by the representatives, to various degrees. For example, the DPE representative felt that Turkey had failed to create a democratic culture, and thereby secure the separation of powers, the freedom of the press, and secularism. The TÜSİAD representative also underlined Turkey's shortcomings in sustaining

---

47 The MGV representative stated: 'Education and democratization' are important in Turkey's accession process. Further, he said: 'Economic growth does not suffice. Turkey is the world's 18th largest economy. We should aim at the same ranking in gender equality, in social development, in literacy rate etc. At least 50% of the population should be graduates.'
48 The MGV and SODEV organize several conferences to introduce the EU and its mechanisms to the public.
49 The ARI and AÇED representatives said that the role of CSOs in the accession process consisted of 'raising public awareness'. By contrast, the TDV representative defined an educative role and mentioned the foundation's project of establishing a university.
50 The MGV representative also mentioned this responsibility and complained about the EU's reluctance to mentor Turkey. By contrast, the TESEV representative found a positive aspect in Turkey acting by its own: 'Europe is not even mentioned in the constitution debate, which is negative and positive. It is negative in that the EU can be a good benchmark or model for what needs to be incorporated in the constitution. On the other hand, what is interesting and positive is that Turkey is doing it for Turkey, not for the EU. Turkey is trying to go to the process of writing its own new constitution, but it is doing it for domestic reasons.'

a culture of liberties. He thought that being undemocratic was against Turkey's interests.

The KAGİDER representative stressed the Cypriot issue and human rights as the most important obstacles to Turkey's accession. Other important issues to be solved included minority rights, the Kurdish issue, freedom of the press, women's rights, and torture. The AÇED and TDV representatives pointed out the EU's and their own expectation of the resolution of the Kurdish issue by peaceful and democratic means, and underlined the issue as an obstacle to accession.

It may be said that the İHD has a more coherent perspective on democratization problems. According to this organization, the most important points for democracy and human rights are the Kurdish problem; freedom of thought, conscience, and religion; and gender equality. The İHD representative claimed that 'democracy does not exist in Turkey ... Pluralism, openness and participation are the essentials of democracy ... Turkey is an anti-democratic country, regulated by the constitution of 1982 made by a coup d'état.' The İHD representative indicated that basic democratic problems of Turkey are thus: 'the emphasis on Turkish ethnic and Sunni-Muslim religious identity; the definition of the minority rights through non-Muslims and its misapplication; torture and ill-treatment; the violations of the right to life; the lack of the freedom of expression and association; the 10% election threshold; the lack of judicial independence, neutrality and supremacy of law; supervision of the central government on local authorities; governance of the Constitutional Court and the Supreme Court on political parties; and effects of the National Security Council on the government'.

In addition, the İHD representative considered Turkey far removed from universal secular values, and stated: 'This is why, the İHD opposed the decision of beginning negotiations in 2004 and forced Verheugen to send a committee to Turkey.' For the İHD, the EU bid is a big opportunity for Turkey's democratization. However, Turkey's delay to apply the Copenhagen criteria properly is considered ruinous to this opportunity:[51] 'Unless a strong movement for social democracy develops ... Turkey's membership will not occur. Nevertheless the continuation of the process would contribute to the democratization of Turkey'.

---

51 The İHD representative said:'The government does not intend to become a member of the EU. Its real objective is to create a moderate Islamic policy.' He also thought that the European parties were aware of this fact, and that they did not intend to accept Turkey in the European Union after all.

The crisis and the future of the European Union

For some interviewees, the crisis is a milestone in EU-Turkey relations. They predict an interruption of the European enlargement process (AÇED, KAGİDER, İHD) and assume that Turkey's accession will not occur in the short term, even though all problems will be solved.[52] Some interviewees foresaw the collapse of the Union (MAZLUMDER), while others expected it to evolve into something different (ARI,[53] ÇYDD, DPE, TAV, TESEV, and TÜSİAD). One interviewee (representing TDV) expected that contrary to the economic crisis in Europe, Turkey, with its growing economy,[54] would come out against EU membership one day, just as Norway did.

The DPE representative stated that 'Europe has created the crisis by itself.' The MGV representative blamed 'big states' for inciting the crisis by accepting undeveloped countries such as Bulgaria and Romania while they had been testing Turkey for many years. The crisis was thus seen as 'a kind of payback'. The SODEV representative too, thought that the EU should have accepted Turkey instead of many Eastern European states, as Turkey would have contributed more to the Union. When asked to analyse the reasons for the crisis, the ARI representative said: 'The EU sacrificed stability for pluralism.' In other words, he believed that the reasons for the crisis were political. The TÜSİAD representative also emphasized the inability of democratic institutions to produce a solution to the crisis – an inability that in turn had been further inhibited by the social unrest. For him, the crisis was not a monetary crisis but a crisis of governance. According to the ARI representative, the crisis was a result of the choice for pluralism to majority rule: 'Europe suffers from pluralism. If the election threshold were 10% in member countries, Greece, Italy, Spain, or Portugal would not be in such as mess today. If there were strong parties and strong governments, authoritarian tendencies would probably emerge, but it is likely that they would not suffer from economic crisis. This would mean compromising democracy, but the economic balance would endure.'

---

52   The MGV and AÇED representatives were more optimistic about Turkey's membership.
53   The ARI representative suggested that 'the EU will not be a political union any longer when Turkey successfully completes the chapters of the *acquis communautaire*.' The DPE representative talked about the shift of technological advantages from Europe to the east, and pointed to India, Brazil, countries in the Far East, and Turkey as being the rivals of the EU.
54   The MGV representative presented the Turkish economy as a good example for European countries: 'We did so many things that Europeans do not dare in Turkey.' The TOBB representative also directed attention to the relatively good condition of the Turkish economy.

In the study sample as a whole, the ARI representative's view was exceptional but not extraordinary: the vision of Turkey as an example to European countries in terms of managing economic problems was sufficiently strong in the minds of most interviewees that they willingly avoided mentioning democratic problems in general. Similarly, the EU's ('big states') economic and political intervention in member countries facing crisis in the name of crisis management did not seem to constitute a democratic problem for most of the interviewees. Rather, leading roles played by founding states, such as Germany and France, were taken for granted: 'Member states realize and accept occasional interventions of the EU in their internal affairs once they sign the Agreement' (TDV). The MGV representative supported the decision-making procedures of the Union:

I think it would be unfair if a lazy country asks for equal right to speak with a hard-working country. The leading EU countries are not usually liked or blessed, but we should acknowledge that they are right in many areas. One who asks for equal rights should stand up to obstacles with same consistency. If you take your pocket money from your father as a grown-up, then you should accept him to ask you to make out the accounts. Greece has no right to take offense. One who does not want to be audited should be able to stand on his own. These are also European values.

Once again, the belief in a poetic justice was expressed implicitly.

The TESEV representative linked the financial crisis to the existence of a monetary union without fiscal union: 'On the one hand, you had a common currency between certain member states but they had no rules and regulations deep enough to govern that single currency.' He continued to explain that this particular reason for the crisis led to a more general crisis in the EU 'because one of these great ideas or great representations of European integration is fake'. Thus, he considered the crisis as an 'existentialist crisis' and expected that the EU would go somewhere else from there: 'We are going to find that there is a small block of the EU having a greater integration and potentially there is going to be a periphery ... There is going to be almost two or maybe three spheres in Europe.' He placed Germany, France, Spain, Italy, and Greece at the core and Britain, Norway, Switzerland, and Central and Eastern European states on the periphery, while Ukraine and Turkey would constitute a field father beyond the periphery. The TAV representative shared the TESEV representative's vision of 'concentric circles'.

The following quotes are representative of the most popular scenario for the future of the EU among four suggested by the TÜSİAD representative:

There are four possible future scenarios for Europe. In the first one, Europe can stand still as a single market as it is today. We call it 'Europa mercātus'. In this scenario, the elimination of some elements of integration that proved to be ill designed seems like a 'must'. In the second scenario, which is called 'Europa nostrum', Europe is considered as a more supranational entity. In this scenario of 'Core Europe', the EU or some of the member states are expected to form a federal state by deepening the supranational/federal characteristics of the EU decision-making and Europeanization of national policymaking. The current monetary union is a good example of this approach. Another scenario, in which Europe is considered unable to move forward, is 'Europa et cetera'. Europe's historical strength and heritage keeps the system alive despite problems, but it is unable to achieve radical changes. There is a fourth scenario combining the first two, which I find most probable. Called 'Europa progressio', this scenario considers Europe as a large circle including actual members and all the newcomers without being able or willing to join the 'Core Europe' group. This means a Europe of variable geometry, where there are several levels of integration. Around a hard core composed by countries such as France and Germany, which are technically and politically most able to go for deeper integration towards a federal entity, takes place a second circle of countries that do not fulfil all the obligations of EU membership, such as the UK, which prefers staying out of the Eurozone, and/or countries such as Switzerland and Norway, which have trade and cooperation agreements with the EU. This probably is not the best, ideal scenario; but it provides a practical solution to the current crisis situation.

Some CSO representatives mentioned the potential damaging effects of the crisis on European democracy. The rise of radical parties in countries facing crisis, the revival of nationalist movements, xenophobia, 'Islamophobia', and intolerance were all accentuated as undesirable developments contradicting the EU's own values (TDV, AÇED, DPE, KAGİDER[55]). Additionally, the SODEV representative was concerned about the occurrence of another war in the name of crisis management, as had occurred before in history.

Despite all the challenges, the belief in an optimistic future for the EU was moderately supported by the interviews. The MGV representative considered that the stage of trouble would be handled eventually, while the AÇED representative believed in the capitalist system's survival capacity. When asked about the EU's

---

55 The KAGİDER representative said:'For an organization defending women rights, it is very problematic that all reductions start from women-oriented budget lines.'

future, he said, 'Another Europe is possible ...The EU in my dreams is something else. Something that presses its periphery for the sake of human rights, and respects and protects labour rights, and does not crush them with useless neoliberal policies. If this happens, it will happen in this continent. The compromise will be achieved in here.'

Conclusions

Our research shows that, to varying degrees, CSOs in Turkey still believe in the European Union as an economic, social, and political project, despite the economic crisis and the ruptures in EU-Turkey relations. In this respect, the dominant view about the Union's future is that it will overcome the crisis and survive regardless. However, it should be acknowledged that the discourse on the EU in civil society contains combined Euro-sceptic and pro-EU arguments and hence seems to be eclectic. This eclectic structure is supported by a nationalist discourse based mainly on the opposition between 'us' and 'them', and on an emotional reaction of victimization. EU can thus be described as the 'peak/climax of democracy' on the one hand, and/or as a villain that is unfair, prejudiced, and insincere towards Turkey on the other hand. Some civil society actors even explain the financial crisis in Europe in terms of divine retribution or imply that the EU has got what it deserved because it integrated financially unstable countries into the Union instead of Turkey.

The majority of interviewees did not mention or underestimate the lack of democracy and human rights as obstacles to Turkey's EU bid. This finding is crucial in a sense that CSOs displaying considerable development, both quantitatively and qualitatively, with the support of the EU are still in the process of internalizing democratic values and structures. There is a need for further research, particularly on CSOs' perceptions and practices of democracy, including their internal operations.

Appendix: Information about the interviewed organizations

Ankara:
Dış Politika Enstitüsü (DPE) [Foreign Policy Institute]: Founded in 1974 by academicians, diplomats, and bureaucrats, the DPE aims to contribute to foreign policy through research, meetings, and publications.

İnsan Hakları Derneği (İHD) [Human Rights Association]: Founded in 1986 by human rights defenders, the İHD aims to protect the right to life, abolish the death penalty, prevent execution, and find missing persons. Organization: 29 branches, 3 offices, and over 10,000 members and activists.

İnsan Hakları ve Mazlumlar İçin Dayanışma Derneği (MAZLUMDER) [Organization of Human Rights and Solidarity for Oppressed People]: Founded in 1991, MAZLUMDER aims to contribute to the global development of a moral and responsible society that values human rights, and to provide an avenue to fight all economic, social, cultural, legal, and psychological oppression. Organization: 22 branches and 7000–8000 supporters.

Türk Demokrasi Vakfı (TDV) [Turkish Democracy Foundation]: Founded in 1987 by politicians, businesspeople, academicians, and journalists, the TDV aims to help establish a stable democracy in which humans can develop freely within the boundaries of basic rights and freedoms. Organization: 1 branch in Istanbul and 1 office in Izmir.

Türkiye İnsan Hakları Vakfı (TİHV) [Human Rights Foundation of Turkey]: Founded in 1990, TİHV aims to provide psychological, medical, and legal support to victims of state torture, and to document and expose the crimes committed by the state. Organization: Approximately 65 members and 300 volunteers.

Türkiye Odalar ve Borsalar Birliği (TOBB) [Union of Chambers and Commodity Exchanges of Turkey]: TOBB is the highest legal entity in Turkey, representing the private sector. TOBB aims at ensuring unity and solidarity between chambers and commodity exchanges, enhancing development of the professions in conformance with general interests, and preserving professional discipline and ethics. Organization: 365 members in the form of local chambers of commerce, industry, commerce and industry, maritime commerce, and commodity exchanges.

Türkiye İşçi Sendikaları Konfederasyonu (TÜRK-İŞ) [Confederation of Turkish Trade Unions]: Founded in 1952, Türk-İş aims to defend and promote the rights and interests of workers in general. Organization: 35 member syndicates, representing approximately 2 million workers.

Istanbul:

Arı Hareketi (ARI) [ARI Movement]: Founded in 1994, ARI aims to build a strong Turkish civil society by establishing a new understanding of volunteerism for Turkish youths and encouraging them to adopt the values of participatory democracy.

Çağdaş Yaşamı Destekleme Derneği (ÇYDD) [Association for the Support of Contemporary Living]: Founded in 1989, ÇYDD aims to promote the development of individuals in the legal, political, economic, cultural, social, and physical spheres, to ensure that they can benefit from all human rights and freedoms, and to realize, protect, and develop the democratic, secular, and social state of law in the society.

Türkiye Kadın Girişimciler Derneği (KAGİDER) [Women Entrepreneurs Association of Turkey]: Founded in 2002 by 38 successful women entrepreneurs, KAGİDER aims to strengthen women entrepreneurship and increase the number of women entrepreneurs in Turkey, and to encourage young girls to have a better education and step into the business life. Organization: 200 members. KAGİDER is the first woman's NGO in Turkey with an office in Brussels.

Marmara Grubu Vakfı (MGV), [Marmara Group Foundation]: Founded in 1985, the MGV aims to improve national and international relations and support the sustainable development of Turkey on issues such as the economy, administration, security, and defence, focusing on the EU, the Middle East, Asia, Cyprus, the Balkans, and the Caucasus.

Sosyal Demokrasi Vakfı (SODEV) [Social Democracy Foundation]: Founded in 1994, SODEV aims to develop and propagate the social democratic ideal.

Türkiye-Avrupa Vakfı (TAV) [Turkey-Europe Foundation]: Established in 2001, TAV aims to build bridges between youths, increase the level of knowledge about the European relations of Turkey and its region. TAV strongly supports Turkey's membership of the EU and promotes peace and stability in the region.

Türkiye Ekonomik ve Sosyal Etdüler Vakfı (TESEV) [Turkish Economic and Social Studies Foundation]: Founded in 1994 to serve as a bridge between academic research and policymaking process in Turkey, TESEV analyses social, political, and economic policy issues facing the country.

Türk Sanayici ve İşadamları Derneği (TÜSİAD) [Turkish Industry & Business Association]: Founded in 1971 by Turkish industrialists and businessmen, TÜSİAD aims to contribute to the formation and development of a social order based on the adaptation of the universal principles of human rights, as well as the rules and regulations of a competitive market economy and environmental sustainability. Organization: 600 members representing Turkey's foremost industrial and service sector institutions; 5 offices abroad, including 1 representative office in Brussels.

Izmir:

Avrupa Çalışmaları Ege Derneği (AÇED) [Aegean Association on European Studies]: Founded in 2010 by scholars involved in European studies, AÇED aims to raise public awareness and prevent disinformation on the EU and Turkey-EU relations. Organization: 40 current members. AÇED encourages the participation of new graduate students.

References

Primary sources

ABGM (2008), 'AB uyum yasalarının iç hukuka etkisi ve katkısı' [The effect and contribution of the harmonisation packages to the internal law], http://www.abgm.adalet.gov.tr/e-kutuphane/AB%20uyum%20yasalar%C4%B1n%C4%B1n%20i%C3%A7%20hukuka%20etkisi%20ve%20katk%C4%B1s%C4%B1.pdf

ABGS (2010), 'Avrupa Birliği Hibe Programları Kapsamında Sivil Toplum Kuruluşlarına Sağlanan Destekler' [EU funds raised for CSOs within the instrument for pre-accession assistance], Republic of Turkey Prime Ministry Secretariat General for EU Affairs, December 2010, http://www.abgs.gov.tr/files/pub/AB_Hibe_Programlari_Kapsaminda_STKlara_SaglananDestekler.pdf

ATAUM (2010), 'Kamuoyu ve Türk Dış Politikası Anketi' [Public opinion and Turkish foreign policy], Ankara University European Research Centre (ATAUM), http://ataum.ankara.edu.tr/anket.pdf

Cengiz, O.K. (2010a), 'Minority foundations in Turkey: From past to future 1', *Today's Zaman*, 16 June 2010, http://www.todayszaman.com/columnists-213210-minority-foundations-in-turkey-from-past-to-future-1.html

Cengiz, O.K. (2010b), 'Minority foundations in Turkey: From past to future 2', *Today's Zaman*, 18 June 2010, http://www.todayszaman.com/newsDetail_getNewsById.action;jsessionid=93FEF317423994C5AD82AD9C8D219452?newsId=213440

EB77 (2012), 'Public opinion in the European Union', *Standard Eurobarometer 77*, Autumn 2012, Factsheets in English: Turkey, http://ec.europa.eu/public_opinion/archives/eb/eb77/eb77_fact_tr_en.pdf

EB76 (2011), 'Public opinion in the European Union', *Standard Eurobarometer 76*, Autumn 2011, Factsheets in English: Turkey, http://ec.europa.eu/public_opinion/archives/eb/eb76/eb76_fact_tr_en.pdf

EB75a (2011), 'Europeans, European Union and the crisis', *Standard Eurobarometer 75*, Spring 2011, http://ec.europa.eu/public_opinion/archives/eb/eb75/eb75_publ_en.pdf

EB75b (2011), 'Europeans, European Union and the crisis', *Standard Eurobarometer 75*, Spring 2011, Factsheets in English: Turkey, http://ec.europa.eu/public_opinion/archives/eb/eb75/eb75_fact_tr_en.pdf

EB74 (2010), 'Public opinion in the European Union', *Standard Eurobarometer 74*, Autumn 2010, http://ec.europa.eu/public_opinion/archives/eb/eb74/eb74_publ_en.pdf

EB72 (2009), 'Public opinion in the European Union', *Standard Eurobarometer 72*, Autumn 2009, Factsheets in English: Turkey, http://ec.europa.eu/public_opinion/archives/eb/eb72/eb72_fact_tr_en.pdf

EB71 (2009), 'Public opinion in the European Union', *Standard Eurobarometer 71*, Spring 2009, http://ec.europa.eu/public_opinion/archives/eb/eb71/eb71_std_part1.pdf

EB67 (2007), 'Public opinion in the European Union', *Standard Eurobarometer 67*, Spring 2007, http://ec.europa.eu/public_opinion/archives/eb/eb67/eb67_en.pdf

EB63.4 (2005), 'Avrupa Birliği'nde Kamuoyu', *Standard Eurobarometer 63.4*, Bahar 2005. Ulusal Rapor: Türkiye [Public opinion in the European Union. National reports: Turkey], http://ec.europa.eu/public_opinion/archives/eb/eb63/eb63_nat_tr.pdf

EB62 (2004), 'Public opinion in the European Union', *Standard Eurobarometer 62*, Autumn 2004. National reports: Turkey, http://ec.europa.eu/public_opinion/archives/eb/eb62/eb62_tr_nat.pdf

Ergin, Sedat (2012), 'Is it only the EU report that was thrown into the waste basket?', *Hurriyet Daily News*, 19 October 2012, http://www.hurriyetdailynews.com/is-it-only-the-eu-report-that-was-thrown-into-the-waste-basket.aspx?pageID=449&nID=32736&NewsCatID=428

EU Delegation (n.d.), Delegation of the European Union to Turkey, 'EU funding in Turkey', http://www.avrupa.info.tr/AB_Mali_Destegi.html

European Commission (n.d.), 'Turkey financial assistance', http://ec.europa.eu/enlargement/instruments/funding-by-country/turkey/index_en.htm

European Commission (2011), 'Turkey 2011 progress report', http://www.abgs.gov.tr/files/AB_Iliskileri/Tur_En_Realitons/Progress/tr_rapport_2011_en.pdf

HaberArtı (2012), 'AB Soveytler Birliği gibi çökecek mi? [Will the EU collapse like the Soviet Union?], 25 April 2012, http://www.haberarti.com/ab-sovyetler-birligi-gibi-cokecek-mi-2248-haberi

HaberTürk (2011), 'Endişeler artıyor! Euro çökecek mi?) [Will Euro collapse?], 23 August

2011, http://ekonomi.haberturk.com/makro-ekonomi/haber/662387-endiseler-artiyor-euro-cokecek-mi

HaberTürk (2012), 'AB'ye destek dibe vurdu' [The support for the EU has fallen down], 19 August 2012, http://www.haberturk.com/dunya/haber/769291-abye-destek-dibe-vurdu

Haber Rüzgarı (2012), 'Euro çökecek mi, çökmeyecek mi? [Will Euro collapse or not?], 29 May 2012, http://www.haberruzgari.com/Ekonomi/40592-EURO-COKECEK-MI-COKMEYECEK-MI.html

Küçükcan, T. (2012), 'AB'nin Geleceği Tehlikede mi?' [Is the future of the EU in danger?] *Sabah*, 16 June 2012, http://www.sabah.com.tr/Perspektif/Yazarlar/kucukcan/2012/06/16/avrupa-birliginin-gelecegi-tehlikede-mi

Milliyet (2012), 'AB Üyeliğine İnanç Kalmadı' [No more belief in EU membership], 23 August 2012, http://m2.milliyet.com.tr/News/NewsArticle.aspx?ID=1584924

Özel, S. (2011), 'AB'nin Geleceği ve Türkiye' [The future of the EU and Turkey], *Haber Türk*, 22 August 2011, http://www.haberturk.com/yazarlar/soli-ozel/661386-abnin-gelecegi-ve-turkiye-1

Today's Zaman (2012a), 'Bağış Promises not to take European Parliament report seriously', 15 October 2012, http://www.todayszaman.com/news-295420-bagis-promises-not-to-take-european-parliament-report-seriously.html

Today's Zaman (2012b), 'Turkey greatly disappointed by EU report, minister Bağış says', 10 October 2012,http://www.todayszaman.com/news-294929-turkey-greatly-disappointed-by-eu-report-minister-bagis-says.html

Yavuz, K. (2012), 'AB Ekonomik Her Anlamda Çökmüş Bir Projedir' [The EU is an economically collapsed project in every sense], Eha EBM Haber Ajansı, 27 December 2012, http://www.ebmhaber.com.tr/HaberYazdir.aspx?HaberId=387

TÜİK (2011), TÜİK Yaşam Memnuniyeti Araştırması [Turkish Statistical Institute, Life Satisfaction Survey 2011], No. 3669, Türkiye İstatistik Kurumu Matbaası, Ankara.

Literature

Ahıska, M. (2003), 'Occidentalism: The historical fantasy of the modern', *The South Atlantic Quarterly*, Vol. 102, Nos. 2/3, pp. 341–379.

Akşit, S., Şenyuva, Ö. and Gürleyen, I. (2011), 'The Turkish parliamentary elite and the EU: Mapping attitudes towards the European Union', *South European Society and Politics*, Vol. 16, No. 3, pp. 395–407.

Bardakçı, M. (2010), 'Turkish parties' positions towards the EU: Between Europhilia and Europhobia', *Romanian Journal of European Affairs*, Vol. 10, No. 4, pp. 26–41.

Diken, Ş. (2006), *Türkiye'de Sivil Hayat ve Demokrasi: Sivil Toplum Sorunlarını Tartışıyor [Civil life and Democracy in Turkey: the Civil Society disscusses its problems]*, Ankara: Dipnot.

Doğanay, Ü. (2011), 'The Turkish Parliament's discourse on Europe', in C. Ramos (ed.), *Ideas of Europe in National Political Discourse*, Bologna: Il Mulino, pp. 263-292.

Ergun, A. (2010), 'Civil society in Turkey and local dimensions of Europeanization', *European Integration*, Vol. 32, No. 5, pp. 507–522.

Eylemer, S. and Taş, İ. (2007), 'Pro-Eu and Eurosceptic circles in Turkey', *Journal of Communist Studies and Transition Politics*, Vol. 23, No. 4, pp. 561–577.

Göksel, D.N. and Güneş, R.B. (2005), 'The role of NGOs in the European integration process: The Turkish experience', *South European Society & Politics*, Vol. 10, No. 1, pp. 57–72.

Heper, M. and Yıldırım, S. (2011), 'Revisiting civil society in Turkey', *Southeast European and Black Sea Studies*, Vol. 11, No. 1, pp. 1–18.

İçduygu, A. (2011), 'Interacting actors: The EU and civil society in Turkey', *South European Society and Politics*, Vol. 16, No. 3, pp. 381–394.

Kejanlıoğlu, B. and Taş, O. (2009), 'Türk Basınında AB-Türkiye İlişkilerinin Sunumu: 17 Aralık 2004 Brüksel Zirvesi [The presentation of EU-Turkey relationship in the Turkish Press: Brussels Summit]', *Kültür ve İletişim*, Vol. 12, No. 1, pp. 39–64.

Kubicek, P. (2005), 'The European Union and grassroots democratization in Turkey', *Turkish Studies*, Vol. 6, No. 3, pp. 361–377.

McLaren, L.M. (2000), 'Turkey's eventual membership of the EU: Turkish elite perspectives on the issue', *Journal of Common Market Studies*, Vol. 38, No. 1, pp. 117–129.

McLaren, L.M. and Müftüler-Baç, M. (2003), 'Turkish parliamentarians' Perspectives on Turkey's relations with the European Union', *Turkish Studies*, Vol. 4, No. 1, pp. 195–218.

Öniş, Z. (2007), 'Conservative globalists versus defensive nationalists: Political parties and paradoxes of Europeanization in Turkey', *Journal of Southern Europe and the Balkans*, Vol. 9, No. 3, pp. 247–261.

Paul, A. (2011), 'The EU-Turkey deadlock', *European Policy Centre*, Commentary, 26 January 2011, http://www.epc.eu/documents/uploads/pub_1220_the_EU-Turkey_deadlock.pdf

Phillips, D.L. (2004), 'Turkey's dreams of accession', *Foreign Affairs*, Sept/Oct, pp. 86–97.

Risteska, M. (2010), 'The effects of the Lisbon Treaty on accession countries', *Turkish Policy Quarterly* Vol. 9, No. 3, pp. 115–122.

Smismans, S. (2003), 'European civil society: Shaped by discourses and institutional interests', *European Law Journal*, Vol. 9, No. 4, September, pp. 473–495.

Warleigh, A. (2001), 'Europeanizing' civil society: NGOs as agents of political socialization', *Journal of Common Market Studies*, Vol. 39, No. 4, pp. 619–639.

Yankaya, D. (2009), 'The Europeanization of MÜSİAD: Political opportunism, economic Europeanization, Islamic Euroscepticism', *European Journal of Turkish Studies*, 9, http://ejts.revues.org/3696#tocto1n2.

Yılmaz, H. (2011), 'Euroscepticism in Turkey: Parties, elites, and public opinion', *South European Society and Politics*, iFirst article, pp. 1–24.

Yiğit, D. (2012), 'Avrupa Birliği'nin Geleceği' [The future of the EU], Institute of Strategic Thinking, 19 June 2012, http://www.sde.org.tr/tr/haberler/1897/avrupa-birliginin-gelecegi.aspx.

A threat to democracy and independence? Perception of the EU in Icelandic discourse

Eiríkur Bergmann

Since gaining independence in 1944 Iceland has been struggling to find its proper place in the world. Mainly on the grounds of guarding its sovereignty, after having struggled for independence from Denmark for more than a century, Iceland has remained outside the European Union (EU). Since then, independence and formal sovereignty have almost been synonymous with democracy in Icelandic public debate.

However, in economic terms Iceland feels the same need as other European states to participate in European co-operation, which may explain its membership of the European Economic Area (EEA) Agreement. The agreement brings Iceland into the European Single Market, but at a cost: Iceland has agreed to adopt the EU's legislation within the boundaries of the agreement, and thus transfer decision-making and domestic governmental power to the EU. Through the EEA, Iceland adopts more than two-thirds of all EU legal acts, and close to one-fifth of all laws passed in the Icelandic Parliament originate from the EU – which is a higher percentage than in many EU member states (NOU 2012:2: 807). The dilemma between economic interests on the one hand and ideas of the sovereignty of the Icelandic nation on the other, and thus democracy, has created a 'rift' between the emphasis on the free and sovereign democratic nation and the reality that Iceland faces in its co-operation with the EU.

It was not until the collapse of its entire financial system in 2008 that the new left-wing government applied for EU membership, in July 2009, as the last country of the 'Nordic five'. The application was in many ways a response to a fundamental systemic flaw Iceland found itself in as an active participant in the European Internal Market but without the collective backup that comes from being a full and formal member of the EU institutions and its political machinery: Iceland had become a participant in a vast legal framework without due democratic representation. In some regard, the financial crisis threw Iceland out of its comfort zone and forced it to face its situation within the European integration process. However, soon after the initial shock had calmed, opposition to membership rose again, even beyond previous levels. Opinion polls indicate increased opposition against the accession negotiations, with a clear majority calling for them to be cancelled and more than two-thirds claiming they would refuse membership in a referendum (Samtök Iðnaðarins, 2012). In an effort to diffuse the issue in the political debate leading up to the Parliamentary elections in April 2013, the government decided to slow down the negotiations. The new right of centre government then immediately halted the negotiations after the elections.

This chapter analyses domestic political discourse in Iceland with regards to (1) the synonymous intertwined understandings of the concepts of sovereignty and democracy; (2) the perception of democracy in the EU; (3) the democratic consequences of participating in the EEA Agreement, and (4) the democratic consequences for Iceland of becoming a full member of the European Union. Previous studies have shown that the inheritance of the struggle for independence still directs the discourse that Icelandic politicians' use in the debate on Europe (Bergmann, 2011). A strong emphasis on formal sovereignty has become the foundation on which Icelandic politics rests. In some respect, participation in the EU's supra-national institutions falls outside the framework of Icelandic political discourse, which highlights Iceland's sovereignty and stresses an everlasting struggle for independence. This chapter adds to the extensive research already done on how national sentiments have influenced Iceland's European integration policy by conducting a discourse analysis of democracy and European integration in parliamentary debates. The analysis maps different ideas on the state of democracy within the triangular relationship between Iceland, EFTA (European Free Trade Association)/EEA, and the EU. Icelandic politics revolve around a double axis: The traditional left/right axis and an internationalist (pro-NATO (North Atlantic Treaty Organization)/EEA/EU)/isolationist (anti-NATO/EEA/EU) axis that relates to Iceland's sovereignty. The main focus is on the four main political parties in Iceland.[1]

---

[1] The party system consists of four main political parties: the Social Democratic Alliance, the Independence Party, the Left Green Movement, and the Progressive Party. The left of centre Social Democratic Alliance (SDA), was founded in 2000 after a merger of the Social Democratic Party (SDP) and the People's Alliance (PA), and is the only party that has consistently campaigned for EU membership. However, until recently the right of centre Independence Party (IP) has been the most influential in Icelandic politics. The IP supported Iceland's membership of EFTA and the EEA but then turned against EU membership. The leftist Left Green Movement (LGM) was founded in 2000 by splinter groups from the PA and its predecessors, and has campaigned against further participation in European integration. The small central Progressive Party (PP) has been split on

This chapter is structured in three parts. The first part provides an overview of Iceland's participation in the European project. The second part provides a historical perspective as a background against which to understand Iceland's national identity. The third part offers a discourse analysis of the debate within the Icelandic Parliament when Iceland decided to apply for EU membership in mid-2009, in the aftermath of the financial collapse of 2008. The narrative on Europe is analysed against Iceland's national myth created in the struggle for independence. The focus is on determining whether the idea of participation in European integration is seen to fit within or violate the boundaries of the nation's political discourse.

The European connection

In order to put Iceland's European relations into perspective it is useful to take a broad look at its foreign policy, which is sorted under three main pillars: the European pillar, the Atlantic pillar, and a pillar representing the rest of the world (Bergmann, 2007). The European pillar is by far the most important and contains most of Iceland's major trade agreements and vital foreign links to underpin the economy, such as its membership of EFTA and the EEA Agreement. Iceland is also a member of the Council of Europe, and is firmly rooted within the heritage of Nordic co-operation. In this context it is also worth mentioning the country's close bilateral trade and cultural relationship with the UK.

The Atlantic pillar is the second most important of the three pillars and contains Iceland's membership of NATO and the defence agreement with the USA since 1951, which resulted in a close bilateral relationship with Washington on foreign policy matters. Icelanders were unified by the struggle for independence, with more than 90% of the electorate agreeing to full independence from Denmark in a national referendum in 1944, thereby ending Iceland's 600 year-long relationship while Denmark was still under Nazi occupation. The feeling of unity was shattered only a few years later after a fierce debate arose on Iceland's membership of NATO and was heightened in violent riots in front of the parliament building.

While Iceland mostly relied on the European pillar to underpin its economy, it relied much more heavily on the Atlantic pillar for its strategic security. However, after the United States Government decided to close its army base in Keflavik in 2006, the Atlantic pillar became less important than before, and gave more weight

---

the European issue and for a long time effectively without a clearly defined policy. After a recent change in the leadership, the party has turned ever more vigorously against EU membership.

to European co-operation in foreign and security policy matters. The third pillar consists of foreign relations with the rest of the world, for example through the United Nations and the World Trade Organisation, to mention just a few.

Icelanders have debated their place in Europe ever since the Treaty of Rome was signed in 1957. Directly resulting from the heritage of the struggle for independence, debates on foreign relations have become more fierce han almost any other political disputes in the country (Bergmann, 2009). Iceland joined EFTA in 1970, one decade after it was established, and together with its EFTA partners it entered into the EEA Agreement in 1994, which resulted in the country becoming a 'de facto member' of the EU. Despite the fact that Iceland is officially outside the European Union, it nonetheless continues, through its co-operation agreement, to participate actively in the European project and is, for example, a full participant in the EU's Internal Market. In some ways, Iceland is more deeply involved in the European integration process than some of the EU's official members. For example, Denmark has many opt-outs from the EU treaties that Iceland is subject to through the EEA, and the EU's border regulation is applied in Iceland through the Schengen Agreement, whereas the UK and Ireland are exempted from that part of EU co-operation (Adler-Nissen, 2008).

The EEA Agreement has facilitated the active Europeanization of Iceland. The agreement brings three of the Member States of EFTA, – Iceland, Liechtenstein, and Norway (collectively EEA EFTA) – into the European Single Market, with those countries agreeing to adopt the regulatory framework of the European Union. The EEA Agreement calls for the constant revision and update of Icelandic law to ensure that the country is in line with the laws and regulations of the European Single Market, as dictated by the EU.

However, the EEA Agreement does not provide access for the EEA EFTA Member States to the EU's institutions and decision-making processes. Further, it does not cover the Common Agricultural Policy and regional cohesion policies, and – perhaps most importantly for Iceland – it does not include the Common Fisheries Policy. EEA EFTA does not participate in the EU's trade policy, monetary policy, tax regimes, foreign affairs, or many of the EU's internal matters, including judiciary affairs that fall outside the Schengen Agreement and Dublin Regulation. However, in sum, Iceland is very deeply involved in Europe and excluded from very few areas. In certain matters, such as those relating to the environment, transport, and food hygiene, the vast majority of all legislation passed in the Icelandic Parliament is initiated through the EEA. Furthermore, the border between what is considered part of the Single Market (and therefore what is relevant with respect to the EEA) and other parts of EU legislation is becoming increasingly blurred.

Thus, the EEA has facilitated the transformation of the Icelandic economy, which has not only grown rapidly but also has become more diversified and internationalised. However, despite the clear economic benefits, the EEA Agreement has also presented grave challenges to Iceland's very small economy and, more importantly, to its cherished democracy.

Democratic challenges

Despite the equality of the EU and EEA EFTA in the formal institutional framework of the EEA Agreement, it has always been clear that the EU is the leading partner. As a result, the automatic implementation of EU legislation is rarely discussed in the Icelandic Parliament. However, according to many legal scholars, this harmonised legal framework is in violation of the Icelandic constitution (Alfreðsson, 1992). When Iceland tries to deviate from joint EU rules, the EFTA Surveillance Authority (ESA) intervenes. On more than a dozen occasions ESA has taken direct action or issued formal infringement procedures against Iceland before the EFTA Court for violation of EU law. The number of cases against Iceland increased substantially after the 2008 economic crash.

Even though EEA legislation needs to be passed through the Icelandic Parliament, it was soon established that the EEA EFTA Member States could not refuse EU legislation without threatening the whole arrangement. If this were to happen, it would go against the overall aim of the EEA Agreement, which is to ensure legal homogeneity in the Single Market, and it would be in the hands of the European Commission to decide whether to suspend the part of the EEA Agreement that refers to vetoed legislation. Vetoing EU legislation could lead to withdrawal from the EEA Agreement, not only for the individual Member State, but also for its other two EEA EFTA partners. Often referred to as the nuclear bomb clause, the formal veto right may be effective, but may not be to anyone's benefit if it were to be used.

However, on a few occasions, EEA directives (i.e. on electricity providers and sewers, and most recently the service directive) have been disputed to the extent that they have prompted a general political debate on the veto right. Furthermore, the Norwegian Parliament refused to implement an EU directive on postal services, which as a result was also of concern for Icelandic authorities.

Economic challenges

In economic terms, the EEA Agreement altered the composition of the Icelandic economy, for example by opening up the international financial market to Icelandic businessmen. However, as was the case accompanying EFTA membership, there were also segments of the economy, such as vegetable and flower growers, that were disadvantaged after entering the EEA.

More importantly, access to the EU financial market rendered Iceland vulnerable, as became evident when the 2008 financial crisis hit. After privatisation and extensive deregulation, the Icelandic banks grew rapidly in the European markets and well beyond Iceland's capability to bail them out when trouble arrived. In order to back up the overinflated banking system in such dire straits, Iceland needed a sizable sum in foreign currency. The Central Bank therefore went knocking on doors in the neighbouring capitals, asking them to open swap lines that could be drawn on in times of need. The objective was to boost confidence in Iceland's capacity to back up the financial system. However, the Icelandic Government was surprised to find that the CB met closed doors in most places. Not only had the banks but also the government been pushed out of international capital markets. Iceland first approached the Bank of England in March 2008 with a request for emergency loan. Initially, the request was positively received, but with a suggestion that the IMF would analyse the need. One month later, the climate had changed, and it had become clear that the central banks of Europe, the USA, and the UK had collectively decided not to assist Iceland.

For the international financial system, the comparatively very small country of Iceland was not considered too big to fail. Though part of the European Single Market, Iceland was left alone in the world when crisis hit. Norway, Sweden, and Denmark finally agreed on a borrowing line, of EUR 500 millions each. However, the offer was only available at an unprecedented cost; the neighbouring states would dictate strict fiscal reform that the Icelandic Government was to implement at home, including changing the country's Housing Financial Fund, a more responsible budget, and changes in union contracts (Rannsóknarnefnd Alþingis 2008, 2010). Although never implemented, this was the most drastic foreign interference in Icelandic domestic affairs since independence in 1944, and was a serious threat to Iceland's cherished sovereignty.

By July 2008, all funding possibilities seemed to have closed, and by October the country's three major banks and virtually the whole of its financial sector were devastated. The whole system collapsed within a week. The Depositors' Guaranty Fund set up on the basis of an EU/EEA directive never had enough funding to cover a systemic collapse and no help came from European institutions that Iceland was not part of. This 'neither in nor out' arrangement – with one foot in the European Single Market and all the obligations that this entailed, and the other foot outside the EU institutions and hence without access to back up from, for example, the European Central Bank – proved to be flawed in the face of a crisis of that magnitude.

The EEA connection did not amount to much when, after the crash, Iceland pleaded access to the IMF programme. IMF assistance was only made available after Iceland gave into the Dutch and the British in the dispute over the Icesave deposit accounts of the fallen Landsbanki.

Operational challenges

Even though the EEA is dynamic, it does not respond to the operational and institutional changes in the EU. Since the Maastricht Treaty was signed in 1992, various political shifts and institutional turns have occurred within the EU, meaning that the political and legal environment in which the EEA operates has changed dramatically.

For example, four new treaties and the eastern EU enlargement have marked a transformation of the EU that has led to the increased influence of the European Parliament and the European Council at the expense of the European Commission. Within the EEA, the Commission is the voice of the EFTA Member States and should speak on their behalf within the EU's institutions. The diminished capacity and influence of the Commission has therefore subsequently further narrowed the influence that EEA EFTA has on the European legislative process.

In addition, the balance of EFTA and the EU within the EEA is being challenged. With only Iceland, Liechtenstein, and Norway representing EFTA, while the EU has grown to 28 member states with a total of c.500 million inhabitants, the influence of the EEA EFTA Member States within the EEA has diminished significantly.

Icelandic officials working within the field of the EEA Agreement are convinced that the EEA is becoming increasingly less important to the EU.[2] This has resulted in the agreement being relegated within the Commission to a lower status than it had enjoyed previously. Increasingly, the European Commission 'forgets' to involve specialists from EEA EFTA when new legislation is being prepared. Consequently, the EEA and the EU clash on an increasingly regular basis. A clear example of this occurred when Iceland was treated as a third state outside the internal trade framework when the EU invoked tariffs on steel in a trade dispute with the United States of America. However, a more serious inci-

---

2   Interviews with senior diplomats within the Icelandic Ministry for Foreign Affairs, 7 February 2011.

dent was the fishmeal crisis in 2000, when the EU unilaterally banned imports of fishmeal for animals in response to the 'mad cow disease' (Bovine spongiform encephalopathy) crisis. It was only by lobbying for support from EU states with similar interests, such as Denmark, that Iceland was able to avoid a comprehensive ban on fishmeal imports, even though the Icelandic product was completely safe.

The eastern EU enlargement almost resulted in the collapse of the EEA Agreement when the EU threatened to halt simultaneous enlargement of the EEA until Iceland, Liechtenstein, and Norway agreed to increase their contribution to the EFTA development fund. The process showed how vulnerable Iceland is in relation to the EU, but the resulting compromise also indicates that when there is a mutual political will to find solutions suitable measures can be found within the framework of the EEA.

The Norwegian connection

As a small country with little more than 300,000 inhabitants, Iceland can only operate a very small administration and has thus been forced to prioritise specific policy areas on which it can focus its limited efforts. It compensates for its lack of resources by relying on both close co-operation with and help from the services of neighbouring countries, especially the other countries in the Nordic region (i.e. Denmark, Finland, Norway, and Sweden). In addition, under the EEA Agreement, the EEA EFTA Member States are meant to harmonise their position and speak with one voice within the EEA. As a result of these two factors, Iceland relies very heavily on Norway.

Iceland's relationship with Norway has not always been a happy one. Senior diplomats in Iceland's Foreign Service claim that occasionally their Norwegian counterparts seem to forget that they have a binding agreement with two smaller partners.[3] Norway, as the largest power within EEA EFTA, tends to operate alone on issues that are of concern to all three of them. The Icelandic Government therefore feels that Norway does not always honour the partnership and tends to voice opinions unilaterally or even enter into negotiation with the European Commission without consulting Iceland.[4]

Despite being linked in the EEA, Iceland and Norway have often been in significantly different positions when it comes to co-operation with Europe and

---

3   *Ibid.*
4   *Ibid.*

operate quite different European policies. It is claimed that after the population of Norway has twice refused to accede to the EU, the Norwegian Government is very concerned with proving itself to be a good European. By contrast, Iceland has never felt the same need to gain that kind of approval in Brussels. As a result, the Icelandic Government feels that Norway prioritises the demands of the EU over the principles of the EEA Agreement and, indeed, the EFTA Convention.

Further tension is also felt over Norway's co-operation with the EFTA Secretariat. Like many small states within the EU that rely on the European Commission more than the larger states that can use resources within their own administration, Iceland tends to rely more on the EFTA Secretariat than Norway. Norway, by contrast, is in a much stronger position to handle EEA-related matters directly. Icelandic officials claim that their Norwegian counterparts systematically bypass the EFTA Secretariat on many EEA relevant issues, thereby avoiding coordination with Iceland.[5]

The relationship between Iceland and Norway in the EEA can perhaps be compared to an arranged marriage between distant cousins. The relationship is not entered into on the basis of 'true love'; instead, there is an uneven balance of power, and ongoing and unresolved tensions between the two parties that are exacerbated by the obligation to make the relationship work.

National identity and Iceland's sense of sovereignty

Various scholars have studied Iceland's relationship with the EU and many factors have been offered to explain Iceland's apparent Euro-scepticism. It is commonly argued that interests related to fisheries have been the main hindrance for Iceland's membership of the European Union. Political science professors Gunnar Helgi Kristinsson and Baldur Thorhallsson (2004) claim that the close relationship between the political elite and the fisheries industry has also factored in Iceland's negative view on EU membership. Similarly, Magnús Árni Magnússon (2011) emphasises these political constraints and agrees with Clive Archer and Ingrid Sogner (1998) when claiming that geopolitical security factors are also at play, in addition to the lack of economic incentives after joining the EEA. Furthermore, Thorhallsson argues that in addition to the fisheries factor, several combined factors are important: special emphasis on Iceland as a small state, its special

---

5   *Ibid.*

security links with the USA, the effects of the Cod Wars, geographical isolation, and an electoral system that favours rural areas (Thorhallsson, 2004).

Even though the above-mentioned factors contribute to explain the position of various social and political groups in Iceland, the rationalist focus on interests can be questioned by referring to the fact that until the collapse of the Icelandic economy in 2008, which followed the global financial crisis, there was never a majority in Parliament to put the fisheries issue to the test in EU accession negotiations. If fisheries, as such, had truly been the main economic obstacle for the parliamentarians otherwise in favour of seeking membership, they should have been willing to test this in the accession negotiations to see whether their concerns would be met with adequate opt-outs; yet until the crash in 2008, they were never willing to do so. Combined with the increased opposition that the accession negotiations faced in the wake of the crisis, this indicates that other factors might have contributed to Iceland's EU policy. I thus maintain that the fisheries situation represents more than merely an economic argument, and that it represents a key element in Iceland's post-independence identity.

Although most students of Icelandic politics acknowledge the importance of the struggle for independence in the development of Iceland's political identity, the importance of the national political identity, the shared discourse of everlasting independence that developed through the struggle and has since been established as the common foundation of Icelandic politics (i.e. what can be referred to as either postcolonial or post-imperial identity), has largely been overlooked in established scholarship on Iceland's EU relations. I maintain that within the parameters of Iceland's national identity EU membership is seen to threaten Iceland's sovereignty and thus its cherished democracy, which Icelanders claim can be traced back to the parliamentary court of the settlement society in the year AD 930: Alþingi (the general assembly).

When studying contemporary Icelandic politics, the legacy of the more than one-century long struggle for independence in the 19th and early 20th centuries (1830–1944) is still present. Thus, a historical account is needed to provide an understanding of the framework to which contemporary political discourse must relate in order to make sense.

Iceland's independence struggle was fought with legal argumentation rather than arms, which emphasised rhetoric over force. Alþingi was resurrected as an advisory body in Reykjavik in 1844, and Iceland received its first constitution from the king of Denmark in 1974, home rule in 1904, formal sovereignty in 1918 (within a personal union with the Danish king as head of state), and full independence in 1944 – against the will of Denmark when it was still under Nazi occupation.

The struggle for independence was led by a small group of Icelandic intellectuals in Copenhagen who, by referring to Iceland's history of independent Vikings, developed a national myth[6] that served as justification for their special emphasis on sovereignty and independence. According to the myth, Iceland is a unique nation and it is the duty of all Icelanders to guard actively its sovereignty and independence. Professor of History Guðmundur Hálfdanarson (2001: 96) explains how Iceland's independence hero Jón Sigurðsson has since become the symbolic father of all Icelanders. Historian Páll Björnsson (2010) claims that all camps in Icelandic politics – conservatives, communists, nationalists, and liberals alike – refer to Jón Sigurðsson to advance and even legitimise their argument.

The myth has created a golden age lasting from the settlement in the year AD 874 (state-like formulation in AD 930) until Iceland fell under foreign rule, first with a treaty with Norway in 1262, then with Danish rule in 1380, and finally with the introduction of absolutism in 1662 (Hálfdanarson, 2001: 28). Iceland's first history professor Jón Jónsson Aðils (1869–1920) describes the golden age as a society superior to all others, in which the unique and pure Icelandic language was the key to its soul. He claimed that Icelanders not only enjoyed the highest standard of living but also that their culture was so rich that it 'only compares to ancient Greece during the highest period of civilisation' (Jónsson Aðils, 1903). According to the myth, Icelandic society started to deteriorate after entering into the treaty made in 1262 with the then king of Norway. A period of humiliation then followed after falling under Danish rule. Jón Jónsson Aðils explains that however weak and humiliated the Icelandic national spirit became, it never died, and at last, in the early 19th century, courageous and wise men finally rose up and reclaimed the nation's own worth and lifted the national spirit by fighting for Iceland's independence in the 19th century. The myth thus creates a u-shaped curve of history, in which emphasis is put on autonomy and avoidance of external influence.

Iceland's independence movement clearly drew its ideas from international trends at the time, most importantly the Enlightenment. However, when the policy of sovereignty and later full independence – Icelandic nationalism – was being developed, its creators looked back one thousand years, to the settlement republic, for arguments and justifications for their claim rather than to current international development (Hermannsson, 2005: 83). The emphasis was on drawing an unbroken link to the golden age rather than on linking the struggle for independence with international ideological developments of the time. Iceland's path to moder-

---

6   The term *myth* is here used in the sense that Iceland's history was creatively interpreted to fit the claim for self-rule for Iceland (see Hermannsson 2005 for further information).

nisation and progress was therefore seen through its own unique past rather than as a part of a larger international trend (Hermannsson, 2005: 252, 292).

Further, Professor Hálfdanarson claims that the sense of nationalism was somewhat stronger than in most other European states at the time, due to the historical conviction that justified the full formal sovereignty and independence of the nation (Hálfdanarson, 2001: 36–39). The nation became almost a concrete natural fact in Icelandic minds. A free and sovereign Icelandic nation became an integral part of the self-image of the nation. Icelandic nationalism was thus created and based on a romantic notion of the natural and pure, or at least special, separate nation. This notion became a vital force in the struggle for independence.

The struggle for external sovereignty and internal democracy was also fuelled by a wish for recognition as an equal partner in Europe. Political scientist Birgir Hermannsson claims that the strive for independence was not only a struggle for sovereignty but also a vehicle for modernisation of a country that had been one of the most backward in Europe for centuries (Hermannsson, 2005: 125–127). Formally, Iceland was not a colony of Denmark but a dependency. The position of the Icelanders in the 19th century was ambiguous. As Kristín Loftsdóttir (2011) explains, they were generally represented as neither complete 'savages' nor integrated as and with 'civilised' people. This ambiguity was reflected in, for example, the protest of Icelandic students in 1905 against being portrayed as colonial subjects in the Danish colonial exhibition in Copenhagen, as they did not want to be associated with colonised people from Greenland and Africa.

Iceland's national myth is not unique. Many nations base their nationhood on similar kinds of myth creation (Smith, 1993). What is interesting in Iceland's case is that after gaining full independence the struggle for independence did not end. Rather, a new one started – an everlasting struggle for independence. A new political idea was born: the notion that the fight for independence is a constant struggle and that it will never end. Accordingly, it is the collective duty of all Icelanders to guard its independence. In his landmark study of Icelandic politics, including the Icelandic political identity, political science professor Ólafur Ragnar Grímsson (1978), now President of Iceland, claimed that this common understanding of Icelandic nationalism, created in the struggle for independence, has since become one of the most important ideas in Icelandic political discourse.

Democracy at risk

In this section, I analyse political discourse on participation in European integration in general and the effects of this participation on Iceland's internal democracy and external independence in particular. In order to illustrate the continuity and how the nationalist discourse travels through in contemporary politics, I present examples from most of the main debating rounds on Europe since the republic was established: first on EFTA (1970), second on the EEA Agreement (1994), and third on possible EU membership. The rhetoric used in foreign relations in the boom years leading up to the collapse of the financial system in autumn 2008 also provides an interesting insight into to the impact of the national identity discourse, including the postcolonial rhetoric, and the one that followed after the crash, on the Icesave dispute with the UK and the Netherlands, and on the involvement of the IMF. The postcolonial emphasis on guarding Iceland's democracy by never again surrendering to foreign authority is seldom explicit in contemporary political discourse, which often makes it difficult to identify specific examples. However, in time of crisis this rhetoric comes to the fore, as was evident in the Icesave dispute.

In the EFTA membership debate (1968–1969) parliamentarians mainly based their argument on the economy, which clearly should be seen in connection with the fact that EFTA was a purely intergovernmental organization. However, the narrative of the struggle for independence and conservative ideas on the nation and its sovereignty was always underlying and in effect formed a base for the economic arguments. For example, in referring to what they called undisputed distinctiveness of the nation, parliamentarians said it was 'only natural that our relationship with EFTA will be marked by that distinctiveness'.[7] This understanding of uniqueness and distinctiveness was then used as an argument for the multiple opt-outs and special solutions that Iceland brought to the negotiating table. Those arguing against further participation in the European integration process feared a loss of identity in such a close relationship with the big nations of Europe. Tapping into the national myth, many referred to the treaty made with Norway in 1262 in their argument against integration with other nations, which was seen to threaten Iceland's long fought for democracy.

In the EEA debate (1989–1994), emphasis on internal democracy and the sovereignty shifted to the forefront in parliament. EEA advocates emphasised the wish of the independence struggle for progress and modernisation, arguing that the agreement would bring Iceland forward as an equal partner in Europe. Minister of

---

7   Tómas Árnason, speech in Parliament on 8 November 1968 (Althingi online archive).

Foreign Affairs Jón Baldvin Hannibalsson (SDP) argued that the EEA would be Iceland's 'passport' to the future and the key to economic prosperity. He referred to Jón Sigurðsson, the main hero of the struggle for independence, to support the claim that the EEA was in some way a continuation of the struggle and would push Iceland further into modernity.[8]

The 'No' camp used the sovereignty argument even more systematically, accusing the pro-EEA side of being unpatriotic. They argued that the EEA threatened Iceland's sovereignty, which would be shifted to undemocratic institutions in Brussels. Thus, with loss of internal democracy, Iceland would fall under foreign rule once again. Further, the 'No' camp claimed that even though the agreement might bring economic benefits, it should be rejected solely on the ground that it violated Icelander's 'sense of sovereignty'.[9] However, in this regard, it is noteworthy that the meaning of sovereignty and what it constitutes were hardly discussed. For example, parliamentarians emphasised protection of the purity of Iceland's identity and language from being contaminated by having too close foreign relations. One parliamentarian claimed that after joining the EEA Icelanders 'would, of course, instantly lose [their] language, culture, and independence in a very short period of time'.[10] This sort of argumentation supports Loftsdóttir's (2010) claim that Icelanders continued to associate national identity with the purity of the nation and its language.

When the debate on possible EU membership started at the beginning of the new millennium, the importance of sovereignty to protect the internal democracy became dominant. One IP parliamentarian claimed that the EU fisheries policy not only violated Iceland's economic interests but also brought 'complete transfer of our nation's sovereignty and authority'.[11] In referring to national heritage and Iceland's unique culture, it was argued that rather than surrendering to the EU, Icelanders should continue to develop a competitive society and strong economy on their own, thus subsequently claiming that it would be a retrograde step of great consequence if Iceland were to lose its self-rule through membership of the EU. Iceland would be locked inside an unproductive trade block and trapped in an undemocratic bureaucracy. Then Prime Minister Davíð Oddsson (IP) described the EU as one of the most 'undemocratic bureaucratic monstrosities man has ever created' (quoted in Friðriksson, 2002). At the other end of the political spectrum, the leader of the LGM similarly remained firmly within the boundaries of the

---

8 Jón Baldvin Hannibalsson, speech in Parliament on 23 October 1991 (Althingi online archive).
9 Jóhann Ársælsson, speech in Parliament on 3 September 1992 (Althingi online archive).
10 Páll Pétursson, speech in Parliament on 9 March 1989 (Althingi online archive).
11 Einar K. Guðfinnsson, speech in Parliament on 8 May 2000 (Althingi online archive).

postcolonial discourse when he said that membership would mean 'diminished independence and sovereignty, loss of distinctiveness'.[12]

In the wake of the '*Pots-and-pans revolution*' in January 2009, the new left wing government (SDA/LGM) decided to apply for EU membership.[13] By promoting the EU as a way forward to protect and strengthen Iceland's sovereignty rather than as a step away from independence, and by continually referring to Jón Sigurðsson to advance their argument, the 'Yes' side also tapped into the postcolonial independence discourse. The same was true of the other side of the argument. For example, one IP parliamentarian remembered Iceland's 65th anniversary of independence: 'We were the poorest nation in Europe after 600 years of co-operation with nations in the south of Europe as we would be if we joined now'.[14] In line with the national myth, he explained that Iceland's misfortune and humiliation had started after it had entered into the treaty with Norway in 1262, and only with independence was Iceland able to change its status to being one of the richest countries. The IP parliamentarian concluded that with EU membership Iceland would again become a 'depopulated poor province in a huge European superstate'.[15] Another IP parliamentarian said that Icelanders should never forget that they are a unique nation, 'tough and hardworking, and with a soul that could never be broken by foreigners'.[16] An MP for the LGM said that he feared that the will of the nation would diminish after joining the EU and concluded that 'he who is glad when beaten to obey becomes a slave' (Jónasson, 2009). In all three debates on advancing further into European integration, the same tropes of the sovereignty argument and impact on democracy was constantly applied.

Around the start of the 21st century, Iceland's new finance-driven economy was taking shape, replacing the old resource-based growth model. With access to the European single market in the mid-1990s and subsequent wide-scale privatisation, Iceland was rapidly rushed towards a neoliberal finance-driven economy: The Icelandic 'Viking capitalist' was born – buying up landmark companies around the world.

Tapping into the national myth deriving from the struggle for independence, a report on the image of Iceland, commissioned by the Prime Minister's Office in 2008, attributed the perceived success to the 'unique characteristics' of the Icelandic nation, 'which separates Icelanders from other nations' (Prime Minis-

---

12 Steingrímur J. Sigfússon, speech in Parliament on 8 May 2000 (Althingi online archive).
13 The PP had left a long-standing coalition with the IP in spring 2007.
14 Pétur Blöndal, speech in Parliament on 10 July 2009 (Althingi online archive).
15 *Ibid.*
16 Árni Johnsen, speech in Parliament on 11 May 2009 (Althingi online archive).

ter's Office 2008). This uniqueness was said to stem from living in harmony with the harsh nature, which had created a special natural force out of the Icelandic nation. The report concludes that on this basis the core of Iceland's image should be 'power, freedom and peace' (Prime Minister's Office, 2008). In this regard, the internationalisation of Iceland's economy is interpreted through a romantic nationalist discourse. Similarly, a report on the future of Iceland, commissioned by the Iceland Chamber of Commerce, published in 2006, suggested that Iceland should 'no longer compare itself with the other Nordic states, as we overreach them in most fields' (Iceland Chamber of Commerce, 2006).

Iceland's president, Ólafur Ragnar Grímsson, provided further credibility to the Viking capitalists. Already at the turn of the millennium, he was predicting 'that the features of the new global economy are such as to allow us Icelanders to prosper as never before and give our global partners access to highly rewarding co-operation' (Grímsson, 2000). He explained that creativity was the backbone of the Icelandic heritage: a creativity that 'centuries ago produced the Icelandic sagas and the Edda poems, unique literary achievements in medieval Europe, and creativity is clearly what confers a competitive edge in the modern global economy and will do so even more in the knowledge-based industries and services of the 21st century' (Grímsson, 2000). Anthropologist Kristín Loftsdóttir (2011) argues that Icelanders have long emphasised the purity of their ethnic origin. The President did not hesitate to explain Iceland's postcolonial success with the unique origin of the nation, thus linking the present with the past. He went on to explain how Icelandic creativity manifests itself not only in literature and the arts but also in running modern companies. In early 2000, he concluded one of his speeches by saying that it was in 'this spirit that we have come to Los Angeles to share with you [The people of America] the excitement of our future' (Grímsson, 2000).

In the coming years, the president directly linked the contemporary Icelandic Viking capitalists with the original Viking settlers in the 9th century AD, claiming that they contained the same qualities and indeed the same spirit. Anthony D. Smith (1993) refers to this claim as 'the myth of a common ancestry'. Although the president may have gone further than most in his speeches, similar rhetoric was widely echoed during the boom years. For example, in 2007 the annual conference of the Iceland Chamber of Commerce (2007) was held under the slogan 'Iceland, best in the world!'

Concerns of the health of the 'Icelandic economic miracle' started to emerge early in 2006. Foreign criticism was often dismissed as ill-willed intervention from abroad. The government responded by launching a defensive PR campaign in London, New York, and Copenhagen. Minister of Industry and Commerce Valgerdur

Sverrisdóttir (PP) said that envy was the root of criticism of the Fitch Ratings in 2006 and dismissed the concerns of the Danish commercial bank Den Danske Bank by asking whether Denmark's self-image had been damaged by Iceland's success (Sverrisdóttir, 2006).

Icelanders felt quite alone in the world when on 8 October 2008 the British government invoked the Anti-Terrorism, Crime and Security Act (2001) to freeze the assets of Landsbanki in the UK and, for a while, all assets of the Icelandic state.[17] The Icelandic state was put on the same 'list' as Al-Qaeda, Burma, the Taliban, Zimbabwe, and North Korea. Within days, the whole financial sector had collapsed in a series of events, which later became known as the 'Crash'. The Icelandic economic miracle was over. Iceland's humiliation was completed when employees of the Danish tabloid *Ekstrabladet* started to hold a sarcastic collection for poor Iceland outside the main landmarks of the Icelandic Viking capitalists in Copenhagen. The fall from grace was heavy. Iceland had all but failed in its eternal quest to uphold a prosperous modern Western democracy.

Tapping into the postcolonial rhetoric, familiar trenches of nationalistic rhetoric were immediately dug. In domestic discourse, Iceland was depicted as a victim of aggressive foreigners who, through conspiracy, had brought Iceland to its knees (Gunnarsson, 2009). An agreement on the Icesave dispute was initially reached in June 2009.[18] The government was immediately accused of high treason by the opposition and pundits.[19] PP leader Sigmundur David Gunnlaugsson, who in spring 2013 replaced Jóhanna Sigurðardóttir as PM, accused Sigurðardóttir of 'humiliating the nation [by] forcing her nation to pay the Icesave debt burden'.[20] Further, he claimed that instead of protecting the nation the government was working on behalf of the British and the Dutch to attack Iceland. Although Iceland was later vindicated of any wrongdoing (EFTA Court Ruling, 2013) the rhetoric used domestically still provides an interesting picture of how the national identity is used in politics. The Icesave dispute was directly linked with the debate on EU membership. After explaining how the EU had forced Iceland to agree to an unjust agreement, one parliamentarian (IP) said it was strange that any Icelander would like 'to join this club that beats us'.[21]

---

17 The Landsbanki Freezing Order 2008, (2008).
18 This agreement was refused by the public in a national referendum in early 2010. Another agreement met the same fate in early 2011 after the President also refused to sign that one.
19 See, for example, Eygló Harðardóttir's speech in Parliament on 6 June 2009 (Althingi online archive).
20 Sigmundur D Gunnlaugsson, speech in Parliament on 5 December 2009 (Althingi online archive).
21 Pétur Blöndal, speech in Parliament on 11 July 2009 (Althingi online archive).

In associating the European Union with a historical enemy of Iceland, the EU was repeatedly referred to as a club of former colonisers, in contrast to Iceland, which had been colonised by one of its fellow members, namely Denmark. An MP for the Citizens Movement, the post crisis protest party, explained: 'Iceland is an old colony and we are negotiating with rooted colonisers who have not shielded their colonies in the past. Are we going to surrender to become their colony?'[22] Similarly, the new IP leader, Bjarni Benediktsson, referred to historically the most important quote of Iceland's struggle for independence: 'We all protest.' His words echoed Jón Sigurðsson, when protesting against the Danish authority after unilaterally closing Iceland's constitutional Assembly in 1851. Benediktsson said that Iceland should send the same message to the UK.[23]

Iceland's misfortune was further attributed to flaws in EU laws on international banking, which it had been made to follow through the EEA Agreement, since Iceland was facing problems 'which the EU had made with bad legislation and by forcing and attacking Iceland because of the Icesave case'.[24]

The Icesave agreement in 2009 emerged in domestic discourse as the most unpopular since the treaty made with Norway in 1262, when according to the national myth Iceland's economy started to deteriorate after falling under foreign rule and the country entered into a period of humiliation after losing independence. The agreement was widely rejected in two national referenda initiated by the president in an extraordinary move in the country's history. As an example, upon becoming Prime Minister, Sigmundur David Gunnlaugsson used the PM's traditional celebratory address on Iceland's national day on 17 June 2013 to remind Icelanders that in the dispute the EU had participated in an illegal attempt at coercing Icelanders to accept enormous burdens (Gunnlaugsson, 2013).

In the rounds of debates, parliamentarians used mainly two sets of arguments: the economic effect on the fisheries industry and how Europe fitted with the idea of the Icelandic nation and Iceland's formal sovereignty. The importance of the nation and its sovereignty came to the fore in the debate on the EEA and continued through a round of debates in the EU. After the collapse of the banks in autumn 2008 and leading up to the EU application in summer 2009, the debate was dominated by harsh nationalistic rhetoric.

The 'No' side used the importance of sovereignty, as developed in the struggle for independence, more directly in their discourse, while the 'Yes' side rather tried

---

22   Margrét Tryggvadóttir, speech in Parliament on 18 June 2006 (Althingi online archive).
23   Bjarni Benediktsson, speech in Parliament on 9 January 2010 (Althingi online archive.
24   Pétur Blöndal, speech in Parliament on 11 July 2009 (Althingi online archive).

to link their economic argument with that part of the sovereignty discourse that has to do with modernisation and economic progress. Both camps used the discourse developed in the struggle in their argumentation, for example by referring to the uniqueness of the Icelandic nation. The sovereignty issue was probably more often used by the 'No' camp, but in the debate on full membership the 'Yes' side made an effort to turn the argument around.

The discourse of uniqueness of the Icelandic nation heard in the boom years echoes the national myth created during Iceland's struggle for independence in the 19th century. The change in the national rhetoric, from the superiority discourse in the boom years to the theory of being under siege by ill-willed foreigners was then quite rapid. On the surface, it might even seem that those two ideas were contradictory. However, on closer inspection, it becomes evident that the harsh nationalistic rhetoric on the EU and the Icesave agreement can be traced to the same origin as the one on the Icelandic economic miracle heard in the first decade of the new millennium. The core of both ideas is found in the common national myth that was created during the struggle for independence in the 19th century, and was written down by Jón Jónsson Aðils in the beginning of the 20th century and kept alive and nurtured by politicians of all ranks throughout the decades and then put into new perspectives by persons such as President Ólafur Ragnar Grímsson.

The national myth, which the Icelandic state is based on and has become evident in almost all debates on foreign relations in the country, is still very much alive. When analysing the discourse on foreign relations, especially on participation in the European project, it can be seen how the national rhetoric travels through all shifts and turns and changing environments. Even though the national myth has taken on different forms in different times and under different circumstances, the basis for it has remained the same. The president's comment after the Icesave referendum in 2009 is a good example of how the nationalistic discourse of the boom years had survived the economic crash of 2008.

Conclusions

When studying Iceland's relationship with the EU through the EEA Agreement it becomes evident that Iceland is a very active participant in the European project. Formally, Iceland is not a member of the EU institutions but in certain areas Iceland participates more actively than some of the official members. Thus, through its agreements with the EU, Iceland has delegated decision rights in important fields of the economy to the EU or bodies that it operates jointly with the EU. It may even be claimed that Iceland is a de facto member of the EU through its close co-operation agreements, despite lacking formal access to decision-making in the EU institutions.

As most reports have stated, the EEA has for the most part functioned in the way that it was meant to function. However, it has also opened up new areas that were not foreseen, for example in the field of the environment and transport, where the vast majority of all legislation set in Iceland now comes directly from Brussels. This is an example of the semi-automatic nature of the co-operation. The parliamentary process in Iceland is therefore only a formal exercise. Furthermore, all policymaking and other decisions on, for example, future development and new regulations, are dealt with within EU institutions, to which the Icelandic Government has very limited access. It can therefore be concluded that in any political understanding Iceland has quite clearly transferred real decision-making to the EU.

The EEA Agreement has clearly proven problematic and has even undermined Iceland's democracy, as it puts limits on member countries' room for making its own legislation and on other kinds of decision-making. However, within this rigid framework, Iceland has been able to find a way to manoeuvre when it comes to its fundamental interests. On a few occasions, Iceland has even been able to negotiate important opt-outs and derogations from EEA relevant acts.

In economic terms, the EEA has both proven instrumental for the boom and bust of the Icelandic economy. A systemic flaw became evident when Iceland's huge financial institutions ran into trouble in the European market in 2008 but found themselves without back up from EU institutions as Iceland was not member of the EU. This flaw was perhaps the main reason for Iceland's EU application in 2009, which the new right of centre government froze after the parliamentary elections in 2013. Having halted the EU accession negotiations, the government will have to revisit its strife for updating the EEA Agreement, providing a stronger safety net for its fragile economy and, perhaps even more importantly, tackling the evident democratic deficit.

This chapter has also analysed the impact of Iceland's colonial past and the national myth created in the struggle for independence. The rhetoric used in the debate on Europe shows clearly that the idea of the Icelandic nation and the importance of formal sovereignty has been central to the debate and suggests that the national factor influences the policies on Europe. Moreover, the sovereignty emphasis and the impact on internal democracy have been central in all discussions on Iceland and the outside world.

As I have shown, the importance of independence and sovereignty has significantly affected the debate on Iceland's role and participation in the European project. The nationalistic emphasis developed in the struggle for independence still influences discourse in Icelandic politics, especially when foreign policy and Iceland's place in the world are debated. As described above, this emphasis on uniqueness, and this holistic and conservative understanding of the Icelandic nation and its sovereignty, make it more difficult for Icelandic politicians to argue for membership of a supranational organisation such as the EU. It can therefore be concluded that the idea of European integration to some extent falls outside the framework of the idea of the sovereign and independent democratic Icelandic nation-state.

However, the political discourse of the struggle for independence has not completely hindered Iceland's involvement in the European project. On the contrary, Iceland is an active participant in European co-operation through EFTA, the EEA, and the Schengen Agreement. Even though Iceland is not formally a member of the EU institutions, it is already deeply involved in the European project. In this regard, there is an interesting rift between the real and practical participation on the one hand and the above-described ideas of the free and sovereign Icelandic nation on the other hand. From this situation, an explanation can be developed.

Like all other open democratic states in Europe, Iceland feels the same economic need and pressure to participate in the European project, as described by neofunctionalism. Accordingly, Iceland has agreed to transfer decision-making in significant fields of the economy to the European level through its participation in the EEA and the Schengen Agreement. The parliamentary discussions have revealed how the neofunctionalist spillover effect puts increasing pressure on Iceland for further participation. At the same time, however, other forces are pulling in the opposite direction. The national political discourse, so deeply rooted in the struggle for independence, has had the effect that Icelanders have been hesitant to agree to the formal transfer of sovereignty, which clearly follows full membership of the European Union. This dilemma can be used to explain why Iceland has been willing to participate actively in the European project through the EEA and the Schengen Agreement while the traditional vision of the Icelandic nation and its sovereignty makes it difficult for Icelandic politicians to argue for full and formal participation in the EU.

References

Primary Sources

Althingi online archive (1845-), retrieved from althingi.is

EFTA Court Ruling (2013), Judgment of the Court 28 January 2013 in Case E-16/11, EFTA Court, retrieved from eftacourt.int

Grímsson, Ólafur Ragnar (2000), speech by the President of Iceland Ólafur Ragnar Grímsson at the Icelandic American Chamber of Commerce's Lunch, Los Angeles 5 May 2000, retrieved from forseti.is

Gunnlaugsson, S. D. (2013), Ávarp forsætisráðherra, Sigmundar Davíðs Gunnlaugssonar, á Austurvelli 17. júní 2013, Reykjavik, retrieved from forsaetisraduneyti.is

Jónasson, Ö. (2009, 11), 'NORRÆN ÞÖGN SAMA OG NORRÆNT SAMÞYKKI', retrieved from ogmundur.is

Samtök Iðnaðarins (SI) (2012), 'Viðhorf almennings til ESB', Reykjavik.

Literature

Adler-Nissen, R. (2008), 'The diplomacy of opting out: A Bourdieudian approach to national integration strategies', *Journal of Common Market Studies*, Vol. 46, No. 3, pp. 663–684.

Alfreðsson, G. (1992), 'Álit Guðmundar Alfreðssonar um EES og stjórnarskrána'. Alþingistíðindi A. Reykjavik: Alþingi.

Archer, C. & Sogner, I. (1998), *Norway, European Integration and Atlantic Security*, London: Sage.

Bergmann, E. (2007), *Opið land: Ísland í samfélagi Þjóðanna*, Reykjavík: Skrudda.

Bergmann, E. (2009), *Hið huglæga sjálfstæði þjóðarinnar: áhrif þjóðernishugmynda á Evrópustefnu íslenskra stjórnvalda* [Sense of sovereignty: How national sentiments have influenced Iceland's European policy], Reykjavik: Faculty of Political Sience, University of Iceland.

Bergmann, E. (2011), *Sjálfstæð þjóð – tryllur skríll og landráðalýður*, Reykjavik: Veröld.

Björnson, P. (2010), 'Jón Sigurðsson forseti of aðild Íslands and Evrópusambandinu', in *Rannsóknir í félagsvísindum IX*, Reykjavik: Félagsvísindastofnun Háskóla Íslands.

Friðriksson, Ó. (2002), 'Davíð Oddsson forsætisráðherra í Morgunblaðsviðtali um ágreining formanna stjórnarflokkanna um Evrópumál, uppgang í efnahagslífinu, kosningar og umdeilda atburði í tengslum við opinbera heimsókn forseta Kína: Ólíkar áherslur hafa ekki úrslitaáhrif á stjórnarsamstarfið', *Morgunblaðið*, 23 June 2002.

Grímsson, Ó.R. (1978), *Icelandic ationalism: A Dissolution Force in the Danish Kingdom and a Fundamental Cleavage in Icelandic Politics: A Draft Framework for Historical Analysis*, Háskóli Íslands: félagsvísindadeild.

Grímsson, Ó.R. (2010), 'Þjóðaratkvæðagreiðslan styrkir lýðræðisþróun – viðtal við forseta Íslands', [TV Interview], Reykjavik: Stöð 2

Gunnarsson, S. (2009), *Umsátrið*, Reykjavík: Veröld.

Hálfdanarson, G. (2001), *Íslenska þjóðríkið: uppruni og endimörk*. Reykjavik: Hið íslenska bókmenntafélag.

Hermannsson, B. (2005), *Understanding Nationalism: Studies in Icelandic Nationalism 1800-2000*, Doktorsavhandling [PhD thesis], Stockholm: Statsvetenskapliga institutionen, Stockholms universitet.

Iceland Chamber of Commerce (2006), *Ísland 2015*. Reykjavik, retrieved from vi.is/
Iceland Chamber of Commerce (2007), 'Ísland, best í heimi! Alþjóðlegt oðrspor og ímynd'. Reykjavik, retrieved from vi.is/
Jónsson Aðils, J. (1903), *Íslenskt þjóðerni*, Reykjavik: Félagsprentsmiðjan.
Kristinsson, G.H. & Thorhallsson, B. (2004), 'The Euro-sceptical political elite', in Thorhallsson, B. (ed.) *Iceland and European Integration: On the Edge*, pp. 145–160. New York: Routledge.
Loftsdóttir, K. (2010), 'The loss of innocence: The Icelandic financial crisis and colonial past', *Anthropology Today*, Vol. 26, No. 6, pp. 9–13.
Loftsdóttir, K. (2011), 'Negotiating white Icelandic identity: Multiculturalism and colonial identity formations', *Social Identities*, Vol. 17, No. 1, pp. 11–25.
Magnússon, M.Á. (2011), *The Engagement of Iceland and Malta with European Integration: Economic Incentives and Political Constraints*, PhD thesis, Reykjavík: Faculty of Political Science, University of Iceland.
NOU 2012:2, *Utenfor og innenfor: Norges avtaler med EU*, Oslo: Utenriksdepartementet [Ministry of Foreign Affairs].
Prime Ministers Office (2008), *Ímynd Íslands: Styrkur, staða og stefna (Skýrsla nefndar)*, Reykjavik, retrieved from forsaetisraduneyti.is
Rannsóknarnefnd Alþingis 2008 (2010), *Aðdragandi og orsakir falls íslensku bankanna 2008 og tengdir atburðir* / Rannsóknarnefnd Alþingis; [ed. Páll Hreinsson, Sigríður Benediktsdóttir, Tryggvi Gunnarsson], Rannsóknarnefnd Alþingis.
Smith, A.D. (1993), *National Identity*, Reno, NV: University of Nevada Press.
Sverrisdóttir, V. (2006), Endalok íslenskrar útrásar', Kópavogur: Blaðið.
B. Thorhallsson (2004), 'Towards a new theoretical approach: Iceland and European Integration', in B. Thorhallsson (ed.) *Iceland and European Integration: On the Edge*, p. 185. New York: Routledge.

Crisis and convergence: Norwegian parliamentary debate on the EU

Lise Rye

In Norway the Eurozone crisis coincided with a new debate on the country's association with the European Union (EU). Due to the divisive nature of the question of EU membership within political parties and governmental coalitions, public debate on the EU in Norway has been dominated by strong civil society organizations (Rye and Steinnes, 2010). The 2007 introduction of half-yearly governmental accounts of important EU and European Economic Area (EEA) affairs to the National Assembly followed by plenary debates represented a change to this pattern. It reflected the National Assembly's aim for a more active role in the formulation of Norwegian policy towards the EU and became a new source for the views of Norwegian political parties on recent developments within the EU and EU-Norway relations.[1] Historically, ideas about the quality of democracy on national and EU levels have had crucial impacts on Norway's relations with the EU. Norway's two rejections of European Communities (EC) and EU membership, in 1972 and 1994 respectively, were the results of popular opposition against political integration. On both occasions voters listed arguments related to national sovereignty, in Norwegian referred to as *'sjølråderett'*, the governing of a country by its own people, as their most important reason for voting 'No' (Ringdal, 1996: 56; Ryghaug and Jenssen, 1999: 19). The idea was that entry into the EC/EU would imply a weakening of national democracy that the benefits of full membership could not outweigh. In 1992, the Norwegian Parliament ratified the EEA Agreement, which granted Norway and other members of the European Free Trade Association (EFTA) access to the EC internal market on equal terms with EC member states. The adoption of the agreement depended on the votes of parliamentarians that were opposed to EC membership but ready to accept the EEA Agreement

---

[1] Recommendation to the Storting from the Standing Committee on Foreign Affairs, Innst. S. nr. 114 (2006–2007), document no. 8:105 (2005–2006).

because it kept formal sovereignty intact. Two decades later, a review showed that the EEA Agreement had served Norwegian economic interests well, but at a price of a steady weakening of domestic democratic institutions (NOU 2012:2).

This chapter investigates whether central ideas of the EU and Norway's relationship with it changed in the context of Eurozone crisis and Europeanization following Norway's EEA association with the EU. Using the parliamentary debates on EU and EEA affairs in the period spring 2007 to spring 2012 as the empirical basis, I ask (1) whether discursive shifts took place and (2) how the respective positions, as communicated in parliamentary discourse, were explained.

On a more general level, the chapter brings new evidence into the larger discussion on whether the political decision-makers' standpoints towards supranational integration mirror domestic or external affairs primarily. In 1992, Alan S. Milward launched his theory of integration as a national choice. He rejected that the process of European integration reflected the ideals of founding fathers or nascent supranational institutions, and claimed that national governments chose integration to facilitate the economic growth needed to finance new and ambitious domestic political programmes. New domestic policies were in turn means to secure popular support – enfeebled by two world wars and an economic crisis – for the nation-state as the dominating framework for political action. Far from being its anti-thesis, the process of European integration after World War II thus became the European rescue of the nation-state (Milward, 1992). Milward based his theory on studies of the period until the early 1960s. The case of Norway illustrates its value for periods beyond that. As a small and highly interdependent state, the EC market was of undisputed importance to Norway. In the early 1970s, the country started, together with its EFTA partners, the quest for an agreement with the EU that would expand relations between the two blocks beyond the dismantling of tariff barriers to trade in industrial products (Kleppe, 2003; Rolstad, 2012). For domestic and foreign political reasons combined, Norway's interests at the time were short of full membership. However, the choice of economic but not political integration that the 1992 decision to enter the EEA constituted became a *national trap* in the sense that it emptied 30 years of pro-EU discourse, conspicuously economic by nature, of its power.

As the end of the Cold War made full membership an option, the previously so coveted EEA Agreement was degraded to the second choice of an increasing number of people and political parties alike. As Norway's economic interests already had been attended to, the question of full membership now became a question of political influence (Rye, 2011). The situation benefited the membership opponents. The core of their argument had always been that a country ought to be governed by its own people and that membership would go against this. The same situation forced the supporters of full membership to construct a new discourse that like the one of the opponents focused on the democratic quality of participation in political decision-making, but at a European level. This chapter demonstrates that while Norway's relations with the EU have changed substantially over the course of the last 20 years, current ideas on the EU and Norway's relations with it are not fundamentally different from the ones that characterized the debate on Norway and the EU in the 1990s. The crisis has nevertheless caused converging positions, as membership proponents and opponents alike now rally round the EEA association.

The chapter is structured in three parts. The first part puts Norway's European policy into historical perspective. The second part identifies the ideas of national and European democracy that were expressed at the time when Norway's current association with the EU was adopted, in October 1992. The third and main part brings new evidence to the table through an investigation of how these ideas have developed after two decades of substantial Europeanization and a period of crisis in which central democratic principles have been put to the test.

Norway and the EU in historical perspective

The EEA Agreement is the major element in a series of agreements between Norway and the EU that ranges from research and development (R&D) and trade to justice and defence. Together, they have made Norway 'as integrated in European policy and economy as any non-member state can be'.[2] While Norway is committed to forming an integral part of the EU internal market, it has chosen to remain outside the process aiming at political unification in Europe. This market-oriented approach may be traced back to the 1960s, when Norway submitted the first of what has since amounted to four applications for European Economic Community (EEC)/EC/EU membership. The approach reflects domestic opposition against political integration, in turn based on long-standing ideas of Europe as 'the other', of Nordic unity, and of the virtues of Norwegian society (Neumann, 2002; Rye, 2011).

The process of European integration initially attracted little interest in Norway. The political elite considered the early moves towards European unity in the

---

2 Council Conclusions on EU relations with EFTA countries, December 2010, http://www.consilium.europa.eu/uedocs/cms_data/docs/pressdata/EN/foraff/118458.pdf

1950s as unrelated to their interests and ideas of post-war Norway. On a number of occasions leading politicians referred to economic, social, and political differences existing between Scandinavia and Britain on the one hand and continental Western Europe on the other hand. While the continental countries were described as advocates of laissez-faire, the British and Scandinavian position gave priority to full employment and social justice (Eriksen and Pharo, 1997). The feeling that Norway belonged with the other Nordic countries, as well as with Great Britain and the United States of America, was strong. At the outset, therefore, Norway had no policy towards integrated Europe. The reappraisal of British policy at the entry of the 1960s turned the tables. Norway submitted its first application for membership of the then EEC in 1962.

The 1962 application marked the beginning of a reactive and guarded approach towards the EEC/EC/EU. The Labour government that submitted it had been in office since 1955 without showing any prior interest in membership. The accompanying letter made it clear that this was not a straightforward application for membership, but an application for 'negotiations on the conditions of admission'.[3] By contrast, Norway's fellow applicant, Denmark, was honoured 'to request the admission of Denmark as a member of the Community'.[4] Like Norway, the Danish Government used the opportunity to direct the attention towards negotiating topics of particular importance for Denmark. Unlike Norway, Denmark chose an opening that left no doubt about the fact that it was aiming for membership.

The second Norwegian application for membership of the EEC was submitted in 1967, following the British Government's decision to reapply (Frøland, 2001). It was launched by a centre-right coalition composed of the Centre Party, the Christian Democratic Party, the Liberal Party, and the Conservative Party. The accompanying letter indicated that the interest in membership in 1967 was stronger than had been the case five years earlier. The government now asked for 'the opening of negotiations with a view to drawing up the agreement mentioned as the basis for accession to Paragraph 2 of Article 237 of the Treaty establishing the European

---

3   Norway's application for membership to the EEC, 30 April 1962, *Bulletin of the European Economic Community*, May 1962, No. 5, Luxembourg: Office for Official Publications of the European Communities.

4   Denmark's application for accession to the EEC, 10 August 1961, *Bulletin of the European Economic Community*, September-October 1961, Nos. 9–10, Luxembourg: Office for Official Publications of the European Communities.

Economic Community'.[5] However, it also signalled a wish for adjustments on the part of the EC in the form of permanent Norwegian exceptions from EC legislation. Referring to the 1962 application, which had identified particular problems related to Norway's geography and economic structure, the Norwegian Government trusted 'that with understanding on both sides' it would be possible to find satisfactory solutions to these problems in the course of negotiations.[6]

Conditioned by British entry and as a consequence of France's repeated veto against it, the first Norwegian applications never led to negotiations. At the end of the 1960s the context changed and at the summit of The Hague in December 1969 principal agreement on enlargement was declared. Against this new backdrop, the four applicants, namely the UK, Ireland, Denmark, and Norway, renewed their 1967 applications and in June 1970 time had come for a joint meeting of foreign ministers in Brussels. For the candidate countries, the meeting represented an opportunity to present their applications in some depth. Norway's foreign minister at the time left no doubt about the fact that Norway had approached the EC for economic reasons: 80% of Norwegian exports went to Europe: '*C'est donc avec un vif intérêt que la Norvège a suivi l'intégration européenne*'.[7] At the same time, the implementation of Community regulations would create considerable problems for Norway, as these could prevent the country from pursuing its policy of regional development, in turn a measure to keep the entire country populated. In order to maintain the present pattern of settlement, satisfactory conditions for agriculture and fisheries were essential. In the area of agriculture, Norway now clearly spelled out what in 1962 had only been indicated: '*D'un point de vue compétitif les désavantages de l'agriculture norvégienne étant permanents, ces solutions devront également être durables.*'[8]

Domestically, the government downplayed the EC's political ambitions. The Community did not aim for a political union, it said, when defending its decision to renew the 1967 application in Parliament in July 1970. Emphasis was placed on the need to secure access to markets. Remaining outside an enlarged EC would mean having to face discrimination in markets receiving 78% of Norwegian exports. Another central, albeit vague, argument was that the EC 'understood

---

5   Norway's second application for membership of the EEC, 21 July 1967, *Bulletin of the European Economic Community*, September-October 1967, Nos. 9–10, Luxembourg: Office for Official Publications of the European Communities.
6   *Ibid.*
7   Svenn Stray, diplomatic conference, Luxembourg 30 June 1970, http://www.cvce.eu/obj/speech_by_svenn_stray_luxembourg_30_june_1970-en-a0529562-8aaa-4ed0-927f-6645b67ee72b html
8   *Ibid.*

Norway's problems in the field of agriculture'.[9] As the government was divided on the issue of membership, it was only the Conservative Party that was able to add that the Norwegian application was not merely a result of economic considerations. For the Conservative Party, it was just as much a result of wider political considerations: Norwegian EC membership would imply more authority and more self-determination than would be the case if Norway remained outside the EC.

As made clear by an advisory referendum on the question of EC membership in September 1972, the majority of the voters held a different opinion. In total, 53.5% cast their votes against Norwegian entry into the EC, stating loss of autonomy as their main motive (Bjørklund, 1982). In the following year, Norway and the other EFTA countries entered bilateral trade agreements with the EC that ensured free trade in industrial products, while the, in the case of Norway more sensitive, primary sector was not included. The free trade agreement on trade in industrial products regulated Norway's relations with the EC until the EEA Agreement became operative in January 1994.

Into the EEA

Norway entered the EEA in order to secure continued non-discrimination in the important EC market. The aim reflected both domestic and external constraints. Domestically, the question of EU membership continued to divide between and within political parties. This was not least the case in the Labour Party, which ran minority governments in the periods 1986–1989 and 1990–1997.[10] Moreover, since the 1970s, official Norwegian policy had been to pursue a common EFTA solution to the question of future relations with the EC. In the Europe of the Cold War, the policy of neutrality of three of the EFTA states made full membership a non-option. Finally, in a context in which the less comprehensive bilateral free trade agreements were considered insufficient and the more comprehensive alternative of full membership was politically impossible, Norway and her fellow EFTA countries took what the stronger part had to offer. The offer reflected the geopolitical realities of the time as well as the then scope of EC-level co-operation, which had not yet extended into the areas of foreign and security policy, and justice and home affairs.

---

9   Parliamentary debate on Norway's relations with Nordic and European market groupings, 24 June 1970, p. 3792.

10   The centre-right coalition in office from autumn 1989 imploded a year later as a result of disagreement on the EU/EEA question.

In their quest to prevent discrimination in the EC market, the EFTA members had to give up their original demand for joint EEA decision-making institutions. Commission president Jacques Delors had indicated the possibility of co-determination in his launching of the EEA, when speaking of 'a new, more structured partnership between the EC and EFTA with common decision-making and administrative institutions'.[11] It turned out that this was the first but also the only time that the EC's top-level representatives mentioned this possibility. As was soon made clear, the EC had no intention of letting outsiders partake in its internal decision-making procedures. The resulting institutional structure was a mechanism for EFTA import of EC internal market regulations that kept the sovereignty of both parties intact: EFTA member states did not gain any role in EC decision-making but maintained the right to reserve themselves collectively against new legislation that they were not ready to adopt.

After two days of debate, the Norwegian Parliament ratified the EEA Agreement in October 1992, with 130 against 35 votes. This was the first and hitherto sole decision taken on basis of the new Paragraph 93 of the Norwegian Constitution. The Norwegian Constitution dates back to 1814, when Norway changed from being subject to Danish rule to having a higher degree of independence in a union with Sweden. The first paragraph of the constitution states that the kingdom of Norway is 'free, independent, indivisible and inalienable'. Paragraph 93 was adopted in 1962 in order to make Norwegian participation in supranational co-operation consistent with Paragraph 1. According to this paragraph, the Storting (Parliament) may,

in order to safeguard international peace and security or to promote the international rule of law and cooperation, consent that an international organization to which Norway belongs or will belong shall have the right, within specified fields, to exercise powers normally vested in the authorities of the State.[12]

The consent requires a three-fourths majority and the presence of at least two-thirds of the parliamentarians. The 1992 use of Paragraph 93 stemmed from the fact that membership of the EEA demanded the surrender of sovereignty to new EFTA institutions for compliance and dispute settlement. To adherents of Norwe-

---

11 Jacques Delors, speech to the European Parliament, 17 January 1989, http://www.cvce.eu/viewer/-/content/39ba5f57-affa-42b0-b18b-830886da5fb9/b9c06b95-db97-4774-a700-e8aea5172233/en
12 The Constitution of the Kingdom of Norway, http://www.stortinget.no/In-English/About-the-Storting/The-Constitution/The-Constitution/

gian EEA membership, this was a surrender of sovereignty that they were ready to accept and an obligation that was considered secondary to the EFTA-EEA block's formal right to reserve itself against new EU legislation.

The 1992 debate crystallized around three positions: one that presented EEA membership as a wanted but *insufficient* solution, one that presented it as a *sufficient* solution and one that presented it as an *unwanted* solution. The first position was taken up by the Conservative Party – the only Norwegian political party whose manifesto at the time included EU membership.[13] In keeping with the party manifesto, party spokespersons made it clear that they did not consider the EEA as an independent alternative for Norway, but as a step towards Norway's full membership of the EU. Norway's entry into the EEA was described as a continuation of Norwegian foreign and commercial political traditions. The Conservative Party's former minister of trade stated: 'Even in 1972, when rejecting EC membership, we chose integration and cooperation, but then through EFTA.'[14] Norwegian entry into the EEA was presented as both an economic *necessity*, enforced by the EC's decision to establish the internal market, and an *improvement* compared to the existing free trade agreements, as the EEA addressed new non-tariff barriers to trade. However, given the lack of decision-making power, the EEA Agreement was also presented as an *unsatisfactory* response to Norway's total challenges, as the agreement attended to the interests of Norwegian industry and commerce while leaving a number of other important issues outside its scope.

The majority of the governing Labour Party, the Christian Democratic Party, the Progress Party, and the Liberal Party defended the second position in the 1992 debate. The Prime Minister, Gro Harlem Brundtland, had come out publicly in favour of EU membership in April that same year. In October she still insisted that her party continued to consider the EEA an *independent* and *sufficient* solution for Norway. The prime minister described the agreement as 'today's best alternative to safeguard Norwegian interests when the internal market comes into force from 1993.' The agreement was not an aim in itself but a tool to 'secure the basis for the further development of the welfare society'. Norwegian employment and welfare in the post-war era had depended on access to the European market. The EEA Agreement was 'about equal access to markets, equal rules and credible

---

13 The Norwegian political system is a multiparty system. In 1992, six parties were represented in Parliament: on a right-left axis there were the two right of centre parties, the Progress Party and the Conservative Party; there were two parties in the political centre, the Christian Democratic Party and the Centre Party; and there were two left of centre parties, the Labour Party and the Socialist Left Party.
14 Kaci Kullman Five, *Stortingsforhandlinger*, 15 October 1992, p. 185.

agreements' – it was 'a free trade agreement for the 1990s'.[15] In lieu of worrying about the lack of decision-making power, the advocates of this position emphasized the agreement's inherent *decision-shaping possibilities*. One of the Labour Party representatives said: 'One of the true advances of the EEA Agreement is the setting up of institutional solutions that offer Norway a place when the shaping of future regulations in our most important trading area is on the table.'[16] The Christian Democratic Party stressed that the EEA Agreement left Norwegian sovereignty and governing of national resources intact: 'The Christian Democratic Party would never waive Norway's right to defend these national resources.'[17]

Together, these two kinds of EEA adherents provided the necessary majority that ratification of the agreement required. Their emphasis on economic arguments stood in stark contrast to the political arguments of the EEA opponents. The anti-EEA position gathered the representatives of the Centre Party, the Socialist Left Party, and a few Labour Party representatives. United in their opposition against the EEA, the Centre Party and the Socialist Left Party differed in their reasons for doing so. The internationally oriented Socialist Left Party argued that entry into the EEA would restrict Norwegian freedom of action in the fields where it was most needed: in the fight against unemployment, as well as in the struggle to achieve a leading role in the global environmental policy. The party also voiced principal objections against the philosophy of growth underpinning the internal market. The growth philosophy would increase environmental problems, further centralization, and weaken the conditions for all forms of popular opposition:

> *Showing splendid contempt for public education and the national will, the parliamentary majority endorses today an agreement that will entail major changes in the Norwegian society and the transfer of power from elected assemblies to the boardrooms of the multinational companies.*[18]

The concern of the more inward-looking Centre Party representatives was with the consequences of the agreement for Norwegian sovereignty. The Centre Party leader declared: 'We do not fight the EEA because we think we are better than others ... but simply because ours is a small country and because a vivid democracy needs to control policy instruments in order to prevent the blind power of

---

15 Gro Harlem Brundtland, *Stortingsforhandlinger*, 15 October 1992, p. 215.
16 Gunnar Skaug, *Stortingsforhandlinger*, 15 October 1992, p. 180.
17 Kåre Gjønnes, *Stortingsforhandlinger*, 15 October 1992, p. 205.
18 Inge Staldvik, *Stortingsforhandlinger*, 16 October 1992, p. 305.

big business and the free play of the market.'[19] The party described an agreement that would impact the governing of the Norwegian society and restrict Norwegian freedom of action in important areas, including agriculture and fisheries, which generally were considered outside the scope of the agreement. A ratification of the EEA Agreement would mean 'a massive transfer of power from Norwegian elected bodies to the EEA system in Brussels and Geneva'.[20]

Two decades after the decision to enter the EEA an Official Norwegian Report demonstrated that the agreement had served Norwegian economic interests well, but at the price of a steady weakening of domestic democratic institutions.[21] This was not least the case for the National Assembly that was as challenged by European integration as parliaments in other European countries but without their access to compensating measures (NOU 2012:2). The report, henceforth referred to as the *EEA Review*, assessed the political, legal, administrative, economic, and other societal consequences of Norway's agreements with the EU. Its conclusion was that 'extensive Europeanization' had taken place. In one way, this was unsurprising, as the dynamic nature of the EEA Agreement had been well known to Norwegian decision-makers from the start. Nonetheless, the lesson learned was that the Europeanization of Norway in a number of areas had proved more extensive and more thorough than had been expected in 1992. One of the new findings was that the institutional set-up of the EEA dampened political debate and engagement, which in turn made it 'difficult to monitor the government and hold it accountable in its European policy'.[22]

Debating the EU and EEA: three sides to one story

Did central ideas of the EU and Norway's relations with it change along with the Eurozone crisis and the new debate on Norway and the EU? Further, if discursive shifts did take place, to what degree did these reflect concern with Norway's EEA association and the EU's handling of the Eurozone crisis respectively? Compared

---

19 Anne Enger Lahnstein, *Stortingsforhandlinger*, 15 October 1992, p. 211.
20 *Ibid.*
21 An Official Norwegian Report (NOU) is 'a thorough investigation into an issue or a field of responsibility prepared by a committee or commission appointed by the Government' (www.stortinget.no).The report in question, NOU 2012:2, was the result of a multidisciplinary and research based review conducted by 12 researchers over a two years period beginning in January 2010.
22 NOU 2012: 2b, Official Norwegian Reports: NOU 2012:2, *Outside and Inside: Norway's Agreements with the European Union*, English summary of Chapter 1, http://www.regjeringen.no/pages/36798821/PDFS/NOU201220120002000EN_PDFS.pdf

with the majority of countries scrutinized in this book, Norway has not been hard hit by the Eurozone crisis. One indication of this is Norway's unemployment rates: as of January 2013, the level of unemployment in Norway was 3.6% compared to an EU average of 10.9%.[23] It is thus the central role that aspects of democracy in general, and state sovereignty in particular, have played in the Norwegian domestic debate on European integration that makes a study of the impact of the crisis on ideas of democracy, and the EU's handling of it, worthwhile. The context, national and European alike, is one in which one would expect reinforced critique from the opponents of Norwegian EU membership. More intriguing is the question of how recent developments have impacted the discourse of EU membership supporters, of EEA critics, and of those that in 1992 defended the EEA Agreement on the grounds that it kept Norwegian sovereignty intact.

At the time when the new debate on Norway and the EU started, Norway was governed by a centre-left majority government composed of the Labour Party, the Centre Party, and the Socialist Left Party. In other words, in 2007 the government consisted of one large and officially pro-EU membership party and two small parties that were declared opponents of membership of both the EU and the EEA. Governing was made possible by a compromise in which the Labour Party agreed not to raise the question of EU membership, while the Centre Party and the Socialist Left Party accepted the EEA Agreement as a basis for governing. The situation did not encourage vivid political debate on Norway and the EU. In a climate with strong and increasing popular opposition against EU membership, the opposition, consisting of the Conservative Party, the Liberal Party, the Christian Democratic Party, and the Progress Party, saw no reason to raise the issues either. In this context, the introduction of parliamentary debates on the EU and the EEA provided a welcome source of insight into the positions of political decision-makers and the arguments used to defend them. As in the 1992 debate on the EEA, the representatives formed three groups: the supporters of EU and EEA membership, the supporters of EEA membership, and the opponents of EU and EEA membership.

The supporters of EU and EEA membership

In 2007 the pro-EU membership camp consisted of the Conservative Party and the Labour Party. One of the characteristic features of the discourse of this group was that it presented supranational integration as a *necessity*: the nation-state

---

23 OECD Harmonised Unemployment Rates, Paris, 15 May 2013, http://www.oecd.org/std/labour-stats/HUR_05e13.pdf

had become 'too small to solve a number of the everyday problems faced by its inhabitants'.[24] The group simultaneously depicted the process of integration as an *intergovernmental* process, driven and controlled by the member states: 'It is the member states that delimit, and provide scope and direction for the further development of EU-level co-operation.'[25] The supporters of full membership described the EU as 'a rallying point of democratic values, [as] the assembly of countries that believe in democracy, in human rights, in a governed market economy, [and] in transparent decision-making'.[26] Given the attraction of membership, the group also depicted the EU as an entity with considerable *democratizing power*. The eastern EU enlargement was held up as the foremost expression of the EU's ability to promote democracy and was described in terms of 'a major solidarity project'[27] and 'the political Marshall-aid of our time'.[28]

The pre-crisis discourse of the advocates of Norwegian EU membership was marked by massive and explicit critique against the EEA association. The economic significance of the EEA Agreement was uncontested. The problem was that it did not give Norway a role in the making of decisions that had substantial and increasing impact on Norwegian society. The question of EU membership had thus 'increasingly become a question of strengthening Norwegian democracy'.[29] A member of the Conservative Party stated: 'We have long held the opinion that membership would facilitate the protection of Norwegian interest and values ... Now there is a new argument: we need to join for the sake of our democracy.'[30]

None of the pro EU parties believed in an imminent change in Norway's association with the EU, and they did not express the will to contribute to such change by raising the membership issue. The Conservative Party made it clear that it did not want a new debate on EU membership until the attitude among the general public rendered a positive outcome of a referendum on the issue likely.[31] Labour Party representatives deplored the EEA Agreement's democratic deficit but saw 'no indications, unfortunately, of a change in our association with the EU in the near future'.[32] The parties agreed that the Lisbon Treaty (which came into effect in 2009) would strengthen EU-level democracy through the extension of the legisla-

---

24 Finn Martin Vallersnes, *Stortingsforhandlinger*, 4 June 2007, p. 3266.
25 Jonas Gahr Støre, *Stortingsforhandlinger*, 4 June 2007, p. 3258.
26 Erna Solberg, *Stortingsforhandlinger*, 23 October 2008, p. 289.
27 Marit Nybakk, *Stortingsforhandlinger*, 24 April 2008, p. 2955.
28 Jonas Gahr Støre, *Stortingsforhandlinger*, 4 June 2007, p. 3261.
29 Finn Martin Vallersnes, Stortingsforhandlinger, 8 November 2007, p. 382.
30 *Ibid.*
31 Finn Martin Vallersnes, *Stortingsforhandlinger*, 8 November 2007, p. 384.
32 Olav Akselsen, Stortingsforhandlinger, 24 April 2008, p. 2962.

tive powers of the European Parliament. At the same time, the treaty would raise new problems for Norway. One reason for this was that the elimination of the columnar structure that had been introduced with the Treaty of Maastricht (which came into effect in 1993), together with the emergence of cross-sector policies, would complicate the process of identifying EEA-relevant legislative processes. Another reason was that the EU's relations with the EFTA-EEA countries were handled by the European Commission, whose influence had diminished in pace with the increase in power of other EU institutions.

The two parties were united in their view of the crisis as one created by states for which the EU could not be blamed:

The countries in the Eurozone and the EU that are having problems have brought these problems upon themselves. It is neither the fault of the EU nor the fault of the Euro-cooperation that they have fallen into trouble.[33]

It is important to emphasize that the crisis that countries are now experiencing is not a crisis created by the EU, but a nationally created crisis. These are countries that have borrowed more than they can repay, countries that have consumed more than they create, countries that have violated the fundamental principle of all economics, namely that you cannot over time spend more than you have.[34]

The main target of the critique was Greece, where 'years of economic misgovernment, crime and corruption' had weakened the general public's trust in democracy.[35]

The attitudes towards southern European countries in crisis contrasted with the unison concern for the situation on Iceland. All political parties spoke up for the need to assist the country consistently referred to as 'our brother nation' in the west. The seriousness of the situation in Iceland required that Norway 'considered all possible ways to express unity and solidarity with our brother nation'.[36] It was considered that Norway ought to assist Iceland 'in a Nordic or European framework, but, of course, on basis of Icelandic requests and needs.'[37] The need for action was explained in terms of 'old historic kinship, proximity and under-

---

33 Ine Marie Eriksen Søreide, *Stortingsforhandlinger*, 18 November 2010, p. 674.
34 Jan Tore Sanner, Conservative Party, *Stortingsforhandlinger*, 22 November 2011, p. 594.
35 Steinar Gullvåg, *Stortingsforhandlinger*, 6 May 2010, p. 3183.
36 Jonas Gahr Støre, *Stortingsforhandlinger*, 23 October 2008, p. 233.
37 Vidar Bjørstad, *Stortingsforhandlinger*, 24 October 2008, p 287.

standing'.³⁸ Norway needed to 'show solidarity when countries in our vicinity, not only the distant ones' experienced difficult times.³⁹ It was time to show both that 'the neighbour cares' and 'the meaning of Nordic solidarity'.⁴⁰

The group in favour of EU membership presented the EU as a *necessary* and *efficient* actor in the process of handling the crisis. While it was within the countries that the road out of crisis had to be found, EU-level co-operation had, according to one Labour Party MP 'in impressively short time' introduced a series of measures 'that shall and will be important contributions to bringing the economies in order as well as to help the countries to conduct responsible economic policies'.⁴¹ In the eyes of the Conservative Party it was clear that

> *the solution to Europe's problems lies in coordination and co-operation. This makes the EU an indispensable factor. The current crisis is simply too deep to be handled by the countries single-handedly.*⁴²

Another prominent representative of the party stated in autumn 2011 that

> *without the EU, I dread that the consequences of this crisis would have been far more severe, and that the danger of the economic crisis developing into a political and social crisis that would strike us all would increase considerably.*⁴³

Unfortunate democratic consequences were linked to developments within the states, but not to the EU: 'Elected governments and parliaments unable to lead way out of the crisis, and thereby becoming part of it, contribute to weaken the faith in democratic institutions'⁴⁴; and 'The political parties have given up and handed the responsibility over to the experts.'⁴⁵ The assuming of office by non-elected experts in Greece and Italy was described as 'a thought-provoking trend'.⁴⁶ However, the Labour Party foreign minister reminded his audience that this solution had been chosen by democratically elected parties in an attempt to regain trust. The most important fact was that the policies of these new governments would

---

38   Erna Solberg, *Stortingsforhandlinger*, 24 October 2008, p. 289.
39   *Ibid.*
40   Anne Margrethe Larsen, *Stortingsforhandlinger*, 24 October 2008, p. 294.
41   Svein Roald Hansen, *Stortingsforhandlinger*, 22 November 2011, p. 580.
42   Ine Marie Eriksen Søreide, *Stortingsforhandlinger*, 22 November 2011, p. 578.
43   Jan Tore Sanner, *Stortingsforhandlinger*, 22 November 2011, p. 593.
44   Steinar Gullvåg, *Stortingsforhandlinger*, 22 November 2011, p. 592.
45   Svein Roald Hansen, *Stortingsforhandlinger*, 22 November 2011, p. 580.
46   Jonas Gahr Støre, *Stortingsforhandlinger*, 17 November 2011, p. 480.

have to pass popularly elected parliaments, described as 'the core of European democracy'.[47]

In their more ideologically inspired assessments, the parties inevitably parted company. The Conservative Party referred to Germany and France, which, under social democratic rule, had been the first to violate the criteria of the Stability and Growth Pact. The party claimed that some countries, mainly those under socialist or social democratic rule, had profited from the low interest rates to expand their own states. The voters were now turning to the right for solutions to the crisis.[48] Labour Party representatives denied that traditional rightist policies would bring Europe out of the crisis. Necessary austerity measures would have to be combined with a strategy for growth. The Labour Party traced Norway's situation to the virtues of social democratic policy: Norway was 'the European contrast', and the most important reason for this was not the country's rich deposits of oil, but its *policy*, the keywords of which were a *restrictive* use of the petroleum revenue fund, the shift to a *viable* pension system, a *sensible* level of taxation, a *just* system of taxation, and a *new* institution for the financing of exports. These elements were in turn linked to the existence of 'a large and responsible trade union movement and a long tradition of co-operation between workers, employers, and government – the jewel in social democratic policy'.[49] Norway was 'a surplus nation, politically and economically'.[50] In contrast to countries in crisis, Norway was also *responsible*: if Norway had been a member of the EU, it would have pursued 'the same responsible economic policy as it had until now, and its situation would have been the same'.[51]

The crisis did not alter the view of the EU and EEA membership supporters of the EU as a stabilizing and democratizing power. In autumn 2011, the leader of the Standing Committee on Foreign Affairs and Defence described the EU as 'the greatest peace and democratization project in Europe in modern history.'[52] Labour Party representatives appeared more reticent and expressed doubt as to whether further integration would bring Europe out of the crisis:

---

47 Jonas Gahr Støre, *Stortingsforhandlinger*, 17 November 2011, p. 480.
48 Ine Marie Eriksen Søreide, *Stortingsforhandlinger*, 22 November 2011, p. 582.
49 Svein Roald Hansen, *Stortingsforhandlinger*, 22 November 2011, p. 581.
50 Jonas Gahr Støre, *Stortingsforhandlinger*, 17 November 2011, p. 479.
51 Svein Roald Hansen, *Stortingsforhandlinger*, 22 November 2011, p. 582.
52 Ine Marie Eriksen Søreide, *Stortingsforhandlinger*, 22 November 2011, p. 579.

> Leading EU bureaucrats obviously believe that increased harmonization and stronger European institutions – in short, more EU and less nation-state, is the solution to the crisis. ... That idea is part of the problem. The EU and the introduction of the euro has enabled countries such as Greece, Italy, Spain, and Portugal to live with an increasing level of debt in the shadow of flourishing economies in Northern Europe. Iceland's handling of the crisis had been impossible within the Eurozone.[53]

The representatives doubted that the way forward went through further and deeper integration, more coordination, and even more cooperation, and linked this to calls for a European identity, the lack of which in turn was identified as the cause of the two Norwegian rejections of EC/EU membership.

Among the advocates of Norwegian EU membership, the crisis entailed a shift towards a stronger defence of the status quo. This shift should be seen in light of the fact that other groups now spoke up for revision and termination of the EEA Agreement respectively. The Conservative Party, which had never concealed its view of the EEA Agreement as insufficient, stated that 'We stand guard over the EEA Agreement'.[54] The party found it 'incomprehensible, in a time when the Norwegian export industry struggles, that someone in earnest may suggest the termination of our most important trade agreement.'[55] Labour Party representatives described the EEA Agreement as 'our most important international agreement'.[56] Referring to the *EEA Review*'s assessment of the EEA Agreement as a stable and predictable framework for Norwegian businesses, the party described it as a paradox that the question of whether the agreement gained Norwegian interests was raised.[57] Full EU membership would have served Norway better, 'but when 70% of the population say that they are not interested, I agree with the Prime Minister that we have other issues to spend time on now.'[58]

The supporters of EEA membership

Of the three parties in favour of the EEA association but without an official pro-EU position, the Progress Party spoke most highly of the EU at the beginning of the new debate. The party described the EU as 'a builder of democracy' as a 'stabili-

---

53 Steinar Gullvåg, *Stortingsforhandlinger*, 22 November 2011, p. 592.
54 Ine Marie Eriksen Søreide, *Stortingsforhandlinger*, 22 November 2011, p 605.
55 Ine Marie Eriksen Søreide, *Stortingsforhandlinger*, 22 November 2011, p. 579.
56 Helga Pedersen, *Stortingsforhandlinger*, 15 May 2012, p. 3369.
57 Helga Pedersen, *Stortingsforhandlinger*, 15 May 2012, p. 3370.
58 Svein Roald Hansen, *Stortingsforhandlinger*, 22 November 2011, p. 582.

zer and a continuous peace process'.[59] By contrast, the Christian Democratic Party depicted a *divided, inaccessible,* and *elitist* EU. Referring to the situation created by the French and Dutch rejections of the Constitutional Treaty, the party leader said the conflict over its future direction was still making its mark on the EU agenda: 'the discussion between leaders behind closed doors is on whether it will be possible to proceed without having to ask the people for advice.'[60] According to the Christian Democratic Party, there were aspects of the EU's structure and practice that were 'clearly inconsistent with important democratic aspects such as popular participation and control from elected bodies', and it questioned whether the Lisbon Treaty would change this situation.[61] While acknowledging the EU's contribution to the dismantling of old European dividing lines, the Liberal Party raised the question of how developments in the EU would impact Norway: 'The EU and the EEA is presenting our democracy with new challenges. A democratic deficit is already manifesting itself in that EEA matters are continuously being passed without genuine political procedures.'[62]

The reform-treaty process and its consequences for Norway, the Eurozone crisis, and the entailed prospect of an Icelandic EU membership were recurrent topics in the new debate on Norway and the EU. Halfway through the period under investigation here, none of these developments had made the EEA proponents change their position. The Christian Democratic Party confirmed in spring 2009 that EEA membership remained its preferred association, 'not a poor substitute'.[63] When explaining its position, the party emphasized the importance of access to the EU market, which in turn was essential for 'value creation, welfare, and employment throughout the country'.[64] The party's defence of the EEA Agreement also resided in the fact that it left important areas out and thus under national control.[65] According to the Liberal Party, there were no realistic alternatives to the EEA Agreement. In his effort to keep eventual opponents of the agreement within the government at bay, the foreign minister could thus 'count on the Liberal Party's full support'.[66] The Progress Party, too, confirmed its support of the EEA Agreement, but pointed

---

59 Morten Høglund, *Stortingsforhandlinger*, 4 June 2007, p. 3265.
60 Dagfinn Høybråten, *Stortingsforhandlinger*, 4 June 2007, p. 3269.
61 Dagfinn Høybråten, *Stortingsforhandlinger*, 24 April 2008, p. 2943.
62 Anne Margrethe Larsen, *Stortingsforhandlinger*, 4 June 2007, p. 3272.
63 Dagfinn Høybråten, *Stortingsforhandlinger*, 7 May 2009, p. 2865.
64 Dagfinn Høybråten, *Stortingsforhandlinger*, 7 May 2009, p. 2862.
65 Dagfinn Høybråten, *Stortingsforhandlinger*, 24 April 2008, p. 2942.
66 Anne Margrethe Larsen, *Stortingsforhandlinger*, 7 May 2009, p. 2863.

out that it (the party) had long been of the opinion that it was time 'to upgrade the agreement in order to adjust it to the legal changes that had taken place within the EU'.[67] In the previous year, the Progress Party had called attention to the 'fundamental challenge residing in the fact that the agreement was written for a different EU than the one that we are currently experiencing'. As a consequence, and despite the fact that the agreement had proved 'remarkably viable', the party wanted 'to make aspects of the EEA Agreement the object of new negotiations'.[68] The core of the problem was, a party representative stated, that for the great majority the agreement remained a compromise solution: 'For most people, this agreement never was and never will be the objective of the relationship with the EU. The EEA is a second-best solution. Fighting for the second best solution is a demanding exercise.'[69]

According to the EEA supporters, the Eurozone crisis 'was mainly homemade' and 'its origins preceded the financial crisis with many years'.[70] Its main cause was an inflated level of public spending combined with the almost total absence of efficiency improvements and fiscal increases in the upswing before 2008.[71] The crisis was simultaneously linked to the existence of a common currency that had 'contributed to the crisis and made it harder to get out of it'.[72] Recovery would require cuts in public expenses and increased revenues. These measures would in turn depend on economic growth. The problem was that the existence of the common currency deprived the countries of the benefit of a declining currency, 'which could have enhanced the competitiveness of their exports and provided opportunities for new growth.'[73] The situation demonstrated what many had long pointed out: launching a common currency without federal budgets large enough to correct regional imbalances and crises that may occur was 'a risky business'. However, this was also a self-imposed weakness, as the member states had opposed increases in EU resources 'at the expense of national government.'[74]

The faith in the EU's potential to solve the crisis clearly was less present within the group of EEA supporters. In autumn 2008, the Christian Democratic Party expressed more faith in governments, both within and outside the EU, that 'had

---

67 Morten Høglund, *Stortingsforhandlinger*, 7 May 2009, p. 2859.
68 Morten Høglund, *Stortingsforhandlinger*, 24 April 2008, p. 2937.
69 Morten Høglund, *Stortingsforhandlinger*, 6 May 2010, p. 3170.
70 Petter N. Myhre, *Stortingsforhandlinger*, 18 November 2010, p. 677.
71 *Ibid.*
72 Dagfinn Høybråten, *Stortingsforhandlinger*, 15 May 2012, p. 3365.
73 Dagfinn Høybråten, *Stortingsforhandlinger*, 22 November 2011, p. 587.
74 Dagfinn Høybråten, *Stortingsforhandlinger*, 6 May 2010, p. 3175.

taken vigorous measures to handle the crisis'. By contrast, the European Union's journey to agreement on a crisis package had not only been far more complicated, but had also necessitated the neglect of Eurozone regulations.[75]

Further, the Christian Democratic Party showed considerable satisfaction with Norwegian politics. Ever since the EEA Agreement came into effect in 1994, Norway, together with Iceland and Liechtenstein, had provided funding to reduce social and economic disparities in the EEA. The Norwegian contribution to the EEA and Norway grants was described as 'considerable' and as proof of Norway's position as 'one of Europe's most solidary nations'.[76] The debate also demonstrated the limits to this solidarity. In a comment to the negotiations on the EEA grants for the period 2009–2014, a representative of the Christian Democratic Party stated that 'new and exorbitant money claims from the EU' would paint an unflattering picture of the European Union: 'I fear this will undermine the general public's confidence in the EU.'[77]

The parliamentarians' interpretations of the effect of the crisis on democratic standards varied within and between parties. For example, in autumn 2011, Progress Party representatives argued that 'democracy, tolerance, and freedom in Europe had not been put to serious test'.[78] Other representatives of the party stated that democratic development in Europe was under pressure, voicing their concern with the installing of technocrat governments in Greece and Italy.[79] Party representatives also called attention to the potential of the crisis to create a new European divide between north and south that could risk the entire idea of the EU, and stated that it was through joint efforts that included Norway that Europe could give back to its youths the hope of a future.

In a context of democracy under pressure, Norway was presented as a role model: as 'one of the countries one looks to, when new democracies are being built around the world'.[80] In this area, Norway was 'among the best in the class.'[81] Several of the countries that struggled had large public sectors, high tax levels, and strong trade unions. The Nordic model thus constituted an insufficient explanation for the relative success of the Nordic countries. To this, the following needed to be added: 'the culture of openness, the lack of corruption, a sense of justice, work

---

75 Dagfinn Høybråten, *Stortingsforhandlinger*, 24 October 2008, p. 292.
76 respectively, Laila Dåvøy, *Stortingsforhandlinger*, 24 April 2008, p. 2953, and Dagfinn Høybråten, *Stortingsforhandlinger*, 6 May 2010, p. 3174.
77 Laila Dåvøy, *Stortingsforhandlinger*, 24 April 2008, p. 2953.
78 Morten Høglund, *Stortingsforhandlinger*, 22 November 2011, p. 582.
79 Karin Woldseth, *Stortingsforhandlinger*, 22 November 2011, p. 593.
80 *Ibid.*
81 *Ibid.*

ethic, frugality, and probably many other qualities'.[82] However, the most important difference between Norway and its neighbours was the enormous income from the petroleum industry that made governing Norway a relatively easy task.[83]

Throughout the period under investigation, the position of the EEA supporters stayed unchanged. Referring to the need for appropriate agreements with important trading partners, the Liberal Party maintained that the EEA Agreement constituted 'a good association between Norway and Europe'.[84] The Christian Democratic Party explained that its continued defence of the EEA Agreement rested partly in that it functioned as 'a viable national compromise', and partly in the doubt that it could be replaced with something better.[85] While the Progress Party continued to argue for an updated EEA Agreement, the crisis also caused a more pronounced defence of the status quo. In autumn 2011, a party representative stated that to question the agreement in times such as those would be reckless. The EEA Agreement was by no means perfect. It was fit to frustrate everyone. To believe that a realistic and equally good alternative could easily be put in place if only Norway wanted this strongly enough was, however, 'totally unrealistic.'[86]

The opponents of EU and EEA membership

The group consisting of EU and EEA opponents interpreted the EU's development and role in ways that differed considerably from the ones of the EU membership supporters. Before the 1994 referendum, the Centre Party had played a pivotal role in the opposition against EU membership, with maintenance of national sovereignty as its leading argument. Together with the Socialist Left Party, the Centre Party now described an increasingly less democratic EU on the road to a federal state. The Treaty of Lisbon, 'the EU's new constitution', prepared for a more supranational EU, in which the competences of EU institutions increased and the member states lost their current right of veto in a number of cases. In spring 2008, one of the Centre Party's MPs stated that the EU consequently was taking 'a major step towards what we can call a central state'.[87]

The distinction between 'us' and 'them' – between the Brussels elite and the people – constituted a central element in the discourse of the EU and EEA

---

82 Christian Tybring-Gjedde, *Stortingsforhandlinger*, 22 November 2011, p. 597.
83 Petter N. Myhre, *Stortingsforhandlinger*, 22 November 2011, p. 600.
84 Trine Skei Grande, *Stortingsforhandlinger*, 15 May 2012, p. 3366.
85 Dagfinn Høybråten, *Stortingsforhandlinger*, 22 November 2011, p. 587.
86 Morten Høglund, *Stortingsforhandlinger*, 22 November 2011, p. 583.
87 Lars Peder Brekk, *Stortingsforhandlinger*, 24 April 2008, p. 2945.

opponents. The process of European integration had 'to a considerable degree been elite-driven'.[88] The Centre Party feared 'that an increasingly federal Europe [would] weaken representative government, [and that] an increasingly stronger Brussels [would] increase the distance between the elite and the people, between the ones that govern and the ones that are being governed.'[89] While EU membership supporters emphasized the EU's democratizing power, the primary expression of which had been the eastern EU enlargement, the Socialist Left Party pointed out that the new members' celebration of the role of the EU and NATO had taken place in more prosperous times. As a result of the financial crisis, they would now be able to 'test this kind of supranationality in a recession'.[90]

The Centre Party and Socialist Left Party, in government with the pro-EU Labour Party since autumn 2005, both had Norwegian EEA exit for the benefit of a less comprehensive free trade agreement in their party manifestos. The Centre Party appeared as the more pragmatic and confident of the two parties. While noting that many unsolved tasks remained and that the impact of EEA legislation on national democracy and on the political room for manoeuvre in social, environmental and industrial policies was considerable, it described Norway's relations with the EU as being 'of a form and with a level of activity with which the party lived well'.[91] Party representatives stated on several occasions that Norway had resources in the form of a market with considerable spending power, and natural resources that would ensure that Norway remained an attractive partner for the EU: 'With sufficient self-confidence in our own policy, there is no need to fear, as some EU membership supporters do, that future enlargements of the EU will make Norway a marginalized country'[92]; and 'The EU is important for Norway, but Norway is also important for the EU.'[93]

The Socialist Left Party was generally less positive. In 2009, the party described the EEA Agreement as 'the festering finger in Norwegian politics'.[94] The party noted that the agreement was the object of increasing critique from the ones that had defended it in 1992, partly because it relegated Norway to a passive recipient of EU legislation, and partly because the EU was developing policies on new areas

---

88   Trygve Slagsvold Vedum, *Stortingsforhandlinger*, 19 November 2009, p. 385.
89   Trygve Slagsvold Vedum, *Stortingsforhandlinger*, 19 November 2009, p. 372.
90   Bjørn Jacobsen, *Stortingsforhandlinger*, 7 May 2009, p. 2867.
91   Alf Ivar Samuelsen, *Stortingsforhandlinger*, 4 June 2007, p. 3271.
92   Dagfinn Sundsbø, *Stortingsforhandlinger*, 8 November 2007, p. 407. For other examples, see Alf Ivar Samuelsen, *Parliamentary Negotiations*, 4 June 2007, p. 3271 and Lars Peder Brekk, *Stortingsforhandlinger*, 24 April 2008, p. 2945.
93   Åslaug Haga, *Stortingsforhandlinger*, 7 May 2009, p. 2862.
94   Rannveig Kvifte Andresen, *Stortingsforhandlinger*, 19 November 2009, p. 370.

that the agreement did not cover. Further, the party expressed the hope that a facts and research based review would provide the ground for 'a more democratic debate on how Norway would be best served in the future'.[95]

According to the EU and EEA opponents, the EU was a *cause for crisis*. Without public support and against professional advice[96], ambitious ideologists had 'pushed the EU very fast forward'[97] and introduced a common currency prior the introduction of joint systems of governance. At the same time, the lack of popular support prevented the introduction of the political harmonization that would have enabled the EU to handle a crisis. The situation had placed European leaders in a straightjacket in the sense that they now had to introduce more integration in a climate in which popular support for such measures was at an all time low: 'The EU has created a self-reinforcing system, in that one continuously has to render more power to Brussels in order for the system to survive. The people oppose this increasingly.'[98] Within this group too, the critique was particularly harsh on Greece, where 'breach of agreement and a highly irresponsible level of consumption' had taken place for years.[99] However, the situation in Greece was not representative of the situation in Europe in general.

On a more general level, the EU and EEA opponents partly described the crisis as a *crisis of modern capitalism*, and partly as a *crisis of democracy*. The internationally oriented Socialist Left Party argued for the need of a new economic policy: 'The debt crisis is on a more fundamental level an inequality crisis, created by mass unemployment and mounting economic and social divides in the Western world.'[100] The Centre Party stated that: 'In addition to a deep economic crisis and a deep social crisis, we are now in a democratic crisis.'[101] European representative government was under a vigorous threat 'when the replacement of politicians by technocrats [was] greeted with joy in both Italy and Greece'.[102] The party rejected the suggestion that further integration was the answer to the current situation, as this would require democracy, which in turn would require a common identity, which did not exist: 'Democracy takes a language, a discussion, the feeling of community and the will to pull in the same direction.'[103] The party described a Europe

---

95 Rannveig Kvifte Andresen, *Stortingsforhandlinger*, 19 November 2009, p. 370.
96 Per Olaf Lundteigen, *Stortingsforhandlinger*, 22 November 2011, p. 603.
97 Trygve Slagsvold Vedum, *Stortingsforhandlinger*, 18 November 2010, p. 682.
98 Trygve Slagsvold Vedum, *Stortingsforhandlinger*, 22 November 2011, pp. 585-586.
99 Snorre Serigstad Valen, *Stortingsforhandlinger*, 15 May 2012, p. 3364.
100 Bård Vegar Solhjell, *Stortingsforhandlinger*, 22 November 2011, p. 584.
101 Trygve Slagsvold Vedum, *Stortingsforhandlinger*, 22 November 2011, p. 585.
102 Trygve Slagsvold Vedum, *Stortingsforhandlinger*, 22 November 2011, p. 606.
103 Trygve Slagsvold Vedum, *Stortingsforhandlinger*, 22 November 2011, p. 586.

in change, where 'an immense political experiment' was about to come asunder.[104] The ultimate consequences of the choice made in the 1990s in favour of free market forces before solid national economies based on production and science were as yet unknown. However, enough had been seen, to warrant change in a different direction: 'Democratic nation states with own currencies is progress'.[105]

The EU and EEA critical position differed from the two EEA-friendly positions in that it called for a change in Norway's relations with the EU. The grouping drew attention to the *EEA Review's* identification of unfortunate democratic consequences of Norway's current relationship with the EU, as well as to the suggested alternative associations that had been listed in another study. The Centre Party argued that the economic and democratic crisis within the EU, together with the *EEA Review's* demonstration of the negative effects of the EEA Agreement on Norwegian democracy 'ought to lead to the replacement of the EEA Agreement with a less comprehensive arrangement'.[106] Both parties argued that opposition against the EEA Agreement was increasing: 'To keep the considerable opposition against the EEA out of the Norwegian debate is a Norwegian variant of what European leaders do too often, namely to debate issues without popular support.'[107]

Conclusion

In autumn 2010, a Centre Party representative said:

I find it astonishing ... that the ones that were EU-membership supporters last year support this option just as strongly this year. It seems as if, regardless of what happens, the EU is the answer. Regardless of what happens, the euro is a good. I sometimes wonder what it will take to say something critical about the development in the Eurozone.[108]

As demonstrated in the present chapter, the ideas of Norwegian political parties on the EU were resilient, regardless of the political persuasions of their carriers. The parties in favour of EU membership maintained their idea of supranational

---

104 Per Olaf Lundteigen, *Stortingsforhandlinger*, 15 May 2012, p. 3376.
105 *Ibid.*
106 Olov Grøtting, *Stortingsforhandlinger*, 15 May 2012, p. 3365.
107 Per Olaf Lundteigen, *Parliamentary Negotiations*, 22 November 2011, p. 603.
108 Trygve Slagsvold Vedum, *Parliamentary Negotiations*, 18 November 2010, p. 681.

integration as a necessity and the one of the EU as a democratizing and solidary power. The parties opposed to Norwegian entry into the EU continued to present the process of integration as a threat to national democracy.

While fundamental conceptions of the EU remained remarkably constant, two changes in ideas on Norway's connection with the EU are worth noting. Within the group of membership supporters, the representatives of the Conservative Party had used the pre-crisis debates to hammer the EEA's inherent lack of political participation. As the crisis led popular support for EU membership to new depths, the Conservative Party stood up as the EEA Agreement's foremost defender. Compared to the positions taken at the time when the agreement was ratified, the analysis also demonstrates a shift in the ideas expressed within the third group, composed of opponents of both EEA membership and EU membership. The new feature in the discourse of this group was the Centre Party's readiness to accept the EEA Agreement – a position that contrasts starkly with the democratic critique that had been levelled by this party against the agreement in 1992. With regard to the third group – the one that supported the agreement but omitted to state a position on the question of full membership – distinct shifts could not be traced. This is a remarkable finding in itself, as it indicates that the findings of the *EEA Review* of the unfortunate impact of the EEA Agreement on Norwegian democratic institutions had no impact on the ideas of the Christian Democratic Party, whose 1992 approval of the agreement had been explained with the fact that it left Norwegian sovereignty intact.

How are the ideas of Norwegian political parties on the EU, and Norway's relationship with it, to be explained? The Conservative Party linked its rallying round the EEA association to the strong opposition against full membership in Norwegian public opinion. The demand for revision or termination called for by some of the smaller parties had also necessitated a stronger defence of the status quo. The Labour Party emphasized the need for predictability. In the context of crisis, putting the agreement into play was presented as associated with great risk. The effect of the European crisis on the discourse of the membership proponents was thus *indirect* in that it strengthened popular opposition and weakened the prospects for improvement of the existing agreement. In the anti-membership camp, the effect was *direct* in the sense that the crisis and the EU's handling of it was presented as yet another instance of the EU's too liberal and anti-democratic character. As for the less expected reconciliation of Centre Party parliamentarians to the EEA Agreement, the material leaves no explanations. A possible interpretation is that they spoke from experience, having been part of the governing coalition since 2005. However, the implication of this is that the findings of the *EEA Review* on the workings of the EEA Agreement were ignored, and that principle opposition had ceded ground to political pragmatism.

To summarize, the European crisis caused Norwegian decision-makers to rally in the middle, around the EEA Agreement. The level of opposition against EU membership clearly diminished the will to stand up for full membership. The democratic weaknesses of the EEA association were not considered important enough to cause a drop in the level of support for the EEA Agreement. The most conspicuous feature of the Norwegian debate on the EU – the gap between ideals and reality – thus remains. On the one hand, there is the wish for more influence, either as a full EU member or as a more independent outsider. On the other hand, there is the current association that relegates Norway to a passive recipient of legislation adopted by others.

References

Primary sources

Bulletin of the European Economic Community, May 1962, No. 5, Luxembourg: Office for Official Publications of the European Communities.

Bulletin of the European Economic Community, September/October 1967, Nos. 9–10, Luxembourg: Office for Official Publications of the European Communities.

Council Conclusions on EU relations with EFTA countries, December 2010, http://www.consilium.europa.eu/uedocs/cms_data/docs/pressdata/EN/foraff/118458.pdf

Jacques Delors to the European Parliament, 17 January 1989, http://www.cvce.eu/viewer/-/content/39ba5f57-affa-42b0-b18b-830886da5fb9/b9c06b95-db97-4774-a700-e8aea5172233/en

OECD Harmonised Unemployment Rates, Paris, 15 May 2013, http://www.oecd.org/std/labour-stats/HUR_05e13.pdf

Parliamentary debate on Norway's relations with Nordic and European market groupings, 24 June 1970.

Stortingsforhandlinger, 15-16 October 1992.
Stortingsforhandlinger, 4 June 2007.
Stortingsforhandlinger, 8 November 2007.
Stortingsforhandlinger, 24 April, 2008.
Stortingsforhandlinger, 23 October 2008.
Stortingsforhandlinger, 24 October 2008.
Stortingsforhandlinger, 7 May 2009.
Stortingsforhandlinger, 19 November 2009.
Stortingsforhandlinger, 6 May 2010.
Stortingsforhandlinger, 18 November 2010.
Stortingsforhandlinger, 17 November 2011.
Stortingsforhandlinger, 22 November 2011.
Stortingsforhandlinger, 15 May 2012.

Recommendation to the Storting from the Standing Committee on Foreign Affairs, Innst. S. No. 114 (2006–2007), document No. 8:105 (2005–2006).
The Constitution of the Kingdom of Norway, http://www.stortinget.no/In-English/About-the-Storting/The-Constitution/The-Constitution/

Literature

Bjørklund, T. (1982), *Mot strømmen: kampen mot EF 1961–1972*, Oslo: Universitetsforlaget.
Eriksen, K.E. and Pharo, H. (1997), *Norsk utenrikspolitikks historie. Bind 5: Kald krig og internasjonalisering, 1949–65*, Oslo: Universitetsforlaget.
Frøland, H.O. (2001), 'The second Norwegian EEC-application, 1967: Was there a policy at all?' in W. Loth (ed.), *Crises and Compromises: The European Project 1963–1969*, Baden-Baden: Nomos, pp. 437–458.
Kleppe, P. (2003), *Kleppepakke: Meninger og minner fra et politisk liv*, Oslo: Aschehoug.
Milward, A. (1992), *The European Rescue of the Nation-State*, London: Routledge.
Neumann, I.B. (2002), 'This little piggy stayed at home: Why Norway is not a member of the EU' in L. Hansen and O. Wæver, (eds.) (2002), *European Integration and National Identity: The challenge of the Nordic States*, Oxford: Routledge, pp. 88-129.
NOU 2012:2 (2012), *Utenfor og innenfor. Norges avtaler med EU*, Oslo: Utenriksdepartementet.
NOU 2012:2b (2012), Official Norwegian Reports, *Outside and Inside: Norway's Agreements with the European Union*, English summary of Chapter 1, http://www.regjeringen.no/pages/36798821/PDFS/NOU201220120002000EN_PDFS.pdf
Ringdal, K. (1996), 'Velgernes argumenter' in A.T. Jensen and H. Valen (eds.), *Brussel midt imot. Folkeavstemningen om EU*, Oslo: Gyldendal, pp. 45-66.
Rolstad, D. (2012), *Integrasjon eller isolasjon? EFTA-landenes tilnærminger mot EF, 1973–1979*, MA thesis, Trondheim: NTNU.
Rye, L. and Steinnes, K. (2010), 'Norway's 1994 quest for EU membership: Ideas of national culture and Europe in Norwegian political discourse' in M. Beers & J. Raflik (eds.), *National Cultures and Common Identity: A Challenge for Europe?*, Brussels: Peter Lang, pp. 267-278.
Rye, L. (2011), 'In search of influence: Norway's 1994 Referendum on EU membership', in C. Ramos (ed.), *Ideas of Europe in National Political Discourse*, Bologna: Societa Editrice Il Mulino, pp. 325-350.
Ryghaug, M. and Jenssen, A.T. (1999), *Den store styrkeprøven: om EU-avstemningen i norsk politikk: sluttrapport fra Folkeavstemningsprosjektet*, Trondheim: Tapir.

Identifying the crisis

George Chabert

The Western world is going through a financial and economic crisis that is reminiscent of the crises initiated by the Wall Street Crash of 1929. The responses to the subsequent social upheavals on both the sides of the Atlantic were varied. The social reforms promoted in the United States of America contrasted starkly with the frantic rearmament in Europe. Yet again, a financial and economic crisis has been met differently in Washington and in Brussels, in this case the one that began in 2008. In the United States of America, President Obama was quick to put in place measures of a magnitude that is simply unthinkable on the other side of the Atlantic. Barak Obama signed a multibillion-dollar plan to help small businesses and the American Recovery and Reinvestment Act, which created as a direct result approximately 755,000 jobs. Moreover, measures were put in place to aid all families at risk of losing their homes, namely the Making Home Affordable Program, and the Helping Families Save Their Homes Act, and in 2009 the Fraud Enforcement and Recovery Act was passed.

What was done in Europe to face the crisis? Well, the culprits were tracked down and quite soon their names became known. This time, they were not to be found in Wall Street, but much closer to home: they were the P.I.G.S. – Portugal, Italy, Greece, and Spain – a transparent reference to those charming creatures that adore reeling in the dirt. What was to be done? Well, nothing, other than to pay the debts of the incompetent and lazy Southerners, wait for better days, and above all do nothing to implement structural and much-needed institutional changes. As neither pigs nor pastors, and fearing that its turn would soon come, the French cried in sympathy for the Greeks and begged the Germans to show more 'fraternity' and pay the bills, and the Germans wondered '*Wird Frankreich das neue Griechenland?*'[1] As a sign of the times, today's 'Jan Palach' is retired Greek pharmacist, Dimitris Christoulas, who on 4 April 2012 shot himself in the head in front of

---

1 *Bild Zeitung*, 31 October 2012.

the Greek Parliament. Allegedly, the successive reductions of his pension[2] imposed by the European Union had driven him to suicide. The following was written in a note found on his body: 'I find no other solution than a dignified end before I start searching through the trash for food.' Today, it is no longer the fear of Soviet tanks and SS 20 missiles threatening our love of freedom and our democracies that haunts us; it is the fear of *'déclassement'* that paralyses most Europeans.

An unidentified political object

Europe is a choice subject for political philosophy. If, after World War II, Europe as a civilization became a topic that was only approached with deep unease, as a political construction Europe is even more intangible. Jacques Delors has thus rightly called Europe *'un objet politique non identifié'*, or UPO. How, then, are we to handle this highly volatile object named Europe?

After the reading of the careful descriptions of the European institutions, mechanisms, party positions, public opinions, and national memories in the preceding chapters of this book, I ask the reader to engage with me in an eclectic wander through a continent at a crossroads. I assure you that, unlike Rousseau, I do not intend to proceed as a 'solitary walker'. On the contrary, I will summon by me at each new perspective and at each new sight, historians, philosophers, sociologists, political scientists, and pedagogues, as well as politicians, writers, and journalists. Moreover, not being bound by statistics or by specific methodologies and theories[3], I will even attempt at the end of my wanderings to provide a solution to the European problem.

To tell my tale, I will not ask from the reader more than the acceptance of three reasonable assumptions. These assumptions are the simple motives that make us act, and as such can be confirmed daily. Together, they form the core of a plausible historical causality and allow us to think the near future. For one thing, people tend to defend their own interests:

---

2   'Even as Greece's economy spirals into free fall, a journalist who revealed the names of over 2000 alleged Greek tax cheats, was arrested for his pains. Kostas Vaxevanis, an investigative reporter, was arrested last week within hours of publishing the secret list of his wealthy compatriots in his *Hot Doc* magazine' (*The Sunday Guardian*, 4 November 2012).

3   Alternatively, not being bound by what François Ricard (2006), in his *Chroniques d'un temps loufoque*, rightly calls '*la frime méthodologique et théorique*'.

All of us are greedy, some for money, some for adulation, some for power, but all greedy nevertheless. Some few among us have the opportunity to act on our greed, while most of us are confined to pursuing our greed in minor ways. (Mesquita and Smith, 2011: 148)

If we combine this assertion with the awareness that, by definition, decisions are made by individuals and not by countries, although the latter is a convenient generalization we so often use and abuse, we will keep our attention focused where it should be – given named politicians – and not on those national reifications painstakingly consolidated in 19th century Europe.

Greed has to be kept within acceptable limits. Hence, we prefer a policed society to the rule of the arbitrary. This second assumption – *Better a well-governed society than an ill-governed one!* – implies a third assumption, namely *the existence of a community*, as there are no politics of the individual. To put it in another way, a political Europe would not exist without a European community of citizens.[4]

The institutionalization of identity

Our difficulty in tackling the crisis is not so much financial or economic. Europe as a whole remains one of the most powerful economies of the world. Our disarray today is a political one in its widest sense. For the first time, Europe finds itself without a self-assumed political community.[5] Any political system needs a community of citizens to operate it, clearly more so in the present case of a democratic political system.

Europeans face the current crisis, a crisis that prefigures the economic world wars of the 21st century, as the only people embracing with alacrity unilateral disarmament, not of weapons but of identity.[6]

---

4   Although Europeans decline to admit it, they share a community of destiny, as once more survival is an open question: '*Nous sommes affrontés au même problème: ne pas mourir, non seulement zoologiquement, mais aussi politiquement, culturellement, intellectuellement. Nous sommes arrivés au moment de la communauté de destin (Schicksalgemeinschaft)*' (Morin, 1987: 195).
5   It is significant that most of the studies in this volume are presented from the periphery of Europe (Portugal, Iceland, Norway, Hungary, and Turkey – although in Turkey's case and tellingly, in a mode of '*us*' and '*them*'), and while professing an institutional and political science approach the authors are constrained to underline the question of national identity and its supposed indissolubility in a larger European identity.
6   We should keep in mind that in human matters *identity* does not imply more than recognition, mutual recognition, and as such no essentialism is here neither involved nor invoked.

Europeans do know without hesitation who they are; indeed, they have never felt the need to agree on a common definition precisely because the sense of vicinity was all too obvious. However, Europeans are entangled in history. Unlike Americans, Europeans are used to living their common identity in recurrent conflict with other Europeans; unlike Americans, they have not only lived through a short Civil War but also have for centuries slaughtered each other by the millions, shooting each other, starving each other, asphyxiating each other, incinerating each other, and bombing each other's cities to rubble. With such a record, it is no wonder that whenever Europeans want to define what a European is they prudently resort to universals.[7]

This apparent munificence of the European, eager to mingle with the rest of mankind into oblivion, is yet another way of preserving themselves from their congenial propensity to conflict. Furthermore, the European universalism articulated ad nauseam as the faithful incarnation of the '*Droits de l'Homme*' is the expression of the European obsession with indicting its past in desperate quest for expiation. Needless to point out, self-hatred is hardly the best cement for making political communities.

Latent, the crises of the European identity shot in the 1990s as the result of two concurrent facts. For one thing, Europe was no longer the exclusive club of the well-off Western Europe. If the integration of Greece had already been problematic, the fall of the Soviet Union opened a new era of almost forgotten problems. The enlargement of the European Communities was not only made of new countries, but also of new minorities. Furthermore, the new ethnic and religious minorities in Europe, particularly in France, Germany, and Great Britain, had by then become a real threat to the political stability of Western Europe. In 1991, Valéry Giscard d'Estaing, former president of France and a major player in European affairs, stated that immigration in France was becoming an 'invasion' of France.[8] Without going that far, the risk of the fragmentation of the social body was by then evident throughout Europe. It was not that Europe was threatened with the loss of its social cohesion as a result of mass immigration; rather, it was that because Europe had renounced the affirmation of its identity and values that it was no longer capable of confronting the problem of large-scale immigration.

---

7 As Victor Hugo put it in 1867, echoing the Kantian understanding of Man, '*Au vingtième siècle il y aura une nation extraordinaire. ... Elle s'appellera l'Europe au vingtième siècle, et, aux siècles suivants, plus transfigurée encore, elle s'appellera l'Humanité.*'
8 *Le Figaro*, 21 September 1991.

One could expect that weakened national communities and national identities[9] would facilitate the constitution of a European community of citizens, but that is not the case. As a result, we seem now stranded in a *no-man's-land* Europe, in an empty shell that we are conceptually inhibited to name.

European metamorphosis

In the aftermath of the fall of Hitler and the dismantling of his concentration camps, Europe, soon to re-emerge as the EU, was supposed to offer a replacement to the old belligerent nation-states. The problem is that we still do not know what this Europe is. Zygmunt Bauman (2004: 140) writes 'Like our ancestors three centuries ago, we are on a rising slope of a mountain pass we have never climbed before and so have no inkling of what sort of a view will open up once we reach the top.'

In truth, we no longer know not just *what* we are, but even *who* we are, as any definition beyond *human kind* brings into our minds all sorts of deleterious associations.[10] We may then wonder: How are we to build a political community of citizens without a certain degree of common acceptance? Hence, the political question par excellence that we are confronted with is: *How can we recreate a self-governed community in Europe?*

Can we remake in the 21st century what poets, historians, archaeologists, geographers, linguists, philosophers, politicians, and above all teachers accomplished in the 19th century? Will we be able to create a people out of the national, regio-

---

9   One example, apparently anecdotal but nevertheless significant, is as follows: one of the most widely read French writers and winner of the prestigious *Prix Goncourt* in 2010, Michel Houellebecq, declared in an interview to the Paris newspaper *Libération* (9 November 2010) that France was no more than a hotel for him, and consequently any political engagement was meaningless. Houellebecq insisted the French are not even national citizens, they are nothing but individuals: '*Je ne suis pas pour l'action politique, au fond. ... Je ne suis pas un citoyen et je n'ai pas envie de le devenir. On n'a pas de devoir par rapport à son pays, ça n'existe pas. Il faut le dire aux gens. ... On est des individus, tous, pas des citoyens ou des sujets. ... On n'a aucun devoir par rapport à son pays. ... La France est un hôtel, pas plus.*' The author of *Les particules élémentaires* [The Elementary Particles], published in 1998, is the perfect example of what Zygmunt Bauman names the 'global elites'.

10 The French writer and essayist Renaud Camus calls the source of this impossibility to mention or even think about our roots without appearing in our own eyes as racists, a *Reductio ad Hitlerum*. In a sense, Hitler is still very much with us. Renaud Camus speaks of 'the second career of Hitler': '*La folie meurtrière d'Hitler a souillé le langage, détourné le sens des mots, changé le cours de la pensée: cela directement, dans un premier temps, indirectement et plus perversement dans un autre, par un effet de miroir, de retournement et d'inversion. Ce deuxième temps dure encore*' (Camus, 2011: 62). The term, *Reductio ad Hitlerum*, was first coined by Leo Strauss in 1951.

nal, urban, and suburban idiosyncrasies? Will we be able to create a transnational European identity without the compulsion that would imply a third world war, or without a catastrophic ecological debacle putting our very survival at risk? The answer is 'probably not', and for many reasons. To name but one, our deep feeling of guilt towards our colonial past has greatly contributed to the spreading of a normative multiculturalism without content and that has become little more than an effective and all-pervasive anti-Europeanism.[11]

However, do we need to engage in a quest for a common identity, national or otherwise? The answer is 'No'. There is a way out from these sterile quests of identity. One simply has to recall two facts. First, national identity does not imply by any means some sort of isomorphism. In any given modern community we are never confronted with individuals that belong to a common origin and sharing the same set of attributes. Second, the feeling of belonging is not the precondition to any political community, but rather the *end result* of a given political community. To apply this to our case study, the construction of Europe is not so much hampered by the lack of a common European identity, but rather a *postulated* European identity can only emerge as a by-product of European state-building.

The history that made us

In the history of Europe the three main political models of a community of citizens were the city-state, the empire, and the nation-state. The city-states eventually became too narrow to contain their vitality, and continuous external wars gave birth to the empire, first Alexander's empire, and then the Rome Empire. The empire was not simply an overgrown city-state, similarly imposing tradition, religion, law, and language within specific borders; the differences were not only in size but also, and mainly, in essence. Leaving behind the exclusiveness of the city-state, the empire did its utmost to combine the diversity it necessarily contained. For that purpose, the empire did not suppress the diversity of cultures and peoples, but accepted foreign cults and concurrent juridical codes. Roman law[12] only prevailed in relations between individuals of different peoples. If Europeans were Roman citizens, they did not need to renounce to their nationality, meaning

---

11 As Jacques Dewitte (2008: 78) points out, if we Europeans could be reconciled with ourselves, with our history and our identity, Europe would again have a bright future.
12 Pierre Legendre (2000) calls it '*cette autre bible de l'Occident*', as Roman law helped us to define the individual, the filiation, and property, i.e. fundamental concepts that ever since have structured our social, political, and economic lives.

their birthplace.[13] Put in modern terms, the empire was a federal structure with a high level of regional autonomy.

As the Roman Church did not succeed in perpetuating the Empire, there was not one model of a political community that prevailed over all other models. Elected or hereditary kingdoms, Italian, Flemish, and Hanseatic cities, and the Holy Roman Empire all coexisted, albeit in continuous instability punctuated by intestine wars and famines. In a long process that was to take more than 1000 years, the European entities sedimented into nation-states. The most important moment in this transformation was not the French Revolution in the 18th century, although a crucial moment in the consolidation of the nation-state, but the Reform two centuries earlier. If French revolutionaries theorized the nation, the reform made it possible through the 'nationalization' of the Christian faith. Some nations embraced the reform – whether Lutheran or Calvinist – in one form or other (Switzerland, England, Netherlands, German princedoms and Scandinavia), while others opted for a counter-reform more or less independent from Rome (France, Spain, and Portugal).

The nation-state, as it were to become solidly founded by the French – One Nation, One People, One Republic[14] – implied internationally recognized frontiers, political centralization, a national economy, and, in most cases and specifically in France, a thorough homogenization leading to the destruction of regional languages and cultures. The nation-state became the sole producer of social bonds. It promoted a society of individuals recognized as equal on a secular level and sacrificed all intermediate bodies on the altar of equality.

As a logical consequence of the efforts for homogenization and the redefining of the every man as a citizen, the new definition of man as individual was closely associated with universalism. Kant speaks of *Weltbürger*, the World Citizen, Ancharsis Cloots of *Citoyen de l'Humanité*, Humanity Citizen, whereas Fichte, echoing Kant and his *Allgemeine Vereinigung der Menschheit*, the universal unification of humanity, announces the impending 'universal mankind'.[15] The exal-

---

13 We should bear in mind that the terms defining our nationalities today are far from being as old as we might expect. After the fall of the Roman Empire, the peoples of Europe were *Europeans* (the oldest script with that designation dates from the 8th century AD). 'National' designations appeared at a later stage: *German* dates from the 10th century, and *Spanish* first appeared one century later.
14 The parallel with the Nazi slogan was first suggested by Alexandre Kojève: '*Le slogan hitlérien* Ein Reich, ein Volk, ein Fürer *n'est qu'une – mauvaise – traduction en allemand du mot d'ordre de la Révolution française* La République une et indivisible' (Kojève, quoted in Benoist, 2002: 465).
15 Could we say that this universalism was already contained in the Bible? That is what Rémi Brague (1992; 2006) thinks of Pierre Manent, when he quotes the words of Saint-Paul: '*Il n'y a ni Juif, ni Grec, il n'y a ni esclave, ni homme libre, il n'y a ni homme ni femme; car tous, vous êtes Un en Christ Jésus*' (Manent, 2010: 244).

ted Parisian revolutionaries could thus proclaim the *Universal Declaration of the Rights of Man and of the Citizen*. Hence, the Jacobin nation-state contained within it the element of its eventual dissolution, as the exclusivism of nationality is contrary to the universalism of individualism.

If the idea of individualism was still new in the beginning of the 19th century, the process of atomization of the European citizen started in the aftermath of the European wars of religion. However, the process did not go far enough, as the old structures of society remained based to a large extent on the theological thought that prevailed. The French Revolution is therefore an event of extraordinary consequences. The 'Old Regime' – *l'Ancien Régime* – was finally and at a stroke entirely subverted. In place of social orders, and in place of ancient corporatism or any other traditional sense of belonging, there were now only individuals. These individuals could no longer appeal to God or appeal to something that transcended them and deeply linked them to a common Humanity. Now, there was nothing but natural rights; theology and canon law were definitely replaced by the allegedly neutral juridical rights. In other words, the long transmutation from the empire to the nation-state comprised the transformation of man as a kin into man as an individual. Again, the nation-state contains in its ideology the end of itself, as a true individual cannot logically defend in the long run the exclusivity of a given nation.

The development can be followed through the willingness to die for one's nation. *Pro patria mori*, common in the Antiquity (although the term '*patria*' referred to little more than one's city), simple vanished during the Middle Ages. The willingness to sacrifice for the common good reappeared with the consolidation of the modern nations.[16] Indeed, in the Age of nation-states the willingness to die for the nation (now more encompassing than the somewhat narrow '*patria*') was again widespread. However, this state of affairs did not last long. The two world wars proved fatal to the exaltation of the nation, and the enthusiasm to sacrifice for the 'motherland' died out,[17] and with it the justification of the great French invention of the obligation to serve the state in arms (*Loi Jourdan* of 1798). The fact that in today's Europe the national armies are once again professionalized, tells Europe's tale. Similarly, a diachronically study of the use of the expression '*rai-

---

16 See Ernest Kantorowics (1951: 472–492).
17 Can we honestly imagine for a second, for example, a French soldier in Afganistan or some other exotic place, literally blown to pieces but with breath left to speak his pain, saying '*Ce qu'il faut souffrir pour la France*'? This was still possible in the first half of the 20th century. See Gueno (1998: 23). As Zygmunt Bauman (2004: 134) writes, 'The *heroic patriotism* ... is clearly *passé*; it is neither on offer nor in demand.'

son d'État' (national interest), would certainly show the inexorable rarefication of the expression.

The question of the *existence* of a people, *even at a national level* – which formerly was incongruous because it was self-evident and tautological – is now earnestly debated. The literature on the creation and the nature of national identities in Europe is by now quite extensive[18], and we ask ourselves: *Are we still an 'us'?*[19] Thus, in the 21st century, after a century of national identity building, and a century of nationalistic armed conflicts, the question is: *Where do we go from here?* Should we abandon the European project in a revival of the nation-states, a position more and more advocated in widened circles well beyond the shores of Great Britain, and one that could become a fact if the euro does not survive the present crisis? Alternatively, should Europe, in the pursuit of its 'unfinished adventure',[20] combine both empire and nation-states through the 1000-year-old cement of the Christian civilization in an unequivocal European state of nations?

Der Mann ohne Eigenschaften

Throughout Europe there is a feeling that democracy is no longer delivering the goods it is supposed to provide, namely *freedom* and *social justice*. In France, a country that prides itself on being the birthplace of human rights, the *'malaise dans la démocratie'* (Raynaud quoted in *Causeur*, January 2011), the 'unease from within democracy', is very much present in the public arena. In a special issue of the monthly magazine *Causeur*[21] entitled 'Democracy, we have loved you so much', Marcel Gauchet maintains that if our freedoms are not in anyway at risk – on the contrary, we have never had so much freedom – we have lost track of the general interest. Elisabeth Lévy adds that the problem is not a democratic deficit, but too much democracy, which she names 'hyper-democracy',[22] echoing Ortega y Gasset's words dating from 1929. In a book published in 2012, Tzevetan Todorov sees in

---

18   Benedict Anderson, Ernest Gellner, and Eric Hobsbawm have by now become almost household names. This is in itself significant: 'The very fact that historians are at least beginning to make some progress in the study and analysis of nations and nationalism suggests that, as so often, the phenomenon is past its peak. The owl of Minerva which brings wisdom, said Hegel, flies out at dusk. It is a good sign that it is now circling round nations and nationalism.' (Hobsbawm, 1990: 192).

19   Title of a conference held by the French philosopher Alain Finkielkraut at the École Polytechnique, reproduced in *Causeur*, November 2011.

20   See Bauman (2004).

21   Monthly magazine *Causeur*, entitled 'Nous l'avons tant aimée, la démocratie', January 2011.

22   Monthly magazine *Causeur*, entitled 'Nous l'avons tant aimée, la démocratie', January 2011: 27.

the excess of individual freedom practised without having in view the interests of the community, the major menace facing democracy.[23] The general feeling can be appropriately summarized in the words of Pierre-André Taguieff (2000: 34), we are living in a 'Democracy with neither *Demos* nor *Cratos*'. Europe is a republic without a people, a republic without a coherent political power; hence, there is a widespread sense of political dispossession among the citizens of the European Union.

Even before existing as a political community, Europe was summoned to refuse any specific identity. The construction of a 'European house' or what Julian Benda called a 'European nation' is made impossible by the European belief that there are only human beings, that nothing separates people from each other, and above all that nothing *must* separate them. For the European, the individual is no longer defined within a specific entity, being seamlessly diluted in an unspecified humanity, a humanity dreamed of by the philosophers of the Age of Enlightenment.[24] No doubt, therein lies one of the major sources of the general disenchantment with the European project.

A fractured Europe

For the Europeans of the 21st century, as it is particularly clear for the French, belonging to the political community is more important than historical roots. In line with Montaigne's thinking, *I am a human being, and only French by accident*. Four centuries later, Louis Dumont provided confirmation of this analysis: a Frenchman is essentially a citizen, France being first of all a democracy, a 'republic'.[25] With Braudel and the Annales School, even historiography points in the direction of the expurgation of nationhood. The 'roman national', Clovis, his conversion to Catholicism and the Vase of Soissons, Louis XIV, the 'Fête de la Fédération'[26] and Napoleon, are now set aside in favour of the '*longue durée*', namely

---

23 See Chapter 4, 'La tyrannie des individus' (Tzvetan Todorov 2012, 105–136).

24 When, in 1785, Kant reiterated his belief in a singular humankind, he added that such a bright future was necessarily many centuries away: 'When human nature has reached its ultimate destiny and its maximum possible perfection ... justice and equity will rule under an internal awareness and not because of any public authority. This is the supreme moral perfection that can reach the human race, the ultimate end to which it was intended, *although* we cannot hope to access *to* that stage in many centuries to come.' Are we to believe our politicians and our established intellectuals in thinking that, if not already a reality, the advent of the Kantian humankind is at hand?

25 '*Le Français se sent tel essentiellement comme citoyen. La France, c'est avant tout, pour lui, la démocratie, la République*'(Dumont, 2011: 259).

26 Hiding from the Nazis in 1940, the historian March Bloch was still able to write: '*Ceux qui ne frissonnent pas à l'évocation du baptême de Clovis et de la fête de la fédération de 1790 ne comp-*

civilizations and economic superstructures. Today, the French state school, the very same one that during the Third Republic hammered the notion of the French collective identity into the skull of fearful French pupils, is busy deconstructing the nation by reducing French history to its minimum for the benefit of world history.[27] Yet again, as the national bond recedes in Europe, only men and women are left behind,[28] atomized individuals without any sort of mediation. Nationality is now an empty word, as there are only citizens, individuals related not by family ties – *horresco referens* – but by affairs (of one sort or the other) and juridical contracts.

In the United States of America the election of a president is always the moment of reaffirming the oneness of the national community. This is not the case in Europe, as we have seen during the recent presidential campaign in France. The Socialist François Hollande assured us that the word 'race' will be eradicated from the French Constitution! It will be his first measure, to thus 're-enchant the French Dream', no less! However, as we have now seen, this is not so much a 'French Dream', but a European idea of a cosmopolitan humanism without frontiers, where 'diversity' is the new synonym for openness, tolerance, and happiness. Let us put behind us the exclusivity of ancestry! Let us renounce once and for all to the elusive reification of nations that take pride in a supposed homogeneity! Aren't we all '*métis*', as Jacques Chirac announced during a visit to the Antilles? Aren't we after all, nothing but 'migrants'?[29] Do we still doubt, as François Hollande so elegantly emphasized in a meeting in Paris on 10 March 2012, that 'there is only one race, one family, and that is the human family'? Do we still doubt that 'diversity is our identity'?

---

    rendront jamais l'histoire de la France.' (Bloch, 1990: 7) Who in France, 70 years later, ever would have trembled at the remembrance of the great pages of the history of France?

27 As the historien Dimitri Casali (in *Le spectacle du monde*, 2011: 49) points out, the removal of the history of France from the school curricula, perceptible since the 1980s, took on a new dimension after the latest school programme reforms in 2008: '*Il y a la volonté de gommer toutes les grandes œuvres de l'histoire de France au profit des grands thèmes compassionnels: lutte pour les droits de l'homme, pour la femme, antiracisme*'. He concludes, '*on veut effacer nos mémoires*'.

28 Probably, this will not be for long, as our French and Swedish 'universalists' are busy removing from the French and the Swedish any reference to gender. Say no more 'Madame' or 'Mademoiselle', and soon you will be asked to forget altogether '*Monsieur*', which is all too discriminating. By Decree n° 5575/SG, dated 21 February 2012, *Mademoiselle, maiden name, patronymic name, name of spouse* and *name of husband* are proscribed from official documents. At 'Egalia' (sic), a Swedish kindergarten, are not treated as according to their gender: they are no longer a *she* (*hon*) or a *he* (*han*), and they are no longer boys or girls, but delightfully equal as 'it' (*hen*). Better still, in 2013 a transgender man in Germany gave birth to an infant and expressed the wish that his child should be registered as being of undetermined gender.

29 Such is the 2012 'cultural project' of the French city of Amiens: 'Cultures du monde: tous migrants'.

Let us not cool down this progressive enthusiasm by reminding our brave Socialist candidate, now president of the French Republic, that universalism and humanism are but synonyms for world liberal economy.[30] Maurice Lévy, a leading French businessman who, in 2008 was bestowed the International Leadership Award for his defence of tolerance and diversity, knows this well. For him, France is but a 'site',[31] and a particular generous one, allowing him to collect a bonus of EUR 16 million for the year 2012 alone. Lévy is the perfect example of the promotion of the individual, a promotion that implied the dilution of the social bond and turned man into a predatory individual, always looking after his best interests. The 'new man' considers those of his kind as nothing more than potential rivals in an endless competition. We may indeed consider the postmodern Western society as a global magma made of 'elementary particles'[32] that comprehend no more than the restrained family circle as a sort of return to the pre-urban society. Thus, the 3000 or so years of ever larger social communities would be no more than a short gap in the history of mankind.

Postmodern Europe is now a fractured Europe, a Europe without frontiers. The European suffers from a severed identity. Indeed, the political and economic deterritorialization[33] of their social life tends to turn Europeans into 'immigrants in their own countries'.[34] That is why the debates on national identities flourish here and there in forcibly aborted debates, as the one that we witnessed in France in 2007. As Zygmunt Bauman points out, the question of identity arises when a person no longer knows where he or she belongs.[35] The imagery of nations has indeed entered its final phase, and those who talk of 'national identity' are generally not even able

---

30 On this topic, see the work of Jean-Claude Michéa, particularly his book *Impasse Adam Smith. Brèves remarques sur l'impossibilité de dépasser le capitalisme sur la gauche*, published in 2002.
31 '*Les entreprises ne réussiront que si le site France sort de la crise et génère de la croissance.*' Maurice Lévy, interviewed for *Le Figaro*, 12 March 2012. Playing on another key the same tune, the French Left have long since abandoned the theme of 'national pride' for the cosmopolitan '*citoyen du monde*'. See Hervé Algalrrondo (2011).
32 See Michel Houellebecq (1998: 68–70). In his concise style, Houellebecq draws in a couple of pages what he coins the passage from a Christian anthropology to a materialistic anthropology that took place in France in the seventies.
33 In the White House and Congress, American politics have a spatial dimension; Europe has not become less puzzling since Kissinger and his hypothetical phone call to the unknown Europe. To the European citizen 'Brussels' is but a word, and as precise as 'them'. The sight of the Europeans quarters in Brussels is the closest one can get to a ghost city.
34 See Peter Sloterdijk (2010: 289).
35 '*On pense à l'identité chaque fois que l'on ne sait pas vraiment où l'on est chez soi ... Identité est le non que l'on a donné à la recherche d'une échappatoire à cette incertitude*' (Bauman, 2003: 34). As in 2007, the questions of identity were central in the French presidential campaign of 2012. The enormous space taken up by the question of halal meat in French supermarkets is rather telling.

to define it. The national model of integration seems to be exhausted, and that is why we are inclined to identify ourselves by referring exclusively to ourselves. In an almost solipsistic self-reference, we are but what we accomplish, which in our consumer societies[36] means *we are what we consume*. Postmodern Europe thus lives under the sign of the hyperbole: hyperdemocracy, hyperindividualism, hyperconsumerism, and, one could certainly add, hyperschizophrenia.

Thus, Europe has not become, the solution but *the* problem. So far, Europe has undermined the national communities *and* the possibility of a community of citizens. Instead of the crystallization of a 'European Europe', and instead of constructing a new political body capable of replacing the aging European nation-states, Europe keeps running before itself, risking a final dislocation in a Euro-Mediterranean[37] or a Euro-Anatolian nebula. Again, Europe cannot be limited to be 'a project', an open system without frontiers.[38] There is no community of citizens and *a fortiori* no democracy outside a certain degree of identification.

Instead of paving the way to a multiple European identity based on a series of identification layers, such as Catalan, Spanish, Latin, Catholic, and European –

---

36 See the thorough analysis of our brave new world made by Baudrillard more than half a century ago (Baudrillard, 1970). Society as consumerism should not be understood metaphorically, but ontologically. Our body is now turned towards the centre of our universe: '*Le corps est devenu objet de salut. Il s'est littéralement substitué à l'âme dans cette fonction morale et idéologique*' (Baudrillard, 1970: 200).

37 The project, initiated by right-wing French President Nicolas Sarkozy is now enthusiastically embraced by the extreme-left haranguer Jean-Luc Mélenchon, for example in his meeting the 14 April 2012 at Marseille. (Here, we can see at work the general rule established by Jean-Claude Michéa: '*Dans une société libérale dévelopée, c'est en effet aux universitaires de gauche qu'il incombe de fournir la véritable bande-son des modernisations capitalistes*' (Michéa, 2011: 156–157).

38 All of the arguments put forward against the possibility or even desirability of such a union are met again and again by the dogma of undifferentiated humankind sharing a universal language of human rights. We can only keep repeating them. Here, in the words of one philosopher: 'On ne reliera pas *ces deux parties du monde l'une à l'autre. Elles se trouvent potentiellement en situation de guerre, et sont destinées à s'exécrer mutuellement. Cette haine se nourrit, ici de mépris, là d'envie, même si ces sentiments hésitent à se proclamer au grand jour, et se dissimulent, ici sous la compassion, là, sous la fierté. Le problème de la rupture entre le monde riche et le monde pauvre passe aussi par une béance entre le refus de la religion, d'une part, et le triomphe de la religion sortie de ses gonds, d'autre part. Ceux qui n'ont plus que la religion voudraient bien posséder autre chose – le bien-être, la liberté, l'éducation -, mais ne le peuvent pas. Ceux qui n'ont plus de religion désireraient bien en être pourvus, mais ne le veulent pas, si paradoxal que cela paraisse. Entre les deux se développe une rivalité acerbe. Les premiers pourront tenter de détruire par dépit le calme bonheur temporel de leurs voisins, bonheur qu'ils n'ont pas su produire semblablement chez eux, et auront ainsi le sentiment d'un triomphe définitif de l'absolu; les seconds tâcheront de soumettre par dédain et par crainte cet* élan *mystique venu d'ailleurs, et de diffuser leur bonheur prosaïque sur toute la terre*' (Delsol, 1996: 243–244).

identity strata that have indeed centuries of cohabitation,[39] – the European Union, true to the inspiration of Monnet and Schuman, has opted for a disincarnated definition of the citizen as a mere consumer of goods and rights, a citizen thus engaged in an endless struggle in the face of aggressive competition. Europe has thus become little more than an extra-territorial concept.

Indeed, there has been from the outset of the European construction in the 1950s a strong unwillingness to settle on the frontiers of Europe. To take just a recent example, the former French president Nicolas Sarkozy had promised to open this most important debate, but nothing was done during his five years' term as head of state. As for the new president, the congenial 'socialist' François Hollande, his declarations indicate that in principle he would be sympathetic to the integration of Martians, if only they deigned to apply for membership.

The lack of frontiers makes it difficult, if not impossible, to define the purpose of the European Union. Is it peace and prosperity? However, are not peace and prosperity the aim of every international organization, from the UN to the OECD? Europeans are thus asked to be 'nationals' of a tariffs, trade, and security agreement. No wonder that Europe is most often seen as synonymous with opacity, democratic deficit, institutional complexity, and international helplessness. No wonder that European citizens feel – as the various national discourses and voting behaviour demonstrate – the European Union is not being built with and for them, but *against* them.

The banning of differentiation

In Europe, the idea of mankind, now mankind without mediation, either of a transcendental God or of the nation, has become self-evident. The problem – *our* problem – is that we, secular Europeans, are alone in ever having seen the new 'God-Mankind'. We react with astonishment and incredulity every time we realize that the world at large does not really agree with us, and we tell them and beg them to believe that we are but equals. After all – and for the first time in history – have we not included them into our all-embracing religion of fraternity and equality?[40]

---

39 Beyond the apparent differences, the identity of Europe is obvious. As Fernand Braudel (2003: 529) wrote, '*Nous entendrons par unités brillantes, les rencontres, les unissons qui donnent à la civilisation européenne, sur le plan le plus élevé de la culture, du goût et de l'esprit, une allure fraternelle, presque uniforme, comme si elle était envahie par une seule et même lumière.*'
40 As Pierre Manent (2010: 209) points out, our democratic lucubrations are simply contradicted by

Free from 'European' quails, the Japanese call their country 'The Land of Gods', a belief candidly expressed in the year 2000 by Mori Hishirô, then Prime Minister of Japan: 'Japan is the land of Gods, and the Emperor is its centre'.[41] More recently and more practically, Turkish Prime Minister Recep Tayyip Erdogan encouraged Turkish women to have at least three babies each[42]. Once in Germany, on 27 February 2012 at Düsseldorf, he exhorted the Turkish community to refuse assimilation: 'Our children must learn German, but they have to learn Turkish first'.[43] Incorrigibly proselyte, the European simply refuses to realize that he or she is alone in his Kantian understanding of mankind. In 1919 Paul Valéry wrote 'We, civilisations, know now that we can die'[44]; we soon may have to paraphrase Valéry: *We, civilizations, know now that we can commit suicide.*[45]

The reluctant European

Attached to our old nations, we do not want to leave, we hear the call to a new Europe that we want to build but do not know how to do this. We feel that invisible European governance more and more replaces our representative governments that neither lead us nor represent us. We know that our nations are no longer truly viable, but we feel incapable of giving sense to our post-national community. How,

---

history: '*La foi démocratique des Européens, la foi dans l'unification de l'humanité est contraire à toute expérience humaine, y compris l'expérience contemporaine, cela n'empêche pas d'être aujourd'hui obligatoire, pour nous, en Europe.*' It is amusing to see that our 18nth century philosophers, that knew nothing more amusing than pointing out the absurdities of the Bible, founded new dogmas contradicted by any observation, however random.

41 Pierre Manent (2010: 239) calls this propensity to exclusivity 'the beautiful lie', without which no human society can survive.
42 *Aftenposten*, 3 April 2012. For a French reader, the 'three-babies recipe' is unmistakably reminiscent of the martial injunction of Maréchal Pétain in 1940.
43 'You Are Part of Germany, but Also Part of Our Great Turkey', *Spiegel Online International*, 28 February 2010. Turkish membership of the EU would not change in any way the Turkish perception of the people of Turkey, which is still felt as self-evident. By contrast, for Europeans, Turkish membership would be a further step in the dematerialization of an eventual 'Peoples of Europe', and thus represent the final burial of a hypothetical United Europe.
44 Valéry's first letter on *the crisis of the mind* opens with the following sentence: '*Nous autres, civilisations, nous savons maintenant que nous sommes mortelles*' (Valéry, 2009: 13).
45 '*L'universalisme démocratique européen se confond, en somme, avec le nihilisme, il est l'accomplissement du nihilisme. Il consiste à dire: l'Europe n'est et ne veut être que la pure universalité humaine; elle ne saurait donc être quelque chose de distinct; en un sens bien réel, elle veut être un rien, une absence ouverte à toute présence de l'autre, être soi-même un rien pour que l'autre, n'importe quel autre, puisse être tout ce qu'il est*' (Manent, 2010: 259).

then, are we to face the present crisis with its daily tragedies?[46] What do we have to do to rapidly overcome the crisis and open new perspectives to our continent?

Our problem is not primarily the malfunctioning of democracy in institutional Europe. Our problem is that we are unable to create a social bond and an identity bond beyond the imaginary interior borders of Europe. Actually, even at the national level we no longer feel the immediacy of being a people; Europe is nothing more than a magnifying glass. Again, our deeply engrained belief in the universality of human kind contradicts any national exclusivity, and World War II soiled forever the remains of national epithets.

The European Union has allegedly worked for a European identity by taking measures to introduce a European flag and a European hymn. However, at the same time, whenever an occasion presents itself – which is daily, and several times a day, – European officials denigrate Europe, naturally guilty of all evils past, present, and future. We have to overcome this self-bashing and learn to be as proud of our old world as the Americans are of their *New World*. It is imperative that our leaders proudly defend our values and do not make any compromises with ideologies that are intrinsically contrary to these values.[47]

Although reluctantly, Europeans we will be. Unwillingly, we will become Europeans, as we know that we live in a world of antagonisms and fierce, and lately every so often lethal, competition. We cannot predict the political contours of the new Europe. Will it be a *Great* Europe, thoroughly federal, or a federation of a 'Europe of the peoples'?[48] We can only guess, but we can imagine the institutional transformations that would greatly contribute to the resolution of the present crisis and further ahead consolidate the Europe we will have to create, if we are to be more than a few successful 'Singapores' coupled with a set of sunny 'Club Med' and 'Euro-Disney' resorts.

---

46 '*En la localidad española de Barakaldo, una mujer se suicidó hoy poco antes de ser desalojada de su vivienda por la imposibilidad de afrontar el pago de la hipoteca. Amaia Engaña, de 53 años, se subió a una silla y se lanzó al vacío desde el cuarto piso del edificio en el que vivía en ese municipio de la provincia de Vizcaya (País Vasco), según fuentes policiales. La fallecida era la esposa de un ex concejal del PSE de Barakaldo. Es la segunda muerte que se registra en ese país por los mismos motivos, después de que el pasado 25 de octubre un hombre apareció ahorcado en la ciudad andaluza de Granada, también antes de ser desahuciado de su morada*' (*Ultima Hora*, 9 November 2012).

47 The literature on the 'merits that distinguish us' (Jacques Dewitte) is now growing, with important names such as Leszek Kolakowski, Cornelius Castoriadis, Emmanuel Levinas, Alain Finkielkraut, Jean-François Mattéi, Peter Sloterdijk, Pierre Manent, Zygmunt Bauman, Rémi Brague, Allan Bloom, George Steiner, Octavio Paz, André Rezsler or Pascal Bruckner.

48 The expression '*La République Européenne des peuples*' was coined by the French politician Jean-Pierre Chevènement (Chevènement, 2011).

The United Nations of Europe

Politics are always to some extent the politics of self-interest. 'In democracies, leaders who fail to deliver the policies their constituents want get deposed. ... If they want to keep their jobs they will deliver the politics that *their people* want' (Mesquita and Smith, 2011: 246). Politicians 'must do what their coalition wants; they are not beholden to the coalition in any other country, just to those who help keep them in power' (Mesquita and Smith, 2011: 281). As long as politicians are elected by national constituencies, no European institution will be able to promote a European general interest.

This is particularly true in the time of crises. Thus, the Dutch Geert Wilders – one example among many possible examples – refused any cooperation with 'Brussels', since for him and his constituency, Netherlands, came first. The Dutch government had to resign, but anything was better than helping out 'the deceitful Greeks'.[49] Mesquita and Smith (2011: 166–167) state: 'Democrats act as if they care about the welfare of *their* people because they need their support. They are not helping out of the goodness of their hearts, and their concern extends only as far as *their own* people – the ones from whom they need a lot of supporters.' We can easily guess that if the Dutch politician had needed the votes of the Greeks to be re-elected, his anthropological perception would automatically have altered.

Today, the European politicians are elected by their national constituencies, and they have to do what is expected of them – to favour their electorate – or else face being sacked. If the electorate is enlarged and transnational constituencies are designed, then, as if by a miracle, our German, French, and even British politicians will become overnight *European* politicians, defending with heartfelt conviction the interests of Europeans.

Thus, simpler to put into place than the improbable construction of new transnational identity half-heartedly suggested by the European institutions, the answer to the European crisis lies in the systematic enlargement of constituencies, constituencies no longer delimitated by national borders. Article 24 of the Treaty on the Functioning of the European Union (TFEU) that came into force on 1 April 2012 on the European Citizens' Initiative (ECI) – which allows 1 million citizens of at least seven countries within predefined thresholds, from Malta's 4500 to Germany's 74,250 to request new EU legislation – points in that direction.

As long as the major elections remain on a national level, the EU will remain but a handy explanation for every shortcoming: The national deficit increases? *The*

---

49   *Libération*, 25 April 2012

Troika! The gap between the very rich and the poor has never been greater? *EU liberal policies!* The Welfare State is being dismantled? *The Commission imposes privatizations on us!* Our politicians are powerless or simply incompetent? *Brussels has tied their willing hands!* Our democracy halts limply? *The opacity of the EU is to blame!* Of course, in the meantime, the list of countries wanting to join the EU does not shrink, and the return to a Europe of nation-states is not even seriously envisaged. *Who would we blame then?*

Again, as long as Europe is governed by politicians elected by national constituencies, truly European policies – beyond the usual regulations that Brussels pesters us with – will be inexistent. In fact, the very opposite seems to be the rule, as policies openly favour specific European states. As long as Europe stands without a true federal government directly elected, and eventually removable, by all Europeans, we will need a whole array of enthusiastic humanists chanting the beauties of a lame Europe just to keep it going.

Let us imagine mathematically designed constituencies to avoid the usual gerrymandering in practice as much in the USA as in European countries; further, imagine transnational constituencies, such as inspired in the now well-known European 'twin cities'. Whatever convictions, whether European, national, or regional, the elected politicians would have to practice a policy without borders if they were to be re-elected. From there on, we would probably glide into 'Europeanism' without even noticing, because, in common with our politicians, our self-interest would win over our ailing national convictions.

Let us now imagine a European president directly elected by the peoples of Europe. It would in fact be the easiest starting point as most presidents in Europe have consultative or representative roles. Already here and there, important politicians promote such a measure. In France for example, the centrist presidential candidate François Bayrou defended it in the name of 'a sovereignty that could no longer be exerted by solitary nations'[50]; the green-spectacled Eva Joly and now justly forgotten French presidential candidate went further, promoting a federal Europe as the only way to overcome the '*infinie faiblesse*', the immense frailty of the European institutions; the old president of France and veteran of European politics, Giscard d'Estaing, has long promoted such an inflection of the institutional Europe as a way to bring European citizens closer,[51] and recently, in a interview given to

---

50 '*Je suis pour l'élection du président de l'UE au suffrage universel*', François Bayrou, *Le Monde*, 10 March 2012.

51 Giscard d'Estaing said:'*Combler le vide spatial qui sépare l'Europe de ses citoyens! L'Europe unie devra trouver de nouveaux moyens d'établir des relations concrètes avec les Parlements des États et leurs commissions. Les nominations des hauts responsables devraient rejoindre les normes démo-*

the French newspaper *Libération* Belgian Prime Minister and Eurodeputy Guy Verhofstadt strongly defended a federal Europe as a means to overcome the present crises.[52] In Italy, the new prime minister Enrico Letta, and in Germany, the popular chancellor Angela Merkel, have both called for a President of the European Union directed elected by all Europeans.

True, a federal Europe is still envisaged – if ever seriously – with utter disbelief and even revulsion. Yet the European nation-states are far from obvious constructions: the form of the existing European states is perfectly hazardous, and has changed many times even in recent history; the 27 member states of the European Union contain between them no less than 80 nations. These 'national marriages' are more often than not problematic and in some cases violent. A federal Europe would allow envisaging, for the first time in history, the peaceful rearrangement of national communities, and for once not to some other nation's detriment.

Basque Country, Catalonia, Corsica, Flanders, Scotland, Northern Ireland, and other Italian Padania, just to mention those in the western part of Europe[53] could be painlessly freed from their historical ties if the national security and the redistribution of riches were conducted at a federal level. In this regard, equidistance to a remote federal authority would be an advantage: it is easier to share the same burden with a large and anonymous community than with one's neighbours. Thus, the Catalans and the Flemish would more willingly contribute to a European entity than to their now fellow countryman in Spain and Wallonia.[54] Hence, a federal Europe could succeed where Woodrow Wilson failed, namely to solve once and for all, and at last painlessly, the question of nationalities in the Old Continent.

---

cratiques. On peut imaginer que le président du Conseil de l'Europe unie soit élu par un Congrès composé par des parlementaires européens des États membres et d'un nombre équivalent d'élus issus des Parlements nationaux' (*Le Point*, 8 April 2012: 64).

52 Guy Verhofstadt, article 'Un saut fédéral pour vaincre la crise', *Libération*, 25 December 2012.
53 With the exception of the Czech and the Slovak Republics, Yugoslavia gave us a telling idea of what we can expect of Eastern European national divorces. Soon enough, we might witness comparable disruptions between Romania and Hungary as a sequel to the Trianon Treaty of 1919.
54 Strangely enough, the European Commission favours the permanency of unwilling nation states within Europe. The European Commission's vice president said recently that Catalonia would have to leave the European Union if it declared independence from Spain. Joaquín Almunia said: 'If one part of a territory of a member state decides to separate, the separated part isn't a member of the European Union' (*The Wall Street Journal*, 16 September 2013) Strangely indeed, in the case of Yugoslavia disintegration was a requisite for admission to the EU, while in the case of Czechoslovakia separation was not an issue. Will we in the near future see Brussels, the very siege of EU, excluded from the Union as a result of Belgium separatism? Some might like to question Joaquín Almunia on such an eventuality.

To summarize, the present crisis that has disrupted so many lives in Europe since 2008 is not primarily a financial crisis. The present crisis – more specifically, the way we are dealing or rather *not* dealing with it – is institutional. At this point in our history, only a federal Europe is viable today in an extended world.[55] With the decisive federalization of Europe we would witness faster than we dared to imagine the emergence of a European '*intérêt général*', and with this newborn common interest the possibility to overcome the present crisis and those to come with minimum sacrifices, due to collective and coordinated action. A community of European citizens would slowly take form, and once again our children would know who they are: *Europeans*.

References

Newspapers and periodicals
Aftenposten
Bild Zeitung
Causeur
Le Figaro magazine
Le Point
Le Monde
Le spectacle du Monde
Libération
Spiegel Online International
The Sunday Guardian
The Wall Street Journal
Ultima Hora

Literature
Algalrrondo, H. (2011), *La gauche et la préférence immigrée*, Paris: Plon.
Baudrillard, J. (1970), *La société de consommation*, Paris: Denoël.
Bauman, Z. (2003), *La vie en miettes. Expérience postmoderne et moralité*, Le Rouergue/Chambon: Rodez.
Bauman, Z. (2004), *Europe: An Unfinished Adventure*, Cambridge: Polity Press.
Benoist, A. de (2002), *Critiques: Théoriques*, Lausanne: L'Âge d'Homme.

---

[55] This conclusion – *A Federal Europe, NOW!* – is no longer the exclusivity of some dreamers of a reconciled Europe as was the case between the 14th century and the last decades of the 20th century. For once – and while strongly disagreeing with many of their historical analysis – I feel thus compelled to embrace without reserve Daniel Cohn-Bendit and Verhofstadt's 'Manifesto for a post national revolution in Europe', in their call for a federal European Union (Cohn-Bendit and Verhofstadt, 2012).

Bloch, M. (1990), *L'étrange défaite*, Paris: Gallimard.
Brague, R. (1992), *Europe, la voie romaine*, Paris: Folio essais.
Brague, R. (2006), *Au moyen du Moyen Âge: Philosophies médiévales en chrétienté, judaïsme et islam*, Paris: Champs essais.
Braudel, F. (2003), *Grammaire des civilisations*, Paris: Flammarion.
Camus, R. (2011), *Le Grand Remplacement*, Paris: Editions David Reinharc.
Chevènement, J.-P. (2011), *La France est-elle finie?*, Paris: Fayard.
Cohn-Bendit, D. and Verhofstadt, G. (2012), *For Europe*, Munchen: Carl Hanser Verlag.
Delsol, C. (1996), *Le souci contemporain*, Paris: La Table Ronde.
Dewitte, J. (2008), *L'exception européenne: Ces mérites qui nous distinguent*, Paris: Éditions Michalon.
Dumont, L. (2011), 'L'idéologie allemande' in J.-P. Chevènement, *La France est-elle finie?*, Paris: Fayard.
Gueno, J.P. (1998), *Paroles de Poilus. Lettres et carnets du front 1914–1918*, Paris: Librio.
Hobsbawm, E.J. (1990), *Nations and Nationalism Since 1780*, Cambridge: Cambridge University Press.
Houellebecq, M. (1998), *Les particules élémentaires*, Paris: Flammarion.
Hugo, V. (1882), *Œuvres completes. Actes et Paroles IV*, Paris: J. Hetzel & Cie, A. Quantin.
Kantorowics, E. (1951), 'Pro Patria Mori in Medieval Thought' in *American Historical Review*, 56, pp. 472–492.
Legendre, P. (2000), *La fabrique de l'homme occidental*, Paris: Éditions Mille et Une Nuits.
Manent, P. (2010), *Le regard politique*, Paris: Flammarion.
Mesquita B. de and Smith A. (2011), *The Dictator's Handbook*, New York: Public Affairs.
Michéa, J.-C. (2002), *Impasse Adam Smith: Brèves remarques sur l'impossibilité de dépasser le capitalisme sur la gauche*, Paris: Flammarion.
Michéa, J.-C. (2011), *Le complexe d'Orphée: La gauche, les gens ordinaires et la religion du progress*, Paris: Climats.
Morin, E. (1987), *Penser l'Europe*, Paris: Gallimard.
Ricard, F. (2006), *Chroniques d'un temps loufoque*, Montréal: Éditions du Boréal.
Sloterdijk, P. (2010), *Colère et Temps*, Paris: Fayard.
Taguieff, P.-A. (2000), *L'effacement de l'avenir*, Paris: Galilée.
Tzvetan Todorov, T. (2012), *Les ennemis intimes de la démocratie*, Paris: Robert Laffont.
Valéry, P. (2009), *Variété I et II*, Paris: Gallimard.